Holocaust Memoir Digest

Holocaust Memoir Digest

A Digest of Published Survivor Memoirs with
Study Guide and Maps

Volume 1

Compiled and Edited by

Esther Goldberg

With an Introduction and
30 new colour maps by

Sir Martin Gilbert

VALLENTINE MITCHELL
LONDON • PORTLAND, OR

Published in 2004 in Great Britain by
VALLENTINE MITCHELL
Premier House
112–114 Station Road
Edgware
Middlesex HA8 7BJ

and in the United States of America by
VALLENTINE MITCHELL
c/o ISBS, 920 N. E. 58th Avenue, Suite 300
Portland, Oregon 97213-3786

Website: http://www.vmbooks.com

British Library Cataloguing in Publication Data
A catalogue record for this book is available.

ISBN 0 85303 528 8

Library of Congress Cataloging-in-Publication Data
A catalog record for this book is available.

Cover illustrations Front cover: At a railway station in the Balkans, a passenger train (left) is opposite a train (right) carrying Jewish deportees from Macedonia to the Treblinka death camp.
Back cover: The spur railway line leading into the Theresienstadt Ghetto, photograph taken in 1996.

Typeset in 11/13pt Ehrhardt by Vitaset, Paddock Wood, Kent
Printed in Great Britain by
MPG Books Ltd, Bodmin, Cornwall

"What does it mean to remember?
It is to live in more than one world,
to prevent the past from fading,
and to call upon the future to illuminate it."

Elie Wiesel

CONTENTS

STUDY GUIDE MAPS

INTRODUCTION BY SIR MARTIN GILBERT

In writing about the Holocaust, two types of source have been used by historians to try to understand the enormity of what happened in German-dominated Europe between 1939 and 1945, the deliberate murder of six million Jews. The first source is the records made at the time of the killings, by the perpetrators, by the victims, and by bystanders. The second source is the memoirs and recollections of those who survived: the survivor memoirs that are the subject of this *Holocaust Memoir Digest*.

The records made at the time – the contemporary records – are voluminous. The material published as a result of the research efforts of the International Military Tribunal during the Nuremberg Trials totals 57 volumes. These appeared in print between 1947 and 1953. Raul Hilberg's pioneering *Documents of Destruction, Germany and Jewry 1933–1945*, which made powerful use of the Nuremberg documents, was first published in 1972.

The publication of contemporary wartime material was, understandably, the main focus of historians in the four decades following the end of the war. As early as 1946, the United Nations Relief and Rehabilitation Administration (UNRRA) published details of the routes of the death marches. In 1958 Edward Kossoy set out the regional origin of Jewish prisoners at Auschwitz, Dachau and other camps. He had already issued a series of detailed single-sheet maps showing deportation routes, death camps, concentration camps and slave labour camps.

Among the pioneers in making the contemporary record known, and thus forming the factual basis of all future discussion of what happened during the Holocaust, were four Polish Jewish historians – themselves survivors – Tatiana Berenshtein, Danuta Czech, Danuta Dabrowska and Szymon Datner, who published between 1952 and 1970 comprehensive lists of the deportations inside Poland. In 1978, Serge Klarsfeld published the details of every deportation from France. My own *Atlas of the Holocaust*, in 1982, presented, in more than 300 maps, the statistics of the Europe-wide deportations, camps, revolts and death marches.

By 1982, in the bibliography of books on the Holocaust, the emphasis was still on the archival record of the war years themselves. The struggle to acquire this factual knowledge was considerable. Because the German records were substantial, this inevitably put the emphasis on the perpetrators. The killers were, in the main, fanatical in listing their "achievements". But even then, in 1982, 40 years after the most intense year of destruction, the voices of the survivors, and their stories, were being incorporated – albeit slowly and sometimes reluctantly – into the Holocaust narrative. In my own atlas that year, a number of maps were based entirely upon survivor testimony, as were details that I included on several maps of Jewish resistance – a topic that the Germans, not surprisingly, played down in their records.

Relatively few survivors published their memoirs in the first two decades after the war. One of the earliest – with which this *Holocaust Memoir Digest* begins – was Vladka Meed, whose memoir of the Warsaw Ghetto, which she entitled *On Both Sides of the Wall*, was first published in 1948, in Yiddish. The English version appeared in 1972. At that time there were fewer than two hundred such memoirs in print. Thirty years later the number of memoirs that had been published was in excess of two thousand.

For many years, historians were reluctant to use the memoirs of survivors. The reasons given for this reluctance were several: memory was fallible, the past was far distant, and the individual had no real picture of the wider context of events. But survivors themselves gradually became more confident, speaking at schools and universities, at Jewish communal events – such as Holocaust commemorations – and increasingly putting down their memories in printed form. Several libraries of Holocaust memoirs were begun, including Vallentine Mitchell's Library of Holocaust Testimonies.

The importance of survivor testimony is considerable. Survivors were the witnesses of the fate of their families, their friends and their towns. They lived through the ghettos, the deportations, the camps, and in hiding. They saw things that were not necessarily recorded by the perpetrators of the crimes. They understood the emotions and pressures and fears and hopes of the daily life – and death – of the Holocaust years, in all their cruel and often grotesque variety. Again and again, the survivors were the only witnesses of an event, the only people through whose recollections that event could become a part of the historical record.

The *Holocaust Memoir Digest* makes these survivor memoirs – with their crucial contribution to our knowledge and understanding of the Holocaust – accessible to students and teachers alike. It takes a particular weakness of almost all memoirs – that they lack an index, either of people, places or events – and turns this to an advantage, providing for each memoir a comprehensive analysis that enables anyone who has the *Digest* to discover the full variety of each memoir.

Using the *Digest*, anyone interested in the Holocaust, teaching about it, or studying it at school or university, can gain an immediate insight into every phase of the fate of the Jews during those terrible years.

Each memoir writer has a different story to tell, and tells his or her story in a different way. The nine memoirs included in this first volume of the *Digest* – of which annual volumes are planned – relate to many aspects of the Holocaust.

Vladka Meed was an eyewitness of that terrible arena of suffering, the Warsaw Ghetto, and of one of the most glorious moments of Jewish defiance, the Warsaw Ghetto revolt. Her memoir, *On Both Sides of the Wall*, introduces the reader to many of the leaders of that revolt, and to the day-to-day torment of the ghetto. Her own personal story is an inspiring one, as she worked on behalf of the Jewish Fighting Organization to find arms, to forge links with the Polish resistance beyond the ghetto, and to make contact with Jews in other ghettos.

The second memoir is *Night* by Elie Wiesel. This is the most widely read of all Holocaust memoirs, and has been so since its first publication in 1960. The *Digest* examines its contents through the prism of the 26 themes through which every memoir in the *Digest* is surveyed. These include pre-war Jewish home and community life, and the coming of war, which, in the case of Elie Wiesel and his family, as with so many families, included the order to wear a yellow star. Elie Wiesel's account of the deportation from Hungary to Auschwitz, and the arrival there, is a powerful one. The *Digest* points also to his account of the death marches, his references to Jewish resistance, and to the Righteous non-Jews – in his case the family servant who offered them a safe refuge.

One of the most important memoirs of the Holocaust era is Rudolf Vrba's *I Cannot Forgive*. This, the third memoir in this *Digest*, was first published in book form three years after Elie Wiesel's *Night*, and was the first to tell the story of Auschwitz in detail, as well as the story of Vrba's own escape from Auschwitz, with a fellow Slovak Jew, to bring the news of the truth about the camp to the West, and to arouse a universal outcry. Vrba also made clear – for the first time in any memoir, and as powerfully as anyone has done since – the massive economic gains made by the Nazi war machine by its destruction of the Jews. His account of the "Canada" section in Auschwitz, where the possessions of the deported and murdered Jews were sorted for despatch to Germany, gives a rare perspective in Holocaust writing, as does his account of Himmler's two visits to Auschwitz.

The fourth memoir in the *Digest* is *Of Blood and Hope*, by Samuel Pisar. The ghetto at the centre of this memoir was one of the largest ghettos set up by the Germans on Polish soil, that of Bialystok. Pisar became Bar Mitzvah while in the ghetto, a friend commenting on that moment: "Today our Wailing Wall is right here". Pisar's account of Auschwitz, of the slave labour camps to which he was sent, of the death marches, and of liberation, has a vividness that belies the fact that this memoir was written 35 years after the war, and is a strong tribute to the ability of a memoir writer to make each reader feel a sense of immediacy.

Bertha Ferderber-Salz published her memoir, *And the Sun Kept Shining …*, in 1980 – the same year as Samuel Pisar's memoir. The fifth memoir in the *Digest*, it centres on another of the larger ghettos, Cracow, and on the slave labour camp at Plaszow. Deportation to Auschwitz followed, and then Bergen-Belsen. Like all memoir writers, Bertha Ferderber-Salz was a witness to mass murder and its immediate aftermath; through that category in the *Digest* the reader can see the savage variety of killing which marked the Holocaust. Walking to her slave labour task outside the Cracow ghetto, Bertha Ferderber-Salz encountered "wagons piled high with corpses". The victims, Jews from the ghetto "whose blood flowed onto the road, were being taken to a mass grave". Even amid the torment and brutality, there were acts of resistance: in common with each memoir writer, Bertha Ferderber-Salz also gives testimony about that bright side of the dark coin, including, in Plaszow, ensuring some "serious defect" in every pair of trousers she was being forced to make for the German Army, and the preparation of unleavened bread on Passover, "the symbol of our emergence from slavery to freedom".

Every memoir is informative, and every memoir is poignant. The *Digest* draws out dozens of examples of both. In *Dry Tears, The Story of Lost Childhood*, first published in 1982, Nechama Tec – later a noted Holocaust scholar – tells of her survival in German-occupied Poland in hiding with her parents and older sister. Her memoir, the sixth in the *Digest*, is rich in descriptions of pre-war Jewish life, and pre-war Polish anti-Semitism in her home town, Lublin, another centre of Jewish life for many centuries. The description of life in hiding, given sanctuary by a Christian family in the central Polish town of Kielce, is particularly well delineated in the *Digest*. It presents a clear picture of the hazards and dangers of life in hiding, in disguise, always at risk of capture or betrayal, a risk shared equally by the rescued and the rescuer. So all-pervasive was Polish anti-Semitism that the family who saved the lives of Nehama Tec and her immediate family begged them to leave town without revealing their true identity. "They did not want anyone to know that they had helped a Jewish family to survive."

Half of all Jews murdered in the Holocaust were murdered in German-occupied Poland, where by far the largest pre-war Jewish community lived. But Jews were to be found in every country and region of Europe, and, just as the memoirs reflect this, so does the *Digest*. Salim Diamond was a Polish Jew, who had gone to Italy before the war to complete his training as a medical doctor. His memoir, the seventh in the *Digest*, was published in 1987. It tells of his internment in Italy from the summer of 1940. After the German occupation of Italy, helped by Italian partisans, he escaped, crossing the British front line to safety. After the war he met soldiers of the recently formed Jewish Brigade: it was they who told him what had happened in wartime Poland. "I knew now that to go to Poland was to visit a graveyard." Dr Diamond's experiences in Italy pointed up an aspect of the Holocaust that the *Digest*, by its use of direct quotation from the memoir, is able to stress: "I never found any Italians who approached me, as a Jew, with the idea of exterminating my race."

The eighth memoir in the *Digest* is a recent one, published in 1998. Entitled *Unveiled Shadows, The Witness of a Child*, it is by a young Viennese girl, Ingrid Kisliuk, who survived with her parents in hiding in German-occupied Belgium, to which they had fled from Austria in 1938, when she was 8 years old. In Vienna, she and her family had witnessed Hitler's arrival in the city, "standing in a convertible, his arm raised in his Nazi salute". As a refugee in Belgium she was a witness to the phenomenon – repeated in several other occupied countries, especially in Western Europe – of the local population hating the German occupier so much that it sided as much as possible with the Jews in its midst. "The Germans were our common enemy." Ingrid Kisliuk also writes of the difficulties of being a child in hiding, forced, while not yet a teenager, to hide her true identity until "I was totally entangled in a fictitious existence". This was never easy: she expresses what so many Hidden Children recall, how "all along there persisted inside the nagging guilt, the feeling of imprisonment in deception". Liberation secured life and freedom, but Ingrid Kisliuk noticed that her parents "remained frozen in sadness". Only later did she learn how many relatives and close friends had been murdered.

The ninth and final memoir in this first volume of the *Digest* is the most recent, published in the year 2000. Entitled *Out of the Ghetto*, its author, Jack Klajman, describes how he survived alone in the Warsaw Ghetto. Whereas Vladka Meed, author of the first memoir in the *Digest*, had been an adult in the ghetto, seeing its horrors through adult eyes, Jack Klajman was an 8-year-old when war came (the same age as Ingrid Kisliuk when Hitler occupied Austria). He survived in the ghetto as a young smuggler. When the ghetto revolt began he became a messenger delivering weapons to the resistance groups. He was just 12 years old. After the revolt had been crushed he survived in "Aryan" Warsaw masquerading as a Christian child, until a Christian Pole who knew that he was Jewish gave him sanctuary: one of the many Righteous Gentiles whose stories emerge in the *Digest*.

Also brought into sharp focus in the *Digest* are the stories that are found in each memoir of many individuals – people who are named, and who cease to be mere statistics of the Holocaust. Jack Klajman's account of the deaths of his parents in the ghetto, of his brother Eli betrayed, and of his brother Menashe and sister Brenda, deported to Treblinka, enable the readers of the *Digest* to see some of the human faces behind the "six million".

With every memoir, the regions, towns and camps involved vary. An important feature of the *Holocaust Memoir Digest* is that each memoir is provided with a map, or if necessary two or three maps, on which are located the places mentioned by the memoir writer.

Published memoirs seldom contain maps. The few that do seldom show more than a few of the places mentioned by the memoir writer. Those who use the *Digest* can familiarize themselves with the geography of the area covered by each memoir writer through the maps, which have been drawn specially for the *Digest*. These maps, in black and white, appear immediately after each memoir. They include a map of the Warsaw Ghetto showing the streets mentioned in Vladka Meed's account, and a map of the region between Auschwitz and the Slovak border, showing the route taken by the first two escapees from Auschwitz, one of them being Rudolf Vrba.

In the Study Guide, readers can see – in specially drawn colour maps – the layout of the death camps, the deportation routes, and the location of the slave labour camps, concentration camps and ghettos of wartime Europe.

The Study Guide provides teachers and students with ways to look at the memoirs in the *Digest*, to ask questions about them, and to examine the various categories of experience that make up the Holocaust, from the sections in each memoir on pre-war Jewish life, to liberation and beyond, culminating in post-war life and career, and the personal reflections of each memoir writer. As a fellow survivor told Samuel Pisar: "We may not have to live in the past, but the past lives in us." In the foreword to Bertha Ferderber-Salz's memoir, Menachem Rosensaft, himself the child of Holocaust survivors, writes, "… the survivors are the only ones who can discuss the experience from a personal, authentic perspective. It is their words which must form the basis for any historical understanding of the event." The *Holocaust Memoir Digest* aims to facilitate that understanding.

Sir Martin Gilbert
Honorary Fellow
Merton College
Oxford
January 2004

EDITOR'S ACKNOWLEDGEMENTS

I am deeply indebted – as are all students of the Holocaust – to the survivors who have had the courage and strength to revisit their Holocaust years and share their experiences by writing their memoirs. A further debt is due to those publishers who have understood how important it is to have written survivor accounts as part of the public record, available to succeeding generations. I hope that the survivors who have not yet done so will write of their experiences, and find publishers who will recognize how important it is to make these memoirs available.

Frank Cass of Vallentine Mitchell has done important work in publishing Holocaust memoirs. I am grateful that he is including the *Holocaust Memoir Digest* among his publications. I am grateful also to Maggie Copeland, Sally Green, and Mike Moran of Vallentine Mitchell for producing such a handsome and usable edition, and to Seth Denbo for his gentle corrections to the manuscript. I hope the *Digest* will encourage readers to get to know the voices of the memoir writers, and explore each memoir in its entirety. I am grateful to the memoir writers for allowing me to include their work in the *Digest*.

In the last three years, many professionals in the field of Holocaust education have been a source of encouragement to me. Without their belief in the value of the *Holocaust Memoir Digest*, it would not have come into existence.

I am grateful to the following librarians who, in the early stages of the *Digest*, welcomed it into their libraries: Aviva Astrinsky, YIVO Institute of Jewish Heritage, New York; Dr Julia Bock, Museum of Jewish Heritage, New York; Shirley Markman, Community Hebrew Academy of Toronto, Ontario; Michael Terry, Dorot Judaica Library, The New York Public Library, New York; Snow Zhu, Rita and Leo Greenland Library and Research Center, Anti-Defamation League, New York; and Mark Ziomek, United States Holocaust Memorial Museum, Washington, DC.

The following scholars encouraged me by their warm reception of the *Digest*: Dr Ilana Abramovitch, Manager of Curriculum, Museum of Jewish Heritage, New York; Peggy Jalenak, Board Member, Jewish Historical Society of Memphis and the Mid-South; Rachel Kostanian, Director, Vilna Gaon Jewish State Museum of Lithuania, Vilnius; Dr Allan Levine, St John's-Ravenscourt School, Winnipeg, Manitoba; Jeff Morey, Director, The Asper Holocaust and Human Rights Studies Program, Winnipeg, Manitoba; Dan Napolitano, Mandel Teacher Fellowship Program, United States Holocaust Memorial Museum, Washington, DC; Adrian Schrek, Associate Director and Director of Education; Holocaust Center of Northern California, San Francisco; Ilene Skolnik, Assistant Director, Education Division, Anti-Defamation League, New York; Dr Lorna Swartz, Psychiatrist, San Diego; Helen Walzer, Assistant Director, Holocaust Resource Center, Kean University, Union, NJ; and Dr Froma Zeitlin, Princeton University, NJ.

The following educators have been generous with their time and their interest in the *Digest*: Dr Michael Berkowitz, University College London, England; Josey Fisher, Librarian, Gratz College, and Director, Augerbach Central Agency for Jewish Education, Philadelphia; Dr Alain Goldschlager, Director, Holocaust Literature Research Institute, University of Western Ontario, London, Canada; Dr Bonnie Hausman, Program Officer, The Partnership for Excellence in Jewish Education, Boston; Darcy Lorin, Assistant Director, Development, Anti-Defamation League, New York; Leonid Saharovici, Founder, Tennessee Commission on Holocaust Education,

Memphis; Paul Shaviv, Director of Education, Community Hebrew Academy of Toronto, Ontario; Ann Shore, President, and Rachelle Goldstein, Vice-President, Hidden Child Foundation, Anti-Defamation League, New York; Evelina Silveira, Community Outreach Coordinator, Holocaust Resource Centre, London Jewish Federation, Ontario; Marc Skvirsky, National Program Director, Facing History and Ourselves, Brookline, MA; Ken Venhuizen, Program Services, Learning Coordinator – Social Sciences (7 to 12), Thames Valley District School Board, London, Ontario; and Barbara Wind, Director, Holocaust Remembrance and Education Council of MetroWest, Whippany, NJ. I owe a special thank you to the students of University of California, San Diego, who used the *Digest* as a text in their Holocaust course, Fall, 2002.

The following professors have been of enormous encouragement with the project: Dr Jack Fischel, Millersville University, Lancaster, PA; The Reverend Father Lawrence Frizzell, Seton Hall University, South Orange, NJ; Dr Steven Norwood, University of Oklahoma, Norman; Dr David Patterson, University of Memphis, Tennessee; Dr Eunice Pollock, University of North Texas, Denton; and Dr Haim Shaked, University of Miami, Coral Gables, FL.

I have also been gratified to receive encouragement from Charlene Abrahamson of San Diego, and Johanna Ernst of Washington, DC – both former teachers – who have visualized the use of the *Digest* in the classroom. Special thanks to Herman Wouk who read the *Digest* and was most encouraging, and to Harvey Sarner who allowed me use of his extensive library.

Gloria Gilbert, Co-chair of the Holocaust Resource and Education Committee of London Jewish Federation, Ontario, and Bernie Zaifman, President of Federation gave me a home through which I could apply for funding. Jeffrey Phillips and the London Jewish Community Foundation gave me seed money to help with printing and distribution costs. In addition, the preparation and publication of this volume was supported by a grant from the Memorial Foundation for Jewish Culture, New York.

Shi Sherebrin brought me into the modern era, designing a program for a Palm Pilot for the data entry, a program for the computer for the report itself, and patiently taught me how to use them. Geoff Cain and Earl Pinsky of Digital Internet Group created and maintain the website (<www.holocaustmemoirdigest.org>). I am grateful to Mark Poznansky for his generous support, which has allowed me to devote my energies to this project. Renee Silberman, Sandra Safran, and Pearl Santopinto have been there for me, as has Sean McCoy.

For more than three decades, Sir Martin Gilbert's maps have brought a geographical facet to our comprehension of history, while his belief in survivor testimony has made him a pioneer in that field. His mapping of the memoirs in this volume, and his maps for the Study Guide, prepared by Tim Aspden, have added enormously to the value of the *Digest* as a teaching tool.

I am grateful to my brother Rick for initially sparking my interest in Holocaust memoirs. My daughter Shoshana's interest in the Holocaust is an inspiration to me; I am grateful to my daughter Mirit, who shared her computer with me, and has encouraged me at every turn.

The *Digest* is dedicated in loving memory of the Byk, Flejsz, Goldberg, and Shapiro families, who never had the chance to write their Holocaust memoirs; their lives were cut short in the forest outside Sarny, and at Babi Yar.

My profound gratitude is due to my mother Helen Goldberg, who has lived with "Zachor" – remembrance – and to my late father Ben Goldberg who always believed, "Better days ahead".

Esther Goldberg
London, Ontario, Canada,
January 2004

USING THE DIGEST

The aim of the *Holocaust Memoir Digest* is to make the contents of each survivor's memoir available to schools, libraries, and institutions that deal with the Holocaust. Using the *Digest*, teachers, students, and researchers will know what is in the memoirs, and will be able to use them easily and effectively.

The memoirs appear in the order of their first publication. The memoirs chosen for this first volume of the *Digest* cover a range of regions and experiences, and include the earliest to the most recently published memoirs. Subsequent volumes of the *Digest* will continue to present a range of regions, and experiences.

Outline

Each entry of the *Digest* covers the following:

Author, Title, Publishing details
Focus of the memoir
Features of the memoir
Topics particular to each memoir, with the page numbers from the memoir (given for every reference), according to the following themes:

1. Pre-war Jewish home and community life
2. Pre-war anti-Semitism
3. The coming of war
4. Life under German occupation
5. Creation of the ghetto
6. Daily life in the ghetto
7. Deportation
8. Mass murder sites
9. Transit camps
10. Death camps
11. Slave labour camps and factories
12. Theresienstadt/Terezin
13. Auschwitz-Birkenau
14. Death marches
15. Concentration camps
16. Witness to mass murder
17. Resistance, ghetto revolts, individual acts of courage and defiance
18. Partisan activity
19. Specific escapes
20. In hiding, including Hidden Children
21. Righteous Gentiles (also known as Righteous Among the Nations)
22. Liberation
23. Displaced Persons camps (DP camps)
24. Stories of individuals, including family members

25. Post-war life and career
26. Personal reflections

Places mentioned, within Europe, including variant names or spellings, are listed with the page number of first reference. These places are also shown on individual maps, specially drawn for the *Digest* by Sir Martin Gilbert, to illustrate each memoir.

Places mentioned, outside Europe, are listed with the page number of first reference.

Memoir Digest

Author: Vladka Meed

Title: *On Both Sides of the Wall, Memoirs from the Warsaw Ghetto*

Publishing details: Holocaust Library, New York. 1979. 269 pages.
ISBN #0-89604-013-5.
Published originally in Yiddish by the Workmen's Circle, New York, 1948, also in Spanish in 1959, in Hebrew in 1968, and in English in Israel in 1972. This translation by Dr Steven Meed. From Elie Wiesel's Introduction: "The book first appeared in Yiddish in 1948. Its publication was an event of significance for it was the first authentic document to reach the free world about the uprising and destruction of the Warsaw ghetto, or about the Holocaust in general."

Focus:

A young woman is actively involved in the Warsaw Ghetto Revolt, and with saving Jews through the Jewish underground; the events described take place between 22 July 1942 and June 1945.

Features:

Foreword: Introduction written by Elie Wiesel, pages 3–8.
Photographs: Photographs of some of the Warsaw Ghetto Fighters, and of the destruction of the ghetto.
Documents: Letter written by Mordecai Anilewicz, 23 April 1943, page 155.
Afterword: Epilogue written by the Author, pages 264–9.
Index: Index of people, pages 271–4; Index of places, pages 274–6.

Contents: (by topic, with page numbers)

Pre-war Jewish home and community life

(212) Shabbat with the Miedzyrzeckis in their hiding place at the Russian Orthodox cemetery in Praga reminds her of pre-war Shabbats at home: "The faces of the family circle had reflected serenity and joy; the table, laden with the Sabbath feast, exuded a spirit of peace. My mother's blessing over the Sabbath candles, my father's benediction, my little brother's chanting …"
(216) The pre-war days of the Bund are recalled: "Little by little, almost in whispers, we recalled the days when such celebrations had been held in vast halls before huge audiences of workers with songs, music, speeches and fluttering flags."

Life under German occupation

(194–5) The pervasive fear of those on the "Aryan" side: "Fear of the Germans, fear of the Poles, fear of the blackmailers, fear of losing one's hideout, fear of being penniless. Fear was a constant companion not only of those who, because of their typically Jewish appearance, had to keep out of sight in Gentile lodgings but also of those of us who had the 'Aryan' features – fair hair, blue eyes and snub nose – which meant the chance to move about the streets."

Daily life in the ghetto

(9–10) 22 July 1942, Warsaw, living in constant fear: "But the more one learned about what was happening in the ghetto, the more anxious one felt." On the other hand, "Why, indeed,

I thought, should we despair? For the two years since our imprisonment in the ghetto, we had endured humiliation and hunger. Why should we now lose hope?"

(15–19) "It was necessary to find work, to obtain an employment card; then, according to the German edict, one could be sure of being permitted to stay in the ghetto. The ghetto put its trust in the printed word; workers would not be deported."

(21–2) The roundups begin: "There was no way of knowing which house or block might next be surrounded and raided by the police. Huge wagons loaded with weeping Jews passed by at intervals, headed for the deportation center, the 'Umschlagplatz', where freight cars stood waiting. Fear of what awaited us there dulled our ability to think about anything except saving ourselves, everything else, even hunger, was unimportant."

(68) Loss of friends after the September 1942 selection: "Only the day before, they had been at work; now their vacant places and idle machines remained as mute testimony to the horror of the last few days. We sat numb and frozen at our places, the oppressive stillness of the room broken only by occasional sobs."

(73–6) "Now and then, beyond the ghetto wall running along Zelazna Street, I could make out the movement of adults and children, women carrying baskets, the rushing tempo of life. But here in the ghetto the streets were dead, life was at a standstill."

(99–100) The smuggling business: "Enterprising Gentiles scaled the ghetto wall to purchase wearing apparel, underwear, shoes, sewing machines, and other items from the Jews who, in their desperation, parted with their few belongings for ridiculously small sums."

Deportation

(11–12) Rumours of deportation: "Like most of the rest of us, my mother assumed that the approaching deportations were merely transfers to some other region. After all, for months now the ghetto had been filled with trucks and horse-drawn wagons, bringing Jews from nearby towns. Now, we imagined, it would be our turn to be moved to another place."

(13–14) The first deportation begins with the emptying of the Jewish prison: "… the inmates – for the most part Jews who had been caught smuggling food."

(20) "Running behind the last wagon, a lone woman, arms outstretched, cried: 'My child! Give me back my child!' … The cries of the pursuing mother became more desperate as the horses pulled away. … The cries of the deportees faded away; only the cry of the agonized mother still pierced the air."

(26–8) Vladka, her mother, and brother go through a roundup at her mother's home: "… those who had neither cash nor employment cards to justify their being allowed to remain in the ghetto were the first to be rounded up. … One group gave thanks to the Lord for His mercy; the other, defeated and resigned to their fate, handed over their sacks and baskets, and climbed slowly into the waiting wagons."

(33) The unwillingness to succumb to the German bribes, to give themselves up voluntarily for deportation: "Fear of the unknown destination of the railroad cars was the main thing that kept us from committing ourselves."

(34–5) Unable to find a place to hide, she is separated from her mother and brother before the roundup: "My thoughts turned to my mother and brother, in their rooms, only three houses away. They would surely be taken in the raid. I berated myself for having allowed us to become separated."

(36–9) She is caught in the roundup but her promisory note for a job at Toebbens allows her to survive the selection: "We all watched the other group in silent anguish." Her mother and brother are among those taken.

(44) The German bribery works: "Three kilos of bread loomed very large in the eyes of a starving man. The temptation, even for once, to still that gnawing hunger eclipsed all other considerations, including the dread of the unknown, the destination of the railroad cars."

(62–5) September 1942: "The announcements posted the next morning ordered all Jews still in the ghetto – in the factories and workshops – to assemble in Mila, Wolynska, and Lubecki Streets, where those still eligible to remain in the ghetto would be designated." She receives a card, her "passport to life".

(67) "The selection continued from September 6 to September 12. ... During that time some 60,000 Jews were deported; another 4,000 perished where they were, from starvation or by shooting." 1942.

(175–80) The American Jewish Joint Distribution Committee had succeeded in getting neutral countries' visas to Jews who were then taken to Vittel, France, and later exchanged with German prisoners of war. This becomes an opportunity for the Germans to sell visas and coax Jews out of hiding, to an assembly point at the Hotel Polski, which is raided, the destination, the Pawiak prison: "Within a few hours it became known in Warsaw that half of the Jews with passports had been shot by the Germans in the prison courtyard; the others were deported to the Bergen–Belsen death camp."

Death camps

(14) Rumours: "… Jews being gassed to death." 1942 at Chelmno.

(58–9) Elie Linder escapes from Treblinka, provides an eye witness account. He had hidden under a pile of clothing in the shower ante-room: "Emerging cautiously, he saw a group of Jewish prisoners nearby burying corpses. He joined them." Eventually he returns to the ghetto, and tells his story: "Though we had long suspected the fate that awaited the Jewish deportees, we had now heard our first eyewitness account."

(113) The Blit twins in hiding with the Dubiels: "The children survived, but their mother was to perish in Maidanek." (Majdanek)

(146) The Jewish Fighting Organization sends a message to the outside: "We will avenge the crimes of … Treblinka and Auschwitz."

Slave labour camps and factories

(16, 57) Factories in the Warsaw Ghetto: Toebbens, the Brush Factory on Swientojerska, Roerich, and Schultz which offered some degree of security.

(47–50) She gets work at the Zilberberg workshop on Muranowska: "… Kuba said that this workshop would be a branch of the Toebbens' factory. …" However they do not get much cloth to work with and the roundups are frequent: "It seemed that nothing could save us from our fate any longer, not even the German workshops, though they were the only places authorized to allow Jews on their premises."

(52–5) The smaller ghetto is liquidated, 10 August 1942: "Only those employed by the Toebbens and Roerich firms were exempt." After 20 August, their shop moves from Muranowska to a former Jewish hospital at Nowolipie 69 where the workers also live.

(134–5) Early spring 1943, Yurek takes her to the Brush Factory which is in an uproar: "'They have just learned that the brush factory is going to be moved out of the ghetto,' he informed me. ... 'New labor camps have been set up in Poniatow and Trawniki – both of which are close to Lublin. At least that is what the Germans want us to believe.'"

(136) As the ghetto prepares for revolt, the Germans give promises of labour camps: "Toebbens and Schultz, the German industrialists, had warned the Jews for their own good to disregard the appeals of the Jewish Fighting Organization and not to resist the orders of the German authorities but to submit to deportation."

(239–43) Helping Jewish slave labourers outside Warsaw, in Pelzery and Rakow near Czestochowa: "Great caution and resourcefulness were needed to safeguard the money I brought to be smuggled in to be distributed among the neediest Jews. Often the recipients were unaware that the assistance came from the Coordinating Committee or even that it came from outside the camp. ... Most of the Jews employed in the factories of Pelzery and Rakow survived the war."

(244–9) Helping the Jews of Radom: "As in all the other camps, the prisoners worked under severe hardship and deprivation. The mortality rate was extremely high. ... One hundred destitute Jews benefited from the preliminary efforts of the relief committee set up by Meltzer and Kotlar and Gruenberg, and others." (With funds from the Coordinating Committee which she brought.)

(250) Ala Margolis is caught trying to help Jews in a factory in Piotrkow: "In the end, she was ransomed with the money that she had brought to relieve the distress of the captive forced laborers."

Concentration camps

(179) Deportations are to Bergen-Belsen, from the Hotel Polski "Visas to France" deception.

(146) The Jewish Fighting Organization sends a message to the outside: "We will avenge the crimes of Dachau ..."

Witness to mass murder

(13–14) Gravediggers bring news of Chelmno to Warsaw: "Several months before, three Jewish gravediggers who by some miracle had escaped from Chelmno had startled the ghetto with tales of Jews being gassed to death." July 1942.

(87–8) On the Aryan side, the sound of gunfire coming from the ghetto does not disrupt the Sunday Krasinski Garden scene: "I looked toward the park. Had the people there heard the gunfire? Some of them had looked over their shoulder, startled and alarmed. But one of them pointed toward the wall, and with his other hand made a motion indicating that there was nothing to worry about. 'That is just for the Jews,' a youthful Pole remarked with a grin – and returned for a second ride on a swing."

(103–4) Zygmunt Klepfisz brings specific news to the Warsaw ghetto: "... Zygmunt met an eyewitness who had just fled Treblinka, Azriel Wallach, a nephew of the Soviet diplomat Maxim Litvinov. It was from him that Zygmunt first learned the terrible facts about Treblinka."

(140–1) The uprising begins, with little help from the Polish Underground: "Thousands of Poles had gathered in the streets near the wall to watch the struggle. They came from all over Warsaw; never before had the city witnessed so bitter a struggle in its very heart. The Poles found it almost impossible to believe that the Jews were confronting the Germans without outside support."

(143–5) The Dubiels' house becomes a vantage point from which to watch the ghetto in flames, even for German officers taking photographs: "The Germans did not even bother to search the place; they went straight to the window and unslung cameras. 'It's a good site for pictures,' one remarked, 'if it weren't for those damned fires.'"

Resistance, ghetto revolts, individual acts of courage and defiance

(31) Deportees send coded messages after their train journeys: "… it was rumored that the seemingly reassuring messages were in fact deliberate misrepresentations, in coded language prearranged between sender and recipient to circumvent the German censorship, conveying the most disquieting information about what was really happening."

(43) The "volunteers" who chose to go to the Umschlagplatz: "In hiding places and work-shops, hearts ached with silent admiration for the strength that had enabled these people to take at least this decisive step. My sister and I could summon no such courage."

(69) Resistance as a possibility, discussed in March 1942, and in July: "The Jewish leaders did not want to assume the responsibility of risking the lives of those who still hoped to survive. … Under the circumstances, how could anyone find it in his heart to jeopardize the lives of the entire Warsaw ghetto for the sake of active resistance?"

(70–3) Individual acts of resistance lead to the recognition of the need for a combined force: "'We must no longer submit to deportation,' Abrasha (Blum) said. 'We must offer armed resistance. By now everyone knows where those freight cars are going.'"

(84–6, 94, 96) Vladka meets the Aryan side Resistance leaders and learns what the goals are: "'… our main tasks are to establish contact with Gentiles, find living quarters for women and children, assist Jews who are in hiding, and, in particular, to find sources of arms.' … From now on I was to be an integral active part of the underground."

(90, 100) Vladka tries to procure metal files: "These files were intended for the use of Jews who had been rounded up and put aboard trains bound for Treblinka. … Armed with a file, a prisoner could make a small gap in the window bars and try to jump to freedom."

(101–2) One package of dynamite is smuggled into the ghetto amid great tension and fear.

(106–9) Vladka sneaks back into the ghetto to meet with the Jewish Fighting Organization. She is given some jewellery to sell in order to obtain weapons: "… the Fighting Organization had been levying 'taxes' on Jews in the ghetto who were known to be wealthy, particularly those who had prospered since the ghetto had been set up. … A tax was levied, as well, upon the 'Judenrat'" (Jewish Council).

(116–18) Grinkraut, her teacher from her "folkshul", now at "Centos" the Orphan Care Center: "… he lived with the last of the ghetto's surviving orphans, trying to be a parent as well as a teacher to them. I ventured that, under the circumstances, teaching must be very difficult. My comment brought a faint fleeting smile to the aged, haggard face. 'One does one's best under the circumstances,' he replied." And to the question of further deportations: "'If there are any, we'll just go together.'"

(119–22) The 18 January 1943 uprising: "The mass of deportees fell upon the German troops tooth and nail, using hands, feet, teeth and elbows. … The clash had been instigated by a group from the Fighting Organization under the command of Mordecai Anilewicz. It was the first time that the Jews had offered organized resistance against deportation."

(123–6) Desperate to procure weapons before the eventual German return to liquidate the ghetto, the Jewish Fighting Organization devised a plan to make homemade bombs, and transport the materials to the ghetto: "Michal, therefore, climbed back over the ghetto wall to organize small 'munition plants' throughout the ghetto under the noses of the Germans.

Wherever groups of the Fighting Organization were to be found, they were taught how to make grenades and mix 'Molotov cocktails'."

(133, 137–9) Vladka's last visit to the ghetto as it prepares for an uprising: "Indeed, the mood of the ghetto had changed. Jews could now resist deportation, go into hiding, defend themselves – at any cost. … The fact that the ghetto was now practically unanimous in its stand against the Germans was in itself heartening. The Fighting Organization was now the spokesman for the ghetto – the agency toward which the eyes of the majority of the ghetto were directed."

(145–8) 19 April 1943, the uprising begins: "On the fifth day of the uprising the Coordinating Committee on the 'Aryan side' issued an appeal in the name of the ghetto. … Written in Polish and signed by the Fighting Organization, the appeal stressed the heroism of the fighters and the ferocity of the struggle. … The insurgents sent their fervent salutations to all those fighting the Nazis. 'We will avenge the crimes of Dachau, Treblinka and Auschwitz,' the appeal proclaimed. 'The struggle for your freedom and ours continues.'" The struggle is unaided by the outside.

(149–52) Kazik (Symcha Ratheiser) gives Vladka an eyewitness account of the uprising: "Afraid to penetrate deeper into the ghetto, the Germans changed their strategy. Their aim now was the total destruction of the ghetto. From outside the walls they rained heavy artillery shells on the ghetto while their aircraft dropped incendiary bombs on pockets of resistance. Entire streets were set afire."

(152–3) Zygmunt Igla gives Vladka his eyewitness account of the fighting in the area of the Schultz factory: "The time when Jews had submitted to deportation without protest was past."

(154–5) 8 May 1943, the bunker at Mila 18 is destroyed: "None would submit to being taken alive. Aryeh Wilner was the first to call for suicide. One by one, the other defenders followed him, turning their weapons upon themselves. Somehow two escaped through a side exit. They were among the very few whose fortitude and idealism inspired the ghetto Jews to challenge and resist the enemy – and who had survived."

(157–9) Vladka's tribute to the ghetto fighters Zalman (Zygmunt) Friedrich, Yurek, Lusiek, Gutta Blones, and Faigele Goldstein who were among the seventy ghetto fighters who were able to escape to the forest, but who were then betrayed and murdered in Pludy: "They still live in my memory, as they were in their brief brave lives. …"

(163–5, 170) Abrasha Blum hides with Vladka but is captured: "Abrasha had been the very soul of every aspect of Bund activity – the public soup kitchens, the supervision of illegal cultural activity, the publication of illegal literature, and finally, the leadership of the uprising in the Warsaw ghetto. Abrasha's indefatigable efforts, his humanity, his indomitable optimism and his sincere concern for his fellow man had gained him recognition not only in the Bund, but throughout the ghetto."

(181–4) Jewish relief efforts carried on by the Jewish Coordinating Committee which, after the uprising, focus on helping those who had survived: "Funds eventually began to reach us through the same underground channels, first mainly from the Jewish Labor Committee in the United States, subsequently from other Jewish organizations and, to some extent, from the Polish government-in-exile as well."

(186–9) The surviving fighters continue their activities and work together: "The bond forged among all members of the resistance forces in the ghetto during the days of the 'Aussiedlung' remained strong even after these people had escaped to the 'Aryan side'." ("Aussiedlung", "resettlement", was a euphemism for deportation, in this case to Treblinka.)

(226–8) The Committee tries to offer protection to those in hiding by producing identification and employment documentation: "In the event of an unexpected raid – or if Jews had to abandon their 'melinas' (hiding places) – they would have at least some identity cards."

(230–4) Vladka serves as a liason between the Coordinating Committee in Warsaw and the remnants of the Czestochowa ghetto insurgents, 23 Jews in hiding, 13 in a barn, the rest in two other hiding places: "After this first visit I traveled to Zelislawice every few weeks, bringing money, clothes, and medication for the hidden group."

(251–60) "Aryan" Warsaw tries to revolt against the fleeing Germans in August 1944, throwing the city and the Committee into chaos: "We, the survivors among the activists to whom the others had looked for aid, were now helpless and without directions. Should we try to hide in the city or should we attempt to escape?"

Partisan activity

(156–7, 161–2) Surviving fighters of the ghetto uprising escape to the Lomianki and Wyszkow Forests to join the partisans: "Deserted by all, without contacts, bereft of leadership and threatened by the treachery of the Polish underground, the Jewish partisans were in constant danger. Some had left, hoping to find other hiding places. Most of them had perished."

(219–25) Vladka visits Jewish partisans south of the Wyszkow Forest, near Tluszcz: "Between encounters with the Germans, the group carried out various acts of sabotage: setting fire to occupied estates, cutting telephone lines, raiding German outposts and, in general, harassing the enemy wherever possible."

(235–8) The Zelislawice group are discovered and attacked by Polish partisans in the Koniecpol woods: "Shortly afterwards, I obtained a document from the Polish underground to the effect that the Jews were under the protection of the 'Armja Krajowa', the right-wing Polish underground organization. This was supposed to safeguard the Jews from any further molestations by the local Polish partisan groups."

Specific escapes

(23–5) At the offices of "Zytos", a ghetto relief agency, she obtains fictitious employment cards which, with a bribe, allow her to leave the building during a raid: "The fictitious cards had been of some help, at least for the moment."

(29–30) "Policemen returned home after engaging in a roundup to find themselves beseiged by grieving, pleading Jews who had come to bargain for the release of their kin. ... A Jewish policeman who sometimes accepted bribes happened to live in our building."

(57–8) Moishe Kaufman and six others escape from the train to Treblinka: "Afraid to venture into the Polish neighborhood, they made their way under cover of darkness back to the ghetto, and to the shop where they were employed. ... Seven people snatched from the jaws of death!"

(60–1) While at the employment office trying to get an identity card, she is caught in a raid but escapes by hiding in a closet: "Then the door opened and I heard a woman's voice, 'We have never seen such hell before!' I emerged cautiously from the closets."

(77–9) While leaving the ghetto with a labour detachment, she is detained and searched, but walks out when the Nazi is distracted: "'You're lucky,' the group leader told me. 'Hardly anyone ever gets out of there unhurt.'"

(91–3) Vladka escapes from three "szmalcownicy", blackmailers, by maintaining her Aryan "character": "'Very well, let's go,' I said with a shrug of anger. 'You'll be called to account for casting suspicion on me and for your attempts to blackmail me.'"

(128–9) Michal Klepfisz betrayed, arrested, deported: "Michal knew he had nothing to lose; the train was headed for Treblinka. For a long time he tinkered with a metal screen over the small window in the car until, with the help of several others, he finally succeeded in breaking through it."

(130–2) Vladka's hiding place is betrayed, she is taken to be arrested: "'When the Germans interrogate you, don't tell them we took any money from you. Understand?' the man with the mustache said to me. I looked at him and pretended amazement, 'Why shouldn't I tell them? You're not afraid are you?'" She is released.

(179) Benjamin Miedzyrzecki hides in an attic of the Hotel Polski and escapes the roundup: "Some four hundred Jews were deported to the Pawiak prison."

In hiding, including Hidden Children

(82–3) Feigele assumes her Aryan identity as Wladyslawa Kowalska – Vladka – and with a few of her resistance friends, begins her life hiding as an Aryan.

(89) In hiding as an Aryan: "It was not easy to maintain the pretence of being a Gentile. One had to be wary of each movement, each word, to avoid giving oneself away. The Poles had no difficulty in recognizing Jews."

(105) On a return visit to the ghetto: "The ghetto was a dreary place, but it was my own, real world where I could be myself. Here I had no need to maintain the forced smile I wore before my Polish neighbors. Here I did not have to listen to snide remarks from the Poles that the Jews had had it coming to them and that Hitler was purging Poland of the 'Jewish plague'. Here I did not have to live in constant fear of being unmasked as a Jewess. I was among my own."

(110–11) Vladka's work to save children still in the ghetto: "We spared neither effort nor expense in trying to persuade Poles to hide Jewish children in their homes."

(111–13) Nellie and Vlodka Blit, 10-year-old twins in hiding with the Dubiel family, see their mother from their window which overlooks the ghetto, and drop notes to her: "Of course, this was a dangerous thing to do. Someone might notice what was going on and report it to the Germans. That would seal the fate not only of the mother but of the daughters and of the Dubiels as well. The girls accepted my warning. … I bowed my head with a sense of guilt; why did I have to be the one to cut off the only source of joy left to these children and their mother?"

(171–4) Vladka hides in the countryside as Mr Dubiel's cousin. A Jew, Berko, comes to their door and is helped: "I yearned to reveal to this sorrowing fellow Jew how deeply I felt with him, but I had to maintain a detached air, without showing the least sign of kinship, posing as a total stranger, lest suspicion be aroused and all of us be endangered."

(196–202) Those who lived as Aryans: Yurek Igra who eventually worked with the underground to help those in hiding, Marie Zilberberg who worked for a German family, Yuzik from Piotrkow who preferred being on his own: "He said he was better off in the open, where he was free and could run for cover in case of danger. … He was the only Jew I met in Warsaw during that time who was not afraid."

(203–8) Vladka tries to help those in hiding: Mrs Mermelstein and her son Stefan, Gutka Hechtman and her mother Clara, Clara Falk and her son Adash, Jadzia Rosenberg and her husband, all of whom live under the most dire conditions: "In dark, dreary cubbyholes, unable to go out for any reason, to do anything for themselves, they remained cooped up day after day, fear and anxiety their constant companions, despondency eating away their spirits. They were afraid to complain or to show any dissatisfaction lest their host evict them from their hideout. This would have been a sentence of death."

(209–10) The creative work of those in hiding: "Dr Emmanuel Ringelblum, the eminent Jewish historian, and Mr Melman, a Jewish teacher from the Medem School in Lodz, were living in that hideout and writing about Jewish history and Yiddish literature. It was from this bunker that the now-historic report of Jewish cultural activities in the ghetto was issued."

(213–16) Vladka finds a new apartment, and a shy neighbour: "She had assumed that I, too, was Jewish, but had cautiously maintained aloofness."

(228–9) Finding and building hiding places: "The next most vital relief project at that time was the creation of hideouts in Gentile homes, where persecuted Jews might find asylum in the event of a surprise German raid or if curious neighbors – or 'szmalcownicy' (betrayers) – became suspicious."

Righteous Gentiles

(81, 217) Anna Wonchalska and sister Marysia Sawicka: "Both were devoted co-workers of ours and were connected with the Polish Socialist underground organization."

(83, 190–1) Wanda Wnorowska, who helps her find a job as a seamstress: "… was aware of my Jewish identity, and received me warmly. As a result, I had a refuge during the day, was earning my keep, and was provided with an identity card."

(92) Mrs Brzeska: "… a friendly, upright, compassionate Polish woman … had given shelter to five Jews in an emergency."

(111–13, 171–3) Dubiel family, hide the Blit twins, take Vladka to the countryside, introduce Vladka: "'She's one of us.'"

(113, 234) Marja Barkowska, takes in 6-year-old Olesh Blum for a short time; helps the Czestochowa people in hiding: "I gave them the address of Marja Barkowska as a contact in Warsaw."

(165–70, 213) Anna Wonchalska: "our Gentile confidant, my 'adopted' mother" rescues Vladka from prison before she is taken to the Gestapo; later Vladka assumes the identity of Anna's daughter Stanislawa: "Anna had arranged with her priest not to report her daughter's death, and assured me that if I would be detained as a Jewess, she would intercede on my behalf. At the same time, she told me the names of grandmothers, aunts and cousins. I was now a full-fledged Aryan with two generations of Gentile forebears."

(187) Mrs Wasowska: "… a courageous woman who herself had participated in the underground movement, knowingly allowed us to hold our conferences in her home."

(191–3) Juliana Larisz: "… the kindhearted Juliana, responding to the pleas of her Jewish friends, began cautiously to smuggle them out of the ghetto. With her help, 21 of them escaped." Mr Pero: "All the Jews who found asylum with Pero survived. He himself died as a Polish officer in the general Warsaw uprising of 1944." Helena Sciborowska: "Many Jews owe their survival to the efforts of this dedicated little woman whose kindness and compassion were pure and selfless."

(211–12) Mr Kartaszew who lived on the grounds of the Russian Orthodox cemetery in Praga, employs Benjamin Miedzyrzecki: "Kartaszew engaged him as his assistant, and agreed to shelter his parents and sister. … In return, Kartaszew allowed the Miedzyrzeckis to observe the religious rules of Judaism to some extent in their hideout."

(217–8) Anna Wonchalska hosts a party for Vladka to celebrate her patron saint, St Stanislaw: "Between Anna and me there was, indeed, a deeply shared affection, apart from our common interests."

(228) Mr Rogozinski, the tailor and Mr Jablonski, the janitor of the building, create a hiding place for two Jews Notke and Mietek: "Both Jews survived." Mr Dankewicz of Pruszkow hid a Jewish woman Zucker, who survived.

(236–7) Mr Romanow helps the Czestochowa Jewish partisans: "'If it weren't for Romanow all of us would probably have starved to death', said Staszek as soon as we were alone."

(242–3) Jan Burst who is her liaison to smuggle money and letters into the Rakow factory in Czestochowa, and carry replies out to her: "True, he was well paid for each letter or package he smuggled in, but his humanity, kindness and reliability far outweighed every other consideration." Mr Mendzec: "… who was attached to the factory at Pelzery. He continued the task of smuggling letters to the Jews in the camp."

(255) Mr Wojciechowski who shelters Haika Belchatowska, Boruch Spiegel, and Jakubek and Maszele Gleitman: "… all friends and former ghetto fighters," until his house burned during the Warsaw uprising of August 1944.

Liberation

(261–3) Vladka and Benjamin return from Grodzisk to Warsaw after it is liberated by the Russians, and return to what had been the ghetto: "Perhaps it is better only to gaze in silence upon this dead and desolate wilderness, where every stone, every grain of sand is sodden with Jewish blood and tears."

Displaced Persons camps

(202) Yuzik from Piotrkow, on his own, unafraid: "After the war, when I was at the Displaced Persons Camp Feldafing in West Germany, I learned that the boy had survived and was living somewhere in the American zone in Austria."

Stories of individuals, including family members

(12) Her father Shlomo had died in the ghetto, as she reports on July 1942: "My father had died of pneumonia a year earlier."

(32–3) Baruch Zifferman survives a slaughter in his home; Raisel Malinowski does not.

(40–3) Her mother Hanna and brother Chaim are taken to the Umschlagplatz: "Time and again, my sister and I had talked about joining our mother and brother and sharing their fate. But somehow we had hesitated, restrained by fear of the unknown."

(45–6) Yurek Blones and his brother Lusiek escape from the train to Treblinka: "Eventually, the two brothers joined the ranks of the resistance organization and distinguished themselves in the Warsaw ghetto uprising."

(46) Her sister Henia, working at the public kitchen, is taken in a raid: "'I'm sorry, but I cannot leave my post.'"

(50–1) Roma Brandes, Manya Wasser's sister, begins a discussion on the Vienna Olympics: "… Roma was deported to Treblinka. But her words – and perhaps even more, her faith in mankind – were to linger in my mind and heart for a long time to come."

(51–2) "At Gesia 13, from the window in the hiding place, I saw the march of the orphanage of Janusz Korczak. … The noted educator, who had maintained his home and school for orphans of the ghetto against the greatest odds, was now accompanying his wards to their deaths."

(56–7) Her four roommates, Yankel Gruszka, Edzia and Henach Russ, Schloima Pav: "We helped one another to stay alive, to carry on, to endure hunger, to cope with the threat of deportation that hung over our heads."

(66–7) While passing through a selection, Vladka and her friends Henach and Edzia help a father to hide his son: "'Why not put on your topcoat and let your son slip underneath? We'll cover you, back and front.' … We anxiously approached the exit. If the ruse were detected, we would all be ordered to the left. We trudged along in silence."

(79–80, 115, 127–32) Stefan Machai initially helps them: "Now a 'ricksha' pusher, the stocky Gentile considered it a an honor to have the former engineer as his guest." Later, he changes: "He was no longer the kindly person who had collaborated with us for so long, no longer the friendly host who had rendered us great service. He was hobnobbing with underworld characters." He is believed to have betrayed their hideouts.

(80–1) Gina Klepfisz, teacher, nurse, resistance fighter, in hiding as a Christian, Kazimiera Juzwiak: "… one of the few Warsaw Jews to be buried in a cemetery at a time when thousands of Jews were being gassed and cremated."

(95) Resistance fighter Yurek (Aryeh Wilner) is betrayed with a quantity of weapons, tortured, imprisoned, he escapes: "Yurek was to die at Mila 18 during the ghetto uprising. …"

(97–8) Tadek (Tovye Shaingut) and his arms dealings: "He was both shrewd and fearless, undeterred by obstacles."

(108) Marek Edelman: "He was the commandant of all the resistance groups in the factory area, and also the Bund's representative in the General Command of the Fighting Organization."

(111) Manya Zygielbojm cannot bring herself to send her son Artek to the Aryan side to potential safety: "'Whatever my fate, it shall also be the fate of my son. We've been through so much together. Perhaps we'll succeed in surviving after all. If not, at least we'll perish together.' And so, Manya Zygielbojm did not part from her son. Both of them were to die in the ghetto uprising."

(113–16) The difficulties of some of the children in hiding: 6-year-old Olesh Blum, 1-year-old Krysia Klog, 6-year-old Else Friedrich, 1-year-old Irena Klepfisz who all survived, and that of 12-year-old Mika Perenson, who did not. He "… shared the fate of many other Jewish children."

(121) Avrom Feiner: "… the energetic leader of the underground Bund youth movement, whose fighting group had used its only revolver to fire the fatal shot, attempted to wrest a more useful carbine from the hands of a German. He paid for his attempt with his life. But the other members of his group succeeded in escaping." January 1943.

(142) Michal Klepfisz obtains a revolver on his birthday, 17 April 1943; he smuggles it into the ghetto and remains to fight until his end on the third day of the revolt.

(185) Zoshka Kersh succeeds in rescuing her brother from the Skarzysko-Kamienna labour camp and getting him back to Warsaw, but the Gestapo, on the hunt for someone else, finds them: "… Zoshka and her brother were immediately removed to the Pawiak prison, where they were put to death."

(221, 224) Gabriel Frishdorf leads a group of the Jewish Fighting Organization to free prisoners at the German headquarters, is killed as a partisan.

Post-war life and career

(264–9) Epilogue: Vladka and Benjamin return to Warsaw: "On January 18, 1978, with several dozen elderly Jewish men and women, and with the representatives of Jewish institutions, we assembled at the monument to mark the 35th anniversary of the first organized resistance in the Warsaw Ghetto."

(post-publication) Vladka and her husband Benjamin Meed founded the Warsaw Ghetto Fighters Association and the American Gathering of Jewish Holocaust Survivors.

Personal reflections

(70) The first encouragement to active resistance is not immediately successful: "But we had learned that even the faintest glimmer of hope for personal survival was more powerful than any fear of selection."

(156) Their hideouts betrayed: "The very ground seemed to scorch our feet."

(158) On the betrayal and murder of five of her friends who were among the last of the ghetto fighters: "The pain of loss was so great it made mourning meaningless. The tragedy lay upon my consciousness like a smothering blanket, choking my emotions."

(194) Able to hide their Jewish identity, but unable to camouflage their fear: "Haunted by fear of betrayal, our eyes betrayed us; and this knowledge only increased our fear."

(218) At a clandestine party with friends: "'The more joy, the more sadness.'"

(262) Upon her return to the devastation of the ruins of the Warsaw ghetto after liberation: "The scene is the same in a thousand other towns, a hundred other ghettos; my sorrow repeated ten thousand times. But the figures, the incredible statistics, how do they compare, how can they express what has happened?"

Places mentioned – in Europe: (page first mentioned)

Auschwitz Main Camp/Auschwitz I (146), Belsen/Bergen-Belsen concentration camp (179), Brushmakers' Factory (Warsaw) (56), Chelmno/Kulmhof death camp (13), Cracow/Krakow/Krakau (81), Czestochowa (230), Dachau concentration camp (146), Daring Factory (Warsaw) (155), Deblin (157), Feldafing Displaced Persons camp (202), Grodzisk (261), Hungary (161), Kalisz (44), Kampinos Forest (164), Kawenczyn slave labour camp (95), Kielce (196), Koniecpol (230), Lodz/Litzmanstadt (57), Lomianki Forest (Warsaw) (153), London, England (187), Lublin (33), Lvov/Lemberg/Lwow/Lviv (69), Majdanek concentration camp (113), Malkinia/Malkin (103), Miedzeszyn (17), Muranow (Warsaw) (150), Pawiak Prison (Warsaw) (95), Pelzery slave labour camp (239), Piotrkow/Piotrkow Trybunalski (182), Pludy (Warsaw) (114), Poniatowa slave labour camp (134), Praga (Warsaw) (59), Pruszkow (228), Radom (244), Radzymin (191), Rakow slave labour camp (239), Roerich Factory (Warsaw) (45), Ryki (157), Schultz Factory (Warsaw) (58), Siedlce (171), Skarzysko-Kamienna slave labour camp (185), Smolensk (43), Sokolow Podlaski (104), Switzerland (175), Tluszcz (219), Toebbens Factory (Warsaw) (16), Transavia Factory (Warsaw) (155), Trawniki slave labour camp (134), Treblinka death camp (31), Umschlagplatz (Warsaw) (22), Vienna/Wien (50), Vilna/Wilno/Vilnius (57), Vittel internment camp (176), Volhynia/Wolyn/Volyn (69), Warsaw Ghetto (9), Warsaw/Warszawa/Warschau (9), Werterfassung Factory (Warsaw) (155), Wloclawek (17), Wyszkow Forest (179), Zamosc/Himmlerstadt (110), Zelislawice (231), Zoliborz (Warsaw) (114)

Places mentioned – outside Europe: (page first mentioned)

Palestine (175), United States of America (181)

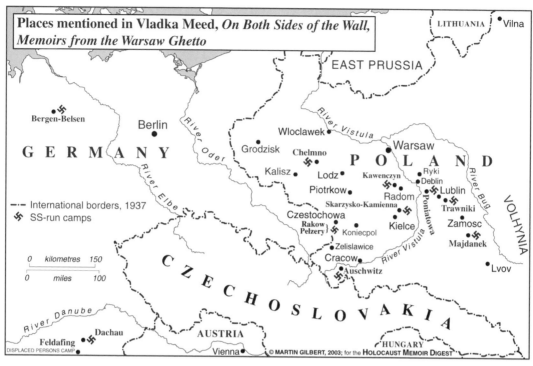

Places mentioned in Vladka Meed, *On Both Sides of the Wall, Memoirs from the Warsaw Ghetto*

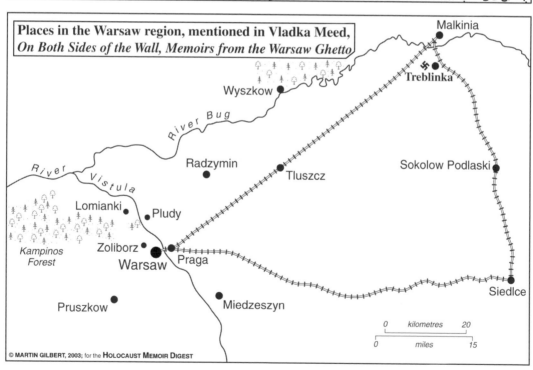

Places in the Warsaw region, mentioned in Vladka Meed, *On Both Sides of the Wall, Memoirs from the Warsaw Ghetto*

© MARTIN GILBERT, 2003; for the HOLOCAUST MEMOIR DIGEST

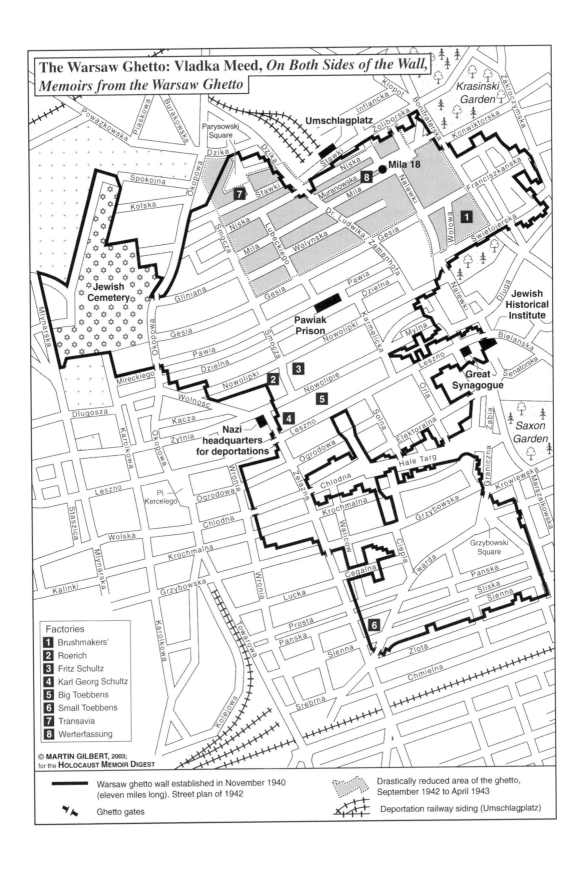

The Warsaw Ghetto: Vladka Meed, *On Both Sides of the Wall,*
Memoirs from the Warsaw Ghetto

Krasinski Garden

Umschlagplatz

Mila 18

Parysowski Square

Jewish Cemetery

Jewish Historical Institute

Pawiak Prison

Great Synagogue

Saxon Garden

Nazi headquarters for deportations

Grzybowski Square

Factories

1. Brushmakers'
2. Roerich
3. Fritz Schultz
4. Karl Georg Schultz
5. Big Toebbens
6. Small Toebbens
7. Transavia
8. Werterfassung

© **MARTIN GILBERT**, 2003;
for the HOLOCAUST MEMOIR DIGEST

Warsaw ghetto wall established in November 1940
(eleven miles long). Street plan of 1942

Ghetto gates

Drastically reduced area of the ghetto,
September 1942 to April 1943

Deportation railway siding (Umschlagplatz)

Author: Elie Wiesel

Title: *Night*

Publishing details: Hill and Wang, New York. 1960. 116 pages.
Library of Congress #60-14910.
First published by Editions de Minuit, France, 1958. Current edition, Random House, New York.
ISBN #0-553-27253-5.
Translated from the French by Stella Rodway.

Focus:

A young religious Hungarian boy survives with his father in Auschwitz and Buchenwald, losing his father before liberation; the events take place between late 1941 and the end of April 1945.

Features:

Foreword: Written by François Mauriac, pages 7–11.

Contents: (by topic, with page numbers)

Pre-war Jewish home and community life

(15–17) A religious life: "We would read together, ten times over, the same page of the Zohar. Not to learn it by heart, but to extract the divine essence from it."
(20) Possibilities to emigrate to Palestine: "I had asked my father to sell out, liquidate his business, and leave. … 'I'm too old to start from scratch again in a country so far away.'"

The coming of war

(20–2) Spring 1944, the Germans enter Hungary, Budapest, Sighet: "However our first impressions of the Germans were most reassuring. … Their attitude toward their hosts was distant, but polite." Then, valuables are confiscated, restrictions begin: "'The yellow star? Oh well, what of it? You don't die of it …' (Poor Father! Of what then did you die?)"

Creation of the ghetto

(22–3) Two ghettos are set up; their home is within the larger ghetto: "We were entirely self-contained. A little Jewish republic."
(24–8) News that the ghetto is to be liquidated is delivered at midnight; the smaller ghetto is emptied the next morning, it becomes: "… an open tomb."

Deportation

(17) 1942, a year and a half before the German invasion of Hungary, foreigners are deported by train: "I heard a Jew behind me heave a sigh. 'What can we expect?' he said. 'It's war. …'"
(28–33) Three days after the smaller ghetto is liquidated in 1944, the remaining Jews are moved into it, then taken to the synagogue for the night: "The following morning, we were marched to the station, where a convoy of cattle wagons was waiting."
(34–7) Two days on the train to leave Hungary: "'From this moment, you come under the authority of the German army.' … Our eyes were opened, but too late."

(37–8) The train comes to a station, a camp: "We had arrived – at Birkenau, reception center for Auschwitz."

Mass murder sites

(18–19) 1942, Moché the Beadle survives the massacre at Kolomyja: "'I wanted to come back, and to warn you. And you see how it is, no one will listen to me. …'"

Slave labour camps and factories

(55–6) Entrance into Buna-Monowitz: "… the work was not difficult. Sitting on the ground, we had to count bolts, bulbs, and small electical fittings. The Kapo explained to us at great length the vast importance of our work."

(56, 59, 61–3) Franek the foreman wants his gold-crowned tooth: "I told him it was impossible, that I could not eat without it. 'What do they give you to eat, anyway?'"

(63–71) Beatings and hangings in Buna: "'Where is God now?' … 'Where is He? Here He is – He is hanging here on this gallows. …'"

(75–8) Surviving a selection: "The head of our block had never been outside concentration camps since 1933." He describes what will happen and adds: "'… the essential thing, don't be afraid.' Here was a piece of advice we should have liked very much to follow."

(78–81) His father faces a second selection: "He would have liked to say so many things. … 'Look, take this knife,' he said to me. 'I don't need it any longer. It might be useful to you. And take this spoon as well. … Take what I'm giving you!' The inheritance." And all of his father's worldly possessions.

(82–5) He has an operation in Buna, pus removed from his foot. As the Russian guns are heard in the distance, another patient tells him: "'I've got more faith in Hitler than in anyone else. He's the only one who's kept his promises, all his promises, to the Jewish people.'"

(85–8) Camp to be evacuated: "The choice was in our hands. For once we could decide our fate ourselves. We could both stay in the hospital. … Or else we could follow the others."

Auschwitz-Birkenau

(39–41) On the platform at arrival at Birkenau (Auschwitz II), passing Dr Mengele's selection with his father: "We did not know yet which was the better side, right or left; which road led to prison and which to the crematory. But for the moment I was happy; I was near my father."

(43–6) First night, Birkenau: "The night was gone. The morning star was shining in the sky. I too had become a completely different person. The student of the Talmud, the child that I was, had been consumed in the flames."

(46–8) "'Work or the crematory – the choice is in your hands.' … Here the word 'furnace' was not a word empty of meaning: it floated on the air, mingling with the smoke. It was perhaps the only word which did have any real meaning here."

(49–51) Entrance at Auschwitz Main Camp, their Polish supervisor: "Drive out despair, and you will keep death away from yourselves. Hell is not for eternity." Elie becomes #A-7713.

(52–4) Three weeks in Auschwitz Main Camp; the possibility that his mother is still alive: "How we should have liked to believe it. We pretended, for what if the other one should still be believing it?"

(54) The four hour walk to reach Buna-Monowitz: "We walked through the villages, many of the Germans stared at us without surprise. They had probably already seen quite a few of these processions."

Death marches

(89–91) Running "forty-two miles" through the night: "Letting oneself be pushed by the mob; letting oneself be dragged along by a blind destiny. When the SS became tired, they were changed. But no one changed us."

(91–3) Stopping to rest in the snow and the cold: "In every stiffened corpse I saw myself. And soon I should not even see them; I should be one of them – a matter of hours."

(95–9) On to Gleiwitz: "We stayed at Gleiwitz for three days. Three days without food or drink." Then pushed on to "an infinitely long train, composed of cattle wagons, with no roofs."

(100–3) Ten days and nights on the train: "The days were like nights, and the nights left the dregs of their darkness in our souls."

(104–5) The train stops at Buchenwald: "A hundred of us had got into the wagon. A dozen of us got out."

Concentration camps

(106–7) Arrival at Buchenwald, his father is very sick, he tries to encourage his father: "I felt that I was not arguing with him, but with death himself, with the death that he had already chosen."

(114–15) At Buchenwald until liberation: "After my father's death, nothing could touch me anymore. ... I spent my days in a state of total idleness." Buchenwald is liberated on 10 April 1945, first by resistance within the camp, and then by American troops.

Witness to mass murder

(42) The pit of flames in Birkenau: "A lorry drew up at the pit and delivered its load – little children. Babies! ... A little farther on was another and larger ditch for adults."

Resistance, ghetto revolts, individual acts of courage and defiance

(40–1) At the platform upon entry to Birkenau (Auschwitz II): "I heard murmurs around me. 'We've got to do something. We can't let ourselves be killed.' ... But the older ones begged their children not to do anything foolish. ... The wind of revolt died down."

(72–5) Rosh Hashanah in Buna, 1944: "Ten thousand men had come to attend the solemn service. ... Thousands of voices repeated the benediction; thousands of men prostrated themselves like trees before a tempest." Yom Kippur: "... there was no longer any reason why I should fast. I no longer accepted God's silence."

(114–15) Resistance within the camp liberates Buchenwald, 10 April 1945: "Armed men suddenly rose up everywhere. Bursts of firing. Grenades exploding. ... The battle did not last long. ... The SS had fled and the resistance had taken charge of the running of the camp."

Righteous Gentiles

(31) Their servant Martha offers them refuge: "... she begged us to come to her village, where she could give us a safe refuge. My father did not want to hear of it."

Liberation

(115–16) Liberated by Americans, 10 April 1945, in Buchenwald: "Our first act as free men was to throw ourselves onto the provisions. ... And even when we were no longer hungry, there was still no one who thought of revenge."

(116) "I wanted to see myself in the mirror hanging on the opposite wall. I had not seen myself since the ghetto. From the depths of the mirror, a corpse gazed back at me."

Stories of individuals, including family members

(15–19) Moché the Beadle: "… was a past master in the art of making himself insignificant, of seeming invisible." As a foreigner, deported; as an eyewitness to slaughter, not believed.

(35–8) Madame Schächter on the train foresees the future: "'I can see a fire!'"

(39) Loss of his mother and younger sister: "'Men to the left! Women to the right!' I did not know that in that place, at that moment, I was parting from my mother and Tzipora forever."

(44) Bela Katz of Sighet, noticed for his strength at Birkenau (Auschwitz II), chosen for the Sonder-Kommando: "… he had himself put his father's body into the crematory oven."

(51–3) Aunt Reizel's husband, Stein of Antwerp, living in hope his family had survived.

(53, 81–2) Friend Akiba Drumer sent to Birkenau after the selection: "… he had no strength left nor faith. Suddenly his eyes would become blank, nothing but two open wounds, two pits of terror. … as soon as he felt the first cracks forming in his faith, he had lost his reason for struggling and had begun to die."

(57) The musicians of Buna-Monowitz: "Louis … complained that they would not let him play Beethoven: Jews were not allowed to play German music."

(58, 76–7) Czech brothers Yossi and Tibi, friends at Buna: "… we would often hum tunes evoking the calm waters of Jordan and the majestic sanctity of Jerusalem." They survive the selection at Buna with him.

(60–1) A French girl offers him kindness: "'I knew you wouldn't give me away.'"

(89–90) Friend Zalman dies on the march from Buna.

(93–5) Rabbi Eliahou looks for his son during the death march: "He was the only rabbi who was always addressed as 'Rabbi' at Buna."

(96–8) Juliek, "The boy from Warsaw who played the violin in the band at Buna…"; played his last Beethoven in Gleiwitz: "… as he said farewell on his violin to an audience of dying men."

(103–4) Father's friend Meir Katz, the gardener at Buna, remains on the train when it reaches Buchenwald.

(107–13) The death of his father, Chlomo, 29 January 1945: "His last word was my name. A summons, to which I did not respond."

Personal reflections

(23) "It was neither German nor Jew who ruled the ghetto – it was illusion."

Places mentioned – in Europe: (page first mentioned)

Antwerp/Antwerpen (51), Auschwitz Main Camp/Auschwitz I (37), Berlin (57), Birkenau/ Brzezinka/Auschwitz II (38), Buchenwald concentration camp (105), Budapest (20), Buna-Monowitz/Monowice/Auschwitz III (66), Czechoslovakia (88), Galicia (18), Gleiwitz/ Gliwice slave labour camp (88), Gross Rosen/Rogoznica concentration camp (88), Holland (57), Kolomyja (18), Kosice/Kassa/Kaschau (34), Paris (60), Sighet/Maramarossziget/ Sighetul Marmatiei (15), Warsaw/Warszawa/Warschau (57), Weimar (116)

Places mentioned – outside Europe: (page first mentioned)

Palestine (20)

Places mentioned in Elie Wiesel, *Night*

Baltic Sea

EAST PRUSSIA

River Elbe

River Oder

River Vistula

Berlin

Warsaw

River Bug

GERMANY

POLAND

River Vistula

Weimar
Buchenwald

SILESIA
Gross Rosen

Gleiwitz

Buna-Monowitz

Birkenau

Auschwitz

GALICIA

Kolomyja

C Z E C H O S L O V A K I A

RUTHENIA

Kosice

TRANSYLVANIA

Sighet

River Danube

AUSTRIA

Budapest

H U N G A R Y

ITALY

ROMANIA

YUGOSLAVIA

BULGARIA

Adriatic Sea

—·—· International borders, 1937
卐 SS-run camps

0   kilometres   75
0   miles   100

© MARTIN GILBERT, 2003; for the HOLOCAUST MEMOIR DIGEST

Author: Rudolf Vrba, with Alan Bestic

Title: *I Cannot Forgive*

Publishing details: Regent College Publishing, 5800 University Boulevard, Vancouver, British Columbia V6T 2E4. 1997. 261 pages.

ISBN #1-57383-096-8.

The result of a series of five articles published in March 1961 in the *Daily Herald* in London, England, the memoir was originally published in 1963, by Sidgwick and Jackson and Anthony Gibbs and Phillips. It has been published also in Germany, France, Holland, the Czech Republic, the United States and Canada.

On doing the newspaper articles, Rudolf Vrba writes: "I was pleased to see that Bestic wrote shorthand faster than I spoke. He transcribed it on his old rickety typewriter. It sounded like machine gun fire ..." On the book: "It was probably the first book on this subject in England addressed to the general public rather than to specialists."

Focus:

A young Slovak Jew survives Majdanek and Auschwitz, escaping with the news that the "unknown destination in the east" was in reality a "death factory": Auschwitz; the Vrba–Wetzler report was the first report about Birkenau to reach the West; the events described take place from March 1942 to September 1944.

Features:

Foreword:	Author's Preface, written by Rudolf Vrba, 22 September 1997, pages iii–x. Preface written by Alan Bestic, October 1963, pages 7–8.
Photographs:	Photograph of Senior Sergeant Rudolf Vrba of the Czechoslovak Army Partisan Units, 1945, front cover.
Documents:	Appendix One: Rudolf Vrba's deposition at the Adolf Eichmann Trial, 16 July 1961, pages 270–3. Appendix Two: Quotations from a report by SS Captain Kurt Gerstein on a gassing at Belzec, with introductory remarks by Rudolf Vrba, pages 274–8. Appendix Three: "The Extermination Camps of Auschwitz (Oswiecim) and Birkenau in Upper Silesia". The statement given by Rudolf Vrba and Alfred Wetzler in Zilina, Slovakia, 25 April 1944, pages 279–317.
Maps:	Martin Gilbert map of the Vrba/Wetzler escape route from Auschwitz to Slovakia, April 1944, page 392 and back cover.
Afterword:	Epilogue written by Rudolf Vrba, pages 262–9. "About the Author", pages 393–4. "The Significance of the Vrba–Wetzler Report on Auschwitz-Birkenau" article written by John S. Conway, Professor of History, University of British Columbia, Vancouver, pages 397–431.
Appendices:	Appendix Four: "Major Post-War Trials of Auschwitz SS Officers" written by Rudolf Vrba, pages 318–21. Appendix Five: "The Role of the Holocaust in German Economy and Military Strategy During 1941–1945" article written by Rudolf Vrba, pages 323–33.

Appendix Six: "The Preparations for the Holocaust in Hungary: An Eye-witness Account" article written by Rudolf Vrba, pages 335–91.

Contents: (by topic, with page numbers)

The coming of war

(21–2) The Protectorate of Slovakia follows the Nazi laws: "… the laws curtailing our rights were introduced discreetly, falling almost imperceptibly around us, like gentle snow." The Jews are removed from schools, from better jobs, moved into ghettos, forced to wear the yellow star, then, deported.

Deportation

(22) "It was only when the deportation laws were passed by the Government that I suddenly rebelled. … by State decree I became overnight a Jew, rather than a Slovak. … Young, able-bodied men would be the first to go. … It was only later, of course, that we learned the real motive was to remove the core of potential resistance."

(40–1) The Jews of Topolcany, his birthplace, prepare for deportation: "In the front garden there was furniture. Here were people about to be deported and as soon as they were gone, the authorities would auction the furniture for peppercorn prices and buy another Quisling by handing him over the house."

(45–6) Their train reaches the Slovak/Polish border: "There the Slovak Hlinka guards left us and the SS took over." Eighty people in their wagon: "They were all imprisoned mentally by unanswerable questions. How had it happened? Why had it happened? What was going to happen to them and to those they had left behind? And, of course, where were they going? Snatched from civilization, yet still attached to it by the umbilical cord of domesticity, they worried, too, about trifles. Had they turned off the gas at the mains? Had they locked the back door? Had they remembered to cancel the milk and the newspapers?"

(51–4) Thirst on the train and the difficulty of having someone at a station get them water: "Looking back, of course, I can understand his attitude. There was an order that any civilian who helped those on the transports would be shot and the SS did not hesitate to carry it out. A bullet in the back is a high price to pay for filling a tin mug."

(57–9) 16 June 1942, just past Lublin, the males aged 16 to 45 are taken from the deportation train from Novaky, and marched to Majdanek. The train, with the women, children, and older people continues on: "I did not know that they were on their way to a place called Belzec. … There they would be gassed with the fumes of exhaust pipes. There their bodies would be burned in open trenches, for crematoria were still in the blue-print stage."

(72–4) Late June 1942, transported by train from Majdanek to Auschwitz: "By the time we had been travelling twenty-four hours, all the food was gone; but that was not our main worry. All the water was gone, too, and, in the stifling heat of that packed waggon, thirst became a torment; nor was there any hope of getting a drink at a station because the security precautions were so stringent that we always stopped well outside them and had to watch the SS men drinking from their water bottles, as we were being counted. In fact the journey lasted two and a half days."

(250–1) Despite the report given to members of the Jewish Council, late April 1944, the deportation of the Hungarians begins: "'They're passing through Zilina in cattle trucks.'"

Transit camps

(34–5) June 1942, in Novaky: "I learned that Novaky was divided into two camps, one the transit section which held those awaiting transport to Poland and the other a labour camp, where the more favoured Jews were supposed to work for the good of the Slovak Government."

Slave labour camps and factories

(106–8) Sixteen hundred prisoners march out of Auschwitz for the Buna Command: "No longer was it simply a question of surviving. It was a question of surviving today without thinking too much about tomorrow."

(109–12) The work at Buna: "Someone dumped a bag of cement on my back. I ran. At the door a kapo thumped me over the kidneys with his club. I stumbled but kept on running. Ten yards farther on a deputy kapo lashed at me. Ahead of me a man went down and a club smashed his skull. I tripped over his body, somehow kept my feet, and dumped my bag by a mixing machine and a bewildering network of heavy wire that soon would be covered in concrete. Josef panted behind me and then we were running back for more cement, more abuse, more blows, in a frantic, nightmare race against a clock we could never beat."

(118) Josef and Rudi at Buna: "Perhaps because of our French protector, perhaps because we were strong and still living off the fat of the SS food store, we stood the pace better than most. In fact, by the fifth week, we were the sole survivors of the sixteen hundred which by chance we had joined on that first day after the fall of Franz."

(119) Why Krupps and I. G. Farben located factories in the Auschwitz region: "In the first place the Silesian coal mines were at their disposal. Secondly, there was plenty of water; and, finally, there was a more than adequate and exceptionally cheap labour force neatly located behind the high voltage wires of the camp."

Auschwitz-Birkenau

(9–15) 17 July 1942, Reichsführer Heinrich Himmler's visit to Auschwitz: "In fact he was far from satisfied with what he had seen, but it was not the appalling conditions which worried him. It was the grossly inefficient methods which were being used to exterminate the Jews who were beginning to arrive in their thousands from all parts of Europe. ... The burning of the bodies in open trenches wasted valuable fuel. ... And so he gave orders for the greatest, most efficient extermination factory the world has ever known. For the modern concrete gas chambers and the vast crematoria that could absorb as many as 12,000 bodies in twenty-four hours and, in fact, did so."

(15–16) January 1943, Himmler's second visit to Auschwitz: "This time I was glad to see him arrive, though not because I still nursed any faint hope that he would improve our lot through benevolence or any sense of justice. His presence was welcome to us all merely because it meant that for one day there would be no unscheduled beatings or killings."

(75–9) 30 June 1942, entrance into Auschwitz: "What were they guarding in this strange camp, with its clean concrete roads and its uplifing slogans, its dogs and its thugs and its double lethal fences? What treasure was stored here, for surely all this vast anti-escape machinery was not designed to corral a few thousand insignificant Jews? ... The security precautions, however, were for us insignificant prisoners. Himmler had ruled that nobody must escape. The world must never know of this place, his most efficient death factory."

(84–5) Upon entering Auschwitz, two prisoners: "... one, a Frenchman, known throughout the camp as Leo, the tattooist, the other a Slovak, called Eisenberg. They were cheerful fellows, who joked about the whole business, asking the cattle politely where they would like their numbers branded – on the left arm or the right, underneath or on top. There was something strangely comical, being given a choice in circumstances such as these; it was rather like asking a man which side he would like his hair parted, before his head was cut off. Anyway, for the record, I chose the top of my left forearm and bear my brand to this day." (#44070)

(86–8) Rudi is chosen by kapo Franz for a work detail: "I followed him, apprehensive of the unknown, but glad in a way for obviously he had singled me out for my health and strength. What I did not know … was that the new kapo with the slap-happy manner was in fact saving my life. Neither did I know that he had bought me from my block senior for a lemon. At that time I knew nothing of the vast black market in the camp. …"

(92–5) Work in the SS food store: "Everywhere I looked I saw food. Mountains of it. … Acres of food and luxuries at that, drawn from all parts of the world and assembled here in the hell hole of Auschwitz."

(116) Sundays: "Health-Through-Joy" day: "Our masters, it seemed, felt that we might grow soft and flabby, lazing around in the sun. … it attracted a substantial audience even from the upper echelons of the SS, who stood around, smiling tolerantly while the sick and the starving, the weak and the dying presented their grotesque pantomime in honour of physical culture."

(120–4) Rudi and Josef survive the 29 August 1942 run which tested for spotted typhus: "Never in my life have I felt less like running. I had been up for twenty-four hours and slaving at Buna for eight of them. For another four hours I had been either marching or almost suffocating in an overcrowded cattle truck; and I had eaten nothing since soup had been dished out in Buna at noon. … We had not been able to run properly because we were starved and exhausted; but Jacob Fries had diagnosed spotted typhus. With a flick of his thumb he had sentenced us both to death and thousands of others, too." But a kapo, Josef's friend, moves the two to the other group. To combat the spotted typhus epidemic, "… half the camp's population had been murdered."

(124–8) Assigned to "Canada": "From what they did not say, I realised that soon I was to learn yet another of Auschwitz's secrets and I had an uneasy feeling that somehow the knowledge was going to be dangerous. … we marched into Canada, the commercial heart of Auschwitz, warehouse of the body snatchers where hundreds of prisoners worked frantically to sort, segregate and classify the clothes and the food and the valuables of those whose bodies were still burning, whose ashes would soon be used as fertiliser."

(129–32) The Canada work routine: "We dumped out trunks and cases and rucksacks on a huge blanket in the store. Immediately they were ripped open or burst open with a sledgehammer and food, clothes, toilet equipment, valuables, documents, pathetic family pictures were emptied out. Specialists fell upon them segregating them, pitching men's clothes to one blanket, women's to another, children's to a third until half a dozen blankets were piled high. The suitcases and trunks were whisked away and burned with all documents. More porters descended on the blankets and carried them away to the women who would classify them by quality and pack them away in the warehouses; and all the time … Graff and Koenig were beating, searching, punishing and bellowing. …"

(132–3) "One week in Canada taught me more about the real purpose of Auschwitz. … It was a sickening lesson, not so much because of the sadism or the brutality or the sporadic deaths, but because of the cold-blooded commercialism of the place. … I was in a death factory; an extermination centre where thousands upon thousands of men, women and children were gassed and burned, not so much because they were Jewish, though that was the primary thought in the sick mind of the Führer, but because in death they made a contribution to Germany's war effort."

(145) Surviving a selection at the hospital, Auschwitz: "I tried to make myself as inconspicuous as possible, not too erect, yet not slouching; not too smart, yet not sloppy; not too proud, yet not too servile, for I knew that those who are different died in Auschwitz, while the anonymous, the faceless ones, survived."

(147–8) Fall 1942, Rudi works the next eight months on the ramp, helps to unload three hundred transports: "The ramp, symbol of Auschwitz for millions because they saw little else except the gas chambers. A huge, bare platform that lay between Birkenau and the mother camp and to which transports rolled from all parts of Europe, bringing Jews who still believed in labour camps. Scene of the infamous selections, where a handful of workers were sent to the right and the rest, the old, the very young, the unfit, were sent to the left, to the lorries, to the crematoria, still believing that somewhere ahead lay a resettlement area."

(177–9) Three criminal Block Seniors at Birkenau: "… a man called Albert Hammerle, but known throughout the camp as Ivan, the Terrible. … 'Monkey' Tyn … a man with the strength and physique of a gorilla; Mietek Katerzynski … would while away their time, seeing who would be the first man to kill a prisoner with one blow of his fist."

(180–2, 184) 7 September 1943, the arrival to Birkenau Camp B of 4,000 deportees from Theresienstadt: "… men, women and children, dressed in ordinary civilian clothes, their heads unshaven, their faces bewildered, but plump and unravaged. The grown-ups carried their luggage, the children their dolls and their teddy bears; and the men of Camp A, the Zebra men who were only numbers, simply stood and stared, wondering who had tilted the world, spilling a segment of it on top of them." In December 1943 they are joined by 4,000 more.

(197–8) 1944, "in January, new railway tracks began edging their way up the broad road that lay between Birkenau 1 and Birkenau 2. … The ramp, it seemed, was to become obsolete. … Here there would be no selections, no weeding out of the young and fit; just a direct line to death." Rudi learns from Philip Müller: "The old trenches, where the bodies were burned before the crematoria were built, were being made ready for action again. New trenches were being dug." The intended victims: "It was the Hungarians whom most of us had thought were reasonably safe."

(199–201) At the July 1942 hanging in Auschwitz of two captured Polish escapees, Oberscharführer Jakob Fries announces: "… 'under their tunics they were found to be wearing civilian shirts. … Any man found planning an escape will be punished by death on the gallows as these two prisoners are about to be punished now.'"

Concentration camps

(60–1) Marched into Majdanek: "The theory of concentration camps was not new to me. For years sinister whispers had been seeping through Czechoslovakia, through Europe, indeed; rumours of ugly, self-contained worlds, where the rule of gun and club and whip prevailed; where the majority died from beating or hunger or shooting; where the emaciated survivors for a day or a week or a month gazed hopelessly at a horizon of barbed wire, while flamingo-legged watch towers hovered over them. Yet the reality, the first sight of a camp in action, shocked me, even though my mind was prepared for it."

(63–4) First impressions of Majdanek: "There were barracks all around me, squalid, wooden affairs. Barracks, barbed wire and beyond that, nothing. … It was depressing, but not nearly so depressing as the sound effects. From the other sections we could hear cries and the sound of beating and occasionally a shot. We could catch glimpses of prisoners scurrying about frantically, one jump ahead of a stick or a bullet. ..."

(69–70) At Majdanek, Rudi volunteers for "farm work": "I was one of the first of about a thousand who volunteered; and I was one of the lucky four hundred chosen. ... Nobody who stayed in Majdanek survived. In fact, from those who went from Majdanek to Auschwitz, I am the only one still alive."

(71–2) Twelve days after his arrival in Majdanek, the 400 are marched out: "I was elated; and I was sad. Somewhere in that sprawling, soulless camp that grew smaller behind me as I marched, was my brother, Sammy. In my heart I knew he could never survive."

Witness to mass murder

(16–19) January 1943, Himmler witnesses a gassing at Auschwitz: "Commandant Hoess, anxious to display his new toy at its most efficient, had arranged for a special transport of 3,000 Polish Jews to be present for slaughter in the modern German way. ... For some minutes Himmler peered into the death chamber, obviously impressed ... and, when everyone inside was dead, he took a keen interest in the procedure that followed. ... Himmler waited until the smoke began to thicken over the chimneys and then he glanced at his watch. It was one o'clock. Lunch time, in fact."

(65–6) Roll call, Majdanek: "Not only were the living counted, but the dead, too. They were piled up neatly behind us, a pathetic heap of corpses, some scraggy with starvation, some blood-stained from beating and some who had died simply because they no longer had the will to live. ... Starvation was a major killer. German scientists reckoned that the rations were sufficient to keep a man alive for three months, but for once they were inaccurate. Beatings and shootings ensured that the death rate remained high, and so did dysentery. It affected many of the newcomers and they were liquidated immediately because they could not work."

(67–8) At Majdanek: "I had noticed that people disappeared from our section, but presumed at first they had been transferred elsewhere. I had watched the daily caravan from the hospital, a pathetic column of the sick and the old and the dying, making their stumbling way to a building some distance away; a building with a tall chimney. Some were able to walk; some had to be helped by those a little stronger; some went in wheelbarrows. I had noticed that they never came back. ... I learned the truth only when I overheard a kapo give a casual order to a prisoner. He said: 'Take those bricks over to the crematorium.' ... Then I knew why those fragments of humanity from the hospital never came back."

(70–1) Rudi quotes SS Erich Mussfeldt's description of the liquidation of Majdanek, the "Harvest Festival", which he witnessed: "'The camp ended on November 3, 1943. ... That day 17,000 people of both sexes were executed at Majdanek. Only three hundred women were left to sort and dispatch the camp property; and three hundred men from Special Detachment 1005 to take the bodies from the graves and burn them. One SS man told me that the Jews from this detachment tried to escape and, as a result, the survivors had to work with chains on their legs.'"

(76) SS Oberscharführer Jacob Fries: "... one of the most brutal men ever spawned by Auschwitz, mother of so many murderers. For me, Fries was Auschwitz and always will be." His post-war Sachsenhausen and Auschwitz war crimes trials sentences are cited.

(79, 141, 146) "Those who could not work, I was soon to learn, were killed, either in the gas chamber or by an injection of phenol in the heart, an operation performed by a member of the SS 'Sanitary Service', Josef Klehr." Auschwitz, early July 1942.

(80–3) The first day at Auschwitz, Rudi watches a cart being filled with corpses: "We newcomers, we to whom work was going to bring freedom, stared at the cart, hypnotised by what we had seen. Two hundred bodies were packed together and the whole operation had taken no more than fifteen minutes. … standing there in our civilian clothes, we felt completely divorced from the scene. This is something which happened to others, to men who came from some other world. We were not hunks of meat. We were people. Our minds were on the run, scattering before a truth which had yet to catch up with us."

(89–90) Kapo Franz saves Rudi from "agricultural work", Auschwitz: "There were 107,000 bodies buried near the camp, including 20,000 Russian prisoners of war who had been murdered. This evidence of mass murder had to be removed, not merely to cover up the crime, but because it was a danger to health; and therefore a special labour force of 1,400 men had been collected to get rid of it. … Of the 1,400, only three hundred were alive when the last body was burned; and these, too, were executed."

(91) "These were the living dead, known for some strange reason as 'Muselmanns', Moslems, the men whose eyes were empty, whose flesh had fled, whose blood was near to water. Off they straggled … for they knew the alternative was hospitalization which meant a dose of phenol in the heart and death." Auschwitz.

(113–15) Returning to Auschwitz after the day at Buna: "… in each group of a hundred, dragging its way along that fine concrete road, there were at least ten limp, lifeless forms. … the journey back to Auschwitz began, with the dead and the dying held upright against the sides of the waggon by the weight of those who had survived another day in Buna. … Up to Block 18, where we stacked our dead neatly. The block registrar was waiting with his notebook to check them. Wearily … he lifted arm after arm, glanced at the number by the light of a match, crossed it off his list and moved on to the next pile. …"

(117–18, 175, 195–7) Philip Müller "cleans up" after Unterscharführer Palitsch's murders in the punishment block: "'No matter what way it's done, my job is always the same: to get rid of the body and clean the blood off the floor before the next customer arrives.'" His job in Birkenau: "Philip stoked the furnaces in the crematorium. By the amount of fuel made available, he could reckon how many bodies were to be burned because the SS never wasted fuel by overloading their fires." He witnesses the deaths of the Czech Family Camp, 7 March 1944.

(150) A transport of French Jews glimpse their fate at the Auschwitz ramp as a truck overloaded with dead comes into view: "… simultaneously from those 3,000 men, women and children, rose a thin, hopeless wail that swept from one end of the orderly queue to the other, an almost inhuman cry of despair that neither threats, nor blows, nor bullets could silence … the lorry cleared the tracks, disappearing out of the arc lights, into the darkness; and then there was silence, absolute and all-embracing. For three seconds, four at the most, those French people had glimpsed the true horror of Auschwitz; but now it was gone and they could not believe what their eyes had told them. Already their minds, untrained to mass murder, had rejected the existence of that lorry; and with that they marched quietly towards the gas chambers which claimed them half an hour later."

(151–3) January 1943, transport of Dutch Jewish mental patients and their nurses: "The SS men were frantic for here was something they could not understand. Something that knew no order, no discipline, no obedience, no fear of violence or death … and everywhere the nurses. Still working. … They fought to bring order out of chaos, using medicines and blankets, gentleness and quiet heroism instead of guns or sticks or snarling dogs. … In unemotional groups they stood around the lorries, waiting for permission to join their patients. … The nurses climbed up after their patients. The lorry engines roared and off they swayed to the gas chambers."

(163–6) A December day in Birkenau, 1942: "… I saw at least ten thousand naked women, lined up in neat, silent rows. … 'It's a typhus inspection. If they don't die of exposure, half of them will die in the gas chambers!' … The air, despite the frost, was slightly warm. … Stretching all around us were ditches vast enough to hold a row of houses, the ditches that spawned that red glow I could see in the sky from the mother camp; great, gaping sores in the forest, not blazing now, but still smouldering. I moved to the edge of one and gazed in. The heat struck my face and at the bottom of this great open oven I could see bones; small bones. The bones of children."

(167–8) 1942, pre-Christmas typhus selection: "… we had to strip in the fierce cold, plunge into hot showers, then dash out into the open air again. As a result, many of those who survived the typhus test contracted pneumonia and died anyway. For two days we were left naked and without food, an ordeal which weeded out a few more."

(173–4) Fred Wetzler, registrar of the mortuary at Birkenau: "One man glanced at an arm and called the tattooed number out to Fred who jotted it down. Another opened the dead mouth with a pair of pliers, hauled out a few gold teeth and dumped them with a clank into a tin can beside him. The remaining two picked up the corpse and sent it whirling through the door towards the lorry."

(175) At Birkenau: "… I was able to see what until then I had only imagined. … Every night I unloaded the waggons and watched the human cargoes line up for selection. … Often I arrived back in camp in time to see them being herded towards the innocent grey building with its mock washrooms, all but a few still believing that they were travelling another section of the road that would bring them to a new life. Here the statistics I had been gathering so carefully, the numbers I held in my head, suddenly became men, women and children, the living, only inches away from death."

(195–6) The destruction of the Czech Family Camp at Birkenau, 7 March 1944: "Philip Müller had been working all night. … 'They sang the Czech and Jewish National Anthems all the time and they just walked straight into the chambers.' 'No resistance?' 'We were waiting for it, but it never came. Had they started a fight we would have joined them. I suppose they were thinking of the children.'"

(248–9) April 1944, Rudi and Fred reach Zilina: "The following day, April 25th, Fred and I were sipping sherry at the Zilina headquarters of the Jewish Council and telling our story to Doctor Oscar Neumann, spokesman for all Slovakia's Jews, Oscar Krasnansky, Erwin Steiner, and a man called Hexner. … For hours I dictated my testimony. I gave them detailed statistics of the deaths. I described every step of the awful confidence trick by which 1,760,000 in my time in the camp alone had been lured to the gas chambers. I explained the machinery of the extermination factory and its commercial side, the vast profits that were reaped from the robbery of gold, jewellery, money, clothes, artificial limbs, spectacles, prams, and human hair which was used to caulk torpedo heads. I told them how even the ashes were used as fertiliser."

(256) Rudi meets with the Papal Nuncio in Slovakia in Svaty Jur near Bratislava: "… I saw that he had a copy of my report in his hand. … He went through the report line by line, page by page, returning time after time to various points until he was satisfied that I was neither lying nor exaggerating; and, by the time we had finished dissecting the horrors about which I had written, he was weeping. 'Mr Vrba,' he said at last, 'I shall carry your report to the

International Red Cross in Geneva. They will take action and see that it reaches the proper hands.'"

Resistance, ghetto revolts, individual acts of courage and defiance

(23–8) Early March 1942, Rudi leaves home to escape to England, gets as far as Budapest, but without the ability to get false documents, he is told to return home and wait for the documents to be brought to him: "I realized then that I was dealing with men who were not only patient but courageous, too."

(54–5) Coded messages sent to relatives: "In some were references to people who were dead or to events which could not possibly have happened; and it was these little nonsenses that made people worry and wonder. ... The letters were written in Auschwitz at pistol point shortly before the writers died. They were written in order to inspire confidence among those yet to be transported, for the Nazis knew that the slightest resistance, created by fear of what lay ahead, could ruin the whole scheme. Sometimes, however, someone managed to slip in a concealed warning by stating the impossible, a tiny act of defiance that took courage; and the tragedy was that those who received these carefully phrased letters invariably managed to explain away discrepancies ... perhaps because they wanted to believe in the resettlement areas."

(99) Rudi recognizes his 17-year-old cousin Eva from Topolcany at Auschwitz and calls out to her: "Her head turned and she gazed, puzzled, unbelieving at me. I saw her frown and then I saw her eyes flood with recognition and life flow into her taut, thin face. 'Rudi!' A whip rose and fell but Eva did not falter. I raised my hand and she raised hers in a gesture of splendid defiance; and, as she passed only ten yards away from me, she shouted once more. 'Good-bye, Rudi. Good-bye.' Again the whip, but it might as well have been a fly swat, for this was no ordinary girl. Her voice was not strong but it sang with courage. Here was no whine, no plea for pity. Here was the spirit of resistance, still smouldering on the edge of death."

(116) Sundays in Auschwitz: "Religious services of all kinds were forbidden. Those found celebrating them were put to death; yet, in spite of this, many brave priests, mostly Poles, held secret Masses for their faithful, and never lacked a congregation."

(142–4) In the Auschwitz hospital, among the patients: "... peaks of courage and islands of incredible dignity in this hell of sickness." And among the doctors: "... I remember feeling, not merely gratitude, but admiration for them, for even among the degradations of Auschwitz, most of them managed to retain their humanity and their professional integrity." Among those facing selection: "Some sagged, certain already that they were going to die; yet again I could sense their spirit, their dignity, their courage."

(161) While Josef Farber cures Rudi's typhus, Rudi learns: "Here in Auschwitz was an underground, a network, a striking force that had even the deputy kapos on its rolls!"

(168–70) Fifteen members of "Canada" command are sent to the punishment block under suspicion of stealing valuables, among them are members of the underground: "The leaders of the underground were fully aware of the danger and took swift evasive action. They smuggled poison into Block Eleven and within a few hours the men in Block Eleven were dead. Rather than risk revealing the names of their comrades, they had committed suicide."

(170–2, 181) Transferred with the "Canada" command to Birkenau, Rudi meets Resistance leaders: Doctor Andreas Milar: "A man who could have evaded Auschwitz, had he kept his wallet open and his mouth shut"; deputy Block Senior of Block 27 David Szmulewski: "Yet still he was only thirty, tall, dark haired, strong and remarkably unscarred for a man who had been at war all his life"; and Fred Wetzler: "He was from my home town Trnava; and, though I had never spoken to him, for he was six years older than I was, I had always admired him. …"

(175–6) Lubomir Bastar from Brno helps Rudi rise in the Resistance ranks: "… soon I found I was being invited to Lubomir's private room, where the cream of the camp's Czech intellectuals gathered sometimes for supper. … These men could have had almost anything they liked, for the traffic in food was brisk. It was clear to me, however, that it would go against their grain to feast while others starved outside."

(176–7) The June 1943 typhus selection causes some reorganization at Birkenau; Rudi becomes an assistant registrar: "It was essential for the underground … to have someone in the new camp who could act as a go-between; and, as Registrar, I would have to move from one camp to the other as part of my regular duties."

(184–7) The organization of Resistance among the Czech Family Camp in anticipation of its destruction planned for 7 March 1944: "… slowly I realized that only by fighting had any of them a chance to survive; then it would depend on how much support they got from other prisoners. How strong was the underground? And how willing? … Would these hardened prisoners, who had seen a million die in their time, risk everything for the sake of 4,000 Czechs?"

(189–93) Szmulewski gives Rudi the orders to pass on to the Czech Family Camp Resistance: "'Tell them we'll fight, if they fight, but that they must start it and start it well. Then call in Fredy and him the role he must play.'" Fredy Hirsch had been chosen to lead the Czechs to resist. He commits suicide.

(258–60) Rabbi Michael Dov Weissmandel whom Rudi meets in Bratislava: "I had heard strange, romantic stories … how, single handed and under the noses of the Nazis, he had saved hundreds of Jews from deportation; how he was … a rare symbol of resistance."

Partisan activity

(260–1) June 1944: "I went to members of the underground … 'My friends, I need a pistol. Some day a bright SS man is going to see through my false papers; and, when that happens, I don't want the argument to be one sided.' To my amazement and fury, they said sternly: 'We don't issue pistols to lads like you.' They grinned and added: 'We issue sub-machine guns!'" Rudi fights with the partisans under Sergeant Milan Uher in a successful attack on the SS in Stara Tura.

Specific escapes

(28–33) Caught returning home from Budapest, he is beaten by the Hungarian border guards as a spy, then arrested by the Slovak border guards as a Jew: "I told them the truth. The guard who had picked me out of the mud frowned and said: 'So you don't want to go to a resettlement area. You don't want to work. You dirty, bloody, Yid, I should beat you so your mother wouldn't recognise you. But that's been done already!'"

(36–9) Spring 1942, he prepares for and escapes from Novaky with his friend Josef Knapp: "There was no sign of the patrolling guard. Knapp and I went under the wire and three minutes later were sliding down the high banks of a stream that trickled down from the nearby forests."

(41–4) In Topolcany he is questioned by a gendarme who had noticed him wearing an extra pair of socks: "I stared at him, unable to speak. To me at that moment, he was not just a gendarme in a country town. He was the Hungarian frontier guards with their rifle butts. He was Novaky in all its dismal squallor. He was a train that had come from God knows where and was going to God knows where." Rudi is arrested and returned to Novaky.

(164) In the back of his mind, he thinks about escaping from Auschwitz: "While on the ramp, I had kept a careful mental note of each transport that arrived and the numbers on board in the hope that sooner or later I would be able to tell the free world about these terrible figures. … With the aid of a school atlas I had found … in 'Canada', I had been able to pinpoint our geographic position fairly exactly. I knew the layout of the mother camp and the strength of its defences; and I was determined to find out whether Birkenau was fortified equally strongly." Fall 1942.

(202) As registrar in Birkenau, Rudi plans an escape: "… I began what was to be my first scientific study: the technique of escape. I began to study every unsuccessful escape attempt, to analyse its flaws and to correct them."

(203–5) Captain Dmitri Volkov, captured as a Russian prisoner of war, escaped from Sachsenhausen near Berlin, recaptured near Kiev, gives Rudi advice in Auschwitz; "He filled in my manual of What Every Escaper Should Know."

(206–8) "… if there ever was a man who seemed indestructible, it was Fero Langer." Yet his planned escape from Auschwitz fails: "It was, it seemed, a simple case of betrayal." His friend and confidant SS Dobrovolny had revealed the plan.

(209–15) Charles Unglick's foiled attempt to escape from Auschwitz: "… we watched the men who normally dragged naked bodies through the mud carry away Charles Unglick with something very like reverence."

(216–18) Different possibilities for escape are cut off, yet: "… I believed that I would escape and I cannot remember ever relinquishing that faith, not even when I saw attempt after attempt end in failure and humiliating death."

(219–20) SS Unterscharführer Pestek offers to smuggle Fred Wetzler or Rudi out; he succeeds in smuggling Lederer to Prague. He returns to smuggle out one of the girls in the Czech camp: "It was a crazy idea, doomed to failure, for by that time he was a wanted man."

(221–4) Slovak friend Sandor Eisenbach and three others try to escape after hiding in the woodpile. Two French Jews also try to escape, they are captured and hung. The four others are captured but do not reveal the woodpile hiding place.

(225–8) Rudi and Fred Wetzler have a perilous journey to escape to the woodpile: "… we had organized two Poles who would replace the planks over our heads as soon as we slid into the hole."

(229–34) "The search was on. The long, meticulous, painstaking search that would continue for three days until every inch of Birkenau had been examined, every known hiding place upended." Their three days hiding in the woodpile ended 10 April 1944.

(234–8) The first 24 hours after leaving their woodpile hideout: "… we wriggled along on our bellies, making use of every hollow, every dip, every ditch we could find." The first five days of their journey: "Though Volkov's advice was useful constantly, he had never managed, however, to teach me how to see in the dark. …"

(241–2) The two escape a German patrol and cross a stream: "Twice I fell and submerged; but at last we made it, hauled ourselves up the bank and lumbered on, gasping for breath, through snow that sometimes reached our waists. We reached the friendly shelter of the trees before the Germans had breasted the hill and now the advantage was with us."

In hiding, including Hidden Children

(252–4) Playing the part of students, Fred and Rudi are sent to Liptovsky Svaty Mikulas to hide out from arrest, May 1944: "We were in fact apprentices in the art of living because for so long we had thought only of survival. We did not fit smoothly and suavely into the world at first, not even into the little world of the train that brought us to our new home."

(255–6) Rudi returns in 1944 to Trnava to see his mother: "'You're a dreadful boy' she said at last. 'You know you never wrote to me once. You never even sent me your address.' 'I'm sorry, Momma,' I said. 'It was a bit difficult. You see we were … very busy all the time.'"

Righteous Gentiles

(33) March 1942, Rudi is arrested crossing into Slovakia from Hungary, and is jailed: "Through the bars fell some cigarettes and some food. News that a Jew had been picked up somewhere along the frontier, it seems, had travelled fast through that Slovak village; and somewhere a Christian woman had thought of him lying alone and maybe hungry."

(87–91) Viennese political prisoner Kapo Franz, Auschwitz: "To the passing SS men he looked and sounded a splendid kapo, heartless, brutal, efficient; yet never once did he hit us. In fact, all the time I knew him, I never saw him strike a prisoner and that in Auschwitz was quite a record."

(98) Rudi avoids the spotted typhus epidemic: "Once again I owed my life to Franz, for, had he not selected me for the food store, I would have been as dirty as the rest of them. Instead I was able to keep myself scrupulously clean because in the store there was plenty of soap and water to ensure that hands which touched the SS food were thoroughly sterlised."

(100–5) Kapo Franz steals a box of marmalade to feed a group of starving girls, Auschwitz: "I saw him walk calmly towards the wire, turn and, with a backward flip of the wrist, send the marmalade flying towards a group of Slovak girls. It shattered at their feet. For a second they gazed at it in amazement, this gold that fell from heaven; and then they fell on their knees and ate it. That marmalade disappeared in less than a quarter of a minute." Franz survives his punishment, and: "He survived the camp and today in his native Vienna, where he owns a hotel, he is known still as Franz Marmalade."

(219–21) Unterscharführer Pestek smuggles Lederer out of Auschwitz; returns to smuggle again and is caught: "… the only honourable SS man I ever met … a man who had not been brainwashed, who saw the vileness that lay beneath those smart, green uniforms and had the courage to strike against it."

(239–41) In the village of Pisarowice, a Polish woman and her daughter give Rudi and Fred food, shelter, and advice: "'The mountains are quite far from here,' she said. 'To reach them you must cross open country which is watched constantly by the Germans because there are partisans in the area. If you attempt to cross those open spaces by day, you will be caught; you must stay here until it is dark.'"

(242–5) Another Polish woman, her grandson, and a partisan sympathizer help them and get them to the border: "Shoving the gun into his pocket, he said: 'You're from a concentration camp, all right. Only really hungry men could eat like that.'"

(246–7) Near Skalite, they meet the Slovak Canecky: "He looked us up and down and grinned. Then he said: 'You'd better come to my place first because you're not going to get far in those clothes.'" He takes them to the town of Cadca, to meet the Jewish leader Doctor Pollak, and he gives them money: "'Poverty's no disgrace I know, but it can be uncomfortable!'"

(256–7) Rudi meets with the Papal Nuncio in Slovakia: "The Papal Nuncio took my report to Geneva. From there it went to Pope Pius XII, to Prime Minister Winston Churchill and to President Roosevelt."

(257–8) "On June 25th 1944, exactly two calendar months after I had dictated my report in Zilina, Monsignor Angelo Rotta, Papal Nuncio in Hungary, handed a letter from Pope Pius to Admiral Horthy, the Regent. … it was undoubtably a protest against the deportation of Hungarian Jews. … The Pope's letter was followed the following day by a note from Mr Cordell Hull, the US Secretary of State, who threatened reprisals against those responsible for the deportations. The King of Sweden offered to help the Hungarian Jews to emigrate; and on July 5th, Professor Karl Burckhardt, President of the International Red Cross, made a personal appeal to Horthy. … On July 7th, Mr Anthony Eden, Britain's Foreign Secretary announced in the House of Commons … By that time, too, the Swiss Government had raised its censorship of the subject in its newspapers; and the world knew at last about Auschwitz."

Stories of individuals, including family members

(9, 12) "Yankel Meisel died because three buttons were missing from his striped, prisoner's tunic. It was probably the first and certainly the last time he had ever been untidy in his life. … His Block Senior spotted the gaping neck of his tunic. Quickly he was clubbed to death and swept, so to speak, beneath the carpet only minutes before the master arrived to inspect the household." Heinrich Himmler's 17 July 1942 visit to Auschwitz.

(20, 22, 255) "My mother was a strong-minded, self-reliant woman, who had built up a small dress-making business from more or less nothing." In March 1942 she says goodbye to her seventeen-year-old son: "Her face showed little emotion and all she said was: 'Take care of yourself. And don't forget to change your socks.'"

(44) Rudi is arrested in Topolcany to be returned to Novaky: "… just as we were about to enter the station, a little, blonde-haired girl darted forward and thrust a parcel into my hands, tears streaming down her face. It was my little cousin, Lici, then only about thirteen. Years later I learned that someone had told her that her Cousin Rudi was being taken away by the police. She dashed into a shop with her few pennies and bought me all that she could afford – cherries."

(45, 205) Fero Langer, who spends four days in a cell with Rudi in Novaky: "He had been conscripted into the Jewish forced labour detachments of the Slovak Army and had used his uniform to bluff his way into Novaky to help a relative who was being transported. 'Trouble was,' he said with his huge grin, 'they posted me as a deserter.'" He is reunited with Rudi in Birkenau in January 1943.

(47–8, 57) The Tomasovs, from his hometown, find Rudi on the deportation train, announce they are newlywed. A party is created: "The Tomasovs, indeed, softened the shell which people had built around themselves for protection; and, after the wedding party, a new, rough courtesy developed, in spite of the fact that we were living under conditions liable to … set neighbour against neighbour."

(49–50) Companions on the deportation train tell of their betrayal: Isaac Rabinowic from Bratislava, Mrs Polanska from a village in central Slovakia, Janko Sokol, and Mr Ringwald from Zvolen: "We listened to these tales with interest. We did not know that they were going to be repeated a million times all over Europe."

(55–6) Izak Moskovic, on the train, foresees future: "'You're fools, if you think you're going to resettlement areas. We are all going to die!' … Soon, in fact, he was forgotten, though later his words were remembered."

(61–2) Kapo Vrbicky in Majdanek: "I knew him well back home. So did everyone in Trnava, for Vrbicky was a character, a man who some liked, some despised and some avoided. … He was about twenty-six, a lorry driver with a somewhat haphazard approach to life. … The respectable Jewish community disliked him because he drank too much and was careless about his wedding vows. The less orthodox – myself among them – could not help liking him. … And now suddenly I saw him wielding a whip with all the savage skill of an SS man."

(62–3) Just at the gate to section five in Majdanek: "… there I saw Erwin Eisler. The long-faced Erwin, whose burly, slow-moving frame held the heart of a keen, if ponderous student. My mind went back to Trnava, to the days when Erwin used to blush when we teased him about girls and always made excuses when we asked him to come for a drink in a cafe." Together they had shared a chemistry book after being forced to turn in all their educational materials; at Majdanek, Erwin tries to warn Rudi to "expect the worst. … I never saw Erwin again and it is certain that he died in Majdanek."

(64) Friend Ignatz Geyer from Trnava, nicknamed "Nazi", enters Majdanek with Rudi, tries to find humour in their situation: "He, too, was sure that he was going to die and, indeed, he was right, for they killed him soon afterwards; but he was determined to die with dignity. He was not going to let them degrade him."

(66–7) Rudi finds his brother Sammy in Majdanek, they arrange to meet: "… although it was nearly dusk, I recognized my brother, the tall, dark Sammy, who was ten years older than I was. He saw me almost simultaneously and we raised our arms in a brief salute." Kapos break up the meeting before it happens. "Next day I was told that Sammy had been moved to another section and I never saw him again. I learned, however, that he had managed to survive as long as Majdanek survived; but when Majdanek died, everyone in it, Sammy included, died with it."

(68–70) Czech Kapo Milan offers Rudi a kitchen job, Majdanek: "He had been a member of the Sokol movement, a quasi-military organization which had been violently anti-Nazi, and had been arrested in 1939. Since then he had seen the inside of Dachau and Sachsenhausen before being sent to Majdanek as a kapo; and though he wanted to keep his soft job, there was still a bright spark of patriotism burning within him."

(73, 89, 96–7, 154–8) On the transport with Rudi from Majdanek to Auschwitz: "Suddenly I spotted a familiar face – Josef Erdelyi who had been with me in Novaky. Not only had we been friends there … I had been to school with his girlfriend." Josef keeps his family photos: "How had they survived when they stripped him, entering Majdanek and again when he left and a third time when he arrived in Auschwitz? What happened to those pathetic pictures when they pummelled him in and out of the showers in both camps?" His death, on his way to Dr Klehr's phenol shot with other typhus patients: "'He fought the kapos and made a break for the wires. They shot him just as he got there.'"

(79, 89, 115, 117–18) Ipi Müller: "… an elderly man who had travelled in the waggon with me from Majdanek. At least to me he seemed elderly, but he could not have been more than forty-five. … I remembered thinking what a fine man Ipi was, a poor Slovak tailor, who paid for his son's violin lessons and, even in that filthy waggon, thought only of him, rather than of himself." His death: "He died in his bunk and I was glad that a man of his calibre was not despatched by beating or shooting or any of the routine degradations of Auschwitz."

(82–3) Otto Pressburger and Ariel Engel in Auschwitz: "'We came in a batch of six hundred from Trnava. … There are only ten of us left.' … Just four months earlier, big, burly Otto, with the dark eyes and the moon face, and I, had been to a dance together, competing with each other for the local girls. Now the flesh had melted from that moon face, making it seem much longer and his massive frame was thin. The change in Ariel Engel, however, was even more frightening. ... The eyes that once had laughed and danced to his own music looked back at me and I saw they were dull with the shadow of death."

(117–18) Ipi and Philip Müller: "... the tough, grey-haired sensitive tailor and the artistic son who was thin, but still vibrant with life ... sweeping away the present, delving into the past, planning a future which Philip knew his father would never see." Philip cleans up after the dead, lies to his father about playing in the orchestra: "'But I'd like him to die, thinking I'm up there on that bloody platform by the gate, playing first fiddle.'"

(124–5, 131, 158–60) Fellow Slovak Laco Fischer, a dentist from Nove Mesto, gets Josef and Rudi work in "Canada": "... when he told us he had been five months in Auschwitz, we looked at him with respect, for here was a man who knew how to survive ..." Laco smuggles Rudi into "Canada" for three days to recuperate from typhus, then gets medication for him.

(134–41, 157, 159) The courtship of kapos Bruno and Hermione in "Canada", and its consequences for Rudi.

(142–4, 146) Rudi's bunk-mates in the Auschwitz hospital, Monek from Mlawa and his young friend who dies: "'Would you mind if we left him in the bunk until the gong sounds? Would you mind ... if we didn't kick him out, like the others?'"

(149) The fate of a young Czech boy working on the ramp at Auschwitz, who tries to warn a woman on a Prague transport of her destination: "He had been taken behind the waggons by two SS men and shot with an air pistol that made no noise and disturbed nobody, except, of course, the prisoner."

(156, 161, 168–70) Ernst Burger: "... the quiet, gentlemanly Registrar of Block 4." "'He's one of us.'" In fact, he was the leader of the underground.

(161–2) Josef Farber, Slovak fighter with the International Brigade in Spain, and with the Auschwitz underground. He gives Rudi injections to combat his typhus, and oversees his recovery.

(182, 190, 192) Fredy Hirsch, in charge of the children's dormitory for the Czech Family Camp at Birkenau, September 1943. Chosen to lead the Resistance, March 1944, he commits suicide: "I looked down at Fredy Hirsch, the German whose heart was too big, who could not bear to see little children suffer; and I realized that I had asked him to do too much."

(183, 187–8, 194–5) From the Czech Family Camp, 22-year-old Alice Munk meets Rudi from across the wire at Birkenau: "We talked of the future, as if there surely was going to be one and all the time I kept my eyes averted from the chimney stack which knew only hearts that were still."

(184, 186–7, 193–6) Helena and Vera Rezek, two sisters from Prague, friends with Alice: "All three were members of the family camp underground ..." Their deaths reported by Philip Müller: "'Three girls made a fight of it and had to be beaten in.' ... I wondered who they might have been; but I asked Philip no more questions."

(209, 214–15) French Army Captain, Charles Unglick, Block Senior in the Quarantine Camp at Auschwitz: "Charles Unglick made a terrible enemy, but a fine friend." He is betrayed attempting escape, and is shot.

Post-war life and career

(270–3) Presented a deposition at the Israeli Embassy, London, for submission at the trial of Adolf Eichmann, 16 July 1961, included as Appendix One.

(323–91) Published two major historical papers based on his experiences, included as Appendices Five and Six.

(393) Professor of Pharmacology, University of British Columbia, Vancouver, has authored more than 50 scientific research papers.

(394) He has been involved with the production of four Holocaust-related films: "(1) 'Genocide' (in the 'World at War' series; directed by Jeremy Isaacs, BBC, London, 1973); (2) 'Auschwitz and the Allies' (directed by Rex Bloomstein, in collaboration with Martin Gilbert; BBC, London, 1982); (3) 'Shoah' (directed by Claude Lanzmann, Paris, 1985); (4) 'Witness to Auschwitz' (directed by Robert Taylor, CBC, Toronto, 1990)"; and has been involved with the bringing to justice of Nazi war criminals and sympathizers.

Personal reflections

(Author's Preface, ix) "I thought I should concentrate upon choosing from my recollection those pieces which in their totality would enable even my honest old milkman to understand the principles used by the Germans to make the unthinkable and unspeakable machinery of Auschwitz a reality."

(77) Auschwitz: "Everywhere I saw neatness and order and strength, the iron fist beneath the antiseptic rubber glove."

(109) "In Buna there were only two types of workers – the quick and the dead."

(133) Auschwitz: "… life in Canada, indeed, was similar in many ways to life in other places. It was not so important what you were, but who you knew."

(171) "… no man in Auschwitz ever thought in terms of living. He thought merely of living a little longer."

(201) At a hanging after the first week, Auschwitz: "I remember thinking: 'When I get out and tell people about this, they probably won't believe me!'"

(254) Within weeks of their escape: "Inevitably, perhaps, there were times when we wondered whether we would ever be happy again or whether Auschwitz, scene of so much death, was immortal and would live in our minds until we, too, died and then live on to haunt those who understood."

(261) "… ever since my childhood … when I was being taught to understand the Scriptures. I remember reading: 'It is evil to assent actively or passively to evil, as its instrument, as its observer or as its victim. …'"

Places mentioned – in Europe: (page first mentioned)

Auschwitz Main Camp/Auschwitz I (9), Austrian Tyrol (16), Batizovce (39), Belzec death camp (59), Berlin (133), Beskid Mountains (239), Bielsko-Biala/Bielitz (239), Birkenau/ Brzezinka/Auschwitz II (123), Bratislava/Posony/Pressburg (20), Brno/Brunn (175), Bucharest (210), Budapest (26), Buna-Monowitz/Monowice/Auschwitz III (106), Cadca (246), Canada/Kanada (Auschwitz II) (124), Cracow/Krakow/Krakau (14), Czechoslovakia (60), Czestochowa (51), Dachau concentration camp (68), Danube River (21), Dnieper River (203), Dunkirk (209), England (20), France (148), Frankfurt-on-Main (123), Galanta (23), Geneva (181), Greece (148), Hungary (22), I. G. Farben Industries (Buna-Monowitz) (119),

Innsbruck (16), Katowice/Kattowitz (51), Kenyermeze (262), Kiev/Kyiv (203), Krupps factory (Buna-Monowitz) (119), Liptovsky Svaty Mikulas/Liptoszentmiklos (252), Lublin (56), Majdanek concentration camp (59), Mlawa (142), Novaky slave labour camp (34), Nove Mesto (124), Paris (210), Piestany (126), Pisarowice (239), Poland (22), Porebka (225), Portugal (137), Prague/Praha (62), Radom (70), Reutte (16), Romania (210), Sachsenhausen concentration camp (Oranienburg) (68), Sered (23), Skalite (246), Slovakia (21), Spain (161), Stara Tura (260), Svaty Yur (256), Sweden (257), Switzerland (137), Tatra Mountains (Eastern) (206), Telgart (45), Theresienstadt/Terezin ghetto/concentration camp (180), Topolcany (37), Trnava (20), Velke Uherce (38), Vienna/Wien (105), Warsaw Ghetto (147), Warsaw/Warszawa/Warschau (70), Yugoslavia (22), Zaporozhe (202), Zilina/Sillein (49), Zvolen (50), Zwardon (46)

Places mentioned – outside Europe: (page first mentioned)

Don River (202), Israel (264), Moscow (202), Palestine (172), Tel Aviv (265), Turkey (258), Washington (D.C.) (218)

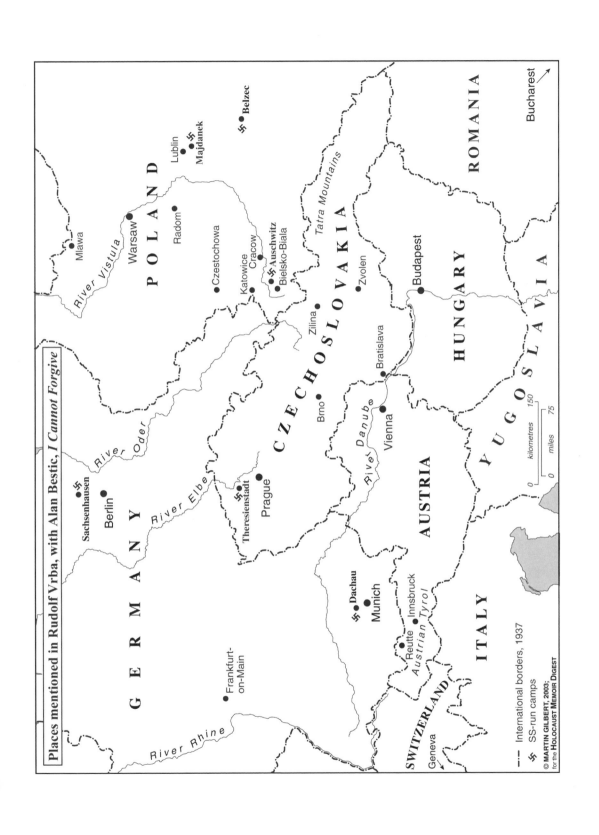

Places mentioned in Rudolf Vrba, with Alan Bestic, *I Cannot Forgive*

GERMANY

Frankfurt-on-Main •

Berlin •
Sachsenhausen ⚜

River Rhine

River Elbe

River Oder

Dachau ⚜
Munich •

Reutte •
Innsbruck •
Austrian Tyrol

SWITZERLAND
Geneva →

ITALY

AUSTRIA

Vienna •

Theresienstadt ⚜
Prague •

CZECHOSLOVAKIA

Brno •

River Danube

Bratislava •

Zilina •

Zvolen •

Tatra Mountains

POLAND

Mlawa •

River Vistula

Warsaw •

Radom •

Czestochowa •

Katowice •
Cracow •
Auschwitz ⚜
Bielsko-Biala •

Lublin •
Majdanek ⚜

⚜ Belzec

HUNGARY

Budapest •

YUGOSLAVIA

ROMANIA

Bucharest →

--- International borders, 1937
⚜ SS-run camps

kilometres 0   75   150
miles   0   75

© MARTIN GILBERT, 2003;
for the HOLOCAUST MEMOIR DIGEST

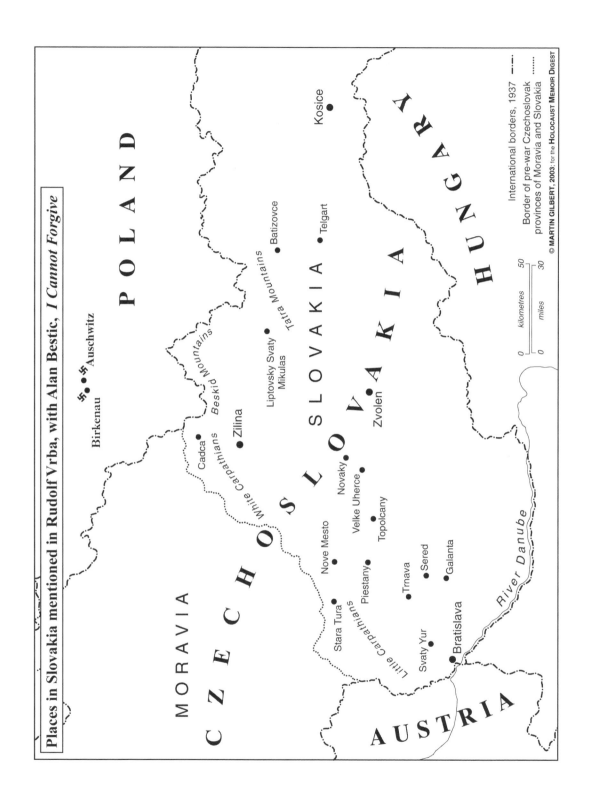

Places in Slovakia mentioned in Rudolf Vrba, with Alan Bestic, *I Cannot Forgive*

POLAND

Auschwitz

Birkenau

MORAVIA

C Z E C H O S L O V A K I A

Beskid Mountains

White Carpathians

Cadca

Zilina

Liptovsky Svaty Mikulas

Tatra Mountains

Batizovce

Telgart

Novaky

Velke Uherce

Topolcany

Zvolen

S L O V A K I A

Nove Mesto

Piestany

Little Carpathians

Stara Tura

Trnava

Sered

Galanta

Svaty Yur

Bratislava

River Danube

AUSTRIA

Kosice

HUNGARY

International borders, 1937

Border of pre-war Czechoslovak provinces of Moravia and Slovakia

© MARTIN GILBERT, 2003: for the HOLOCAUST MEMOIR DIGEST

50
kilometres

30
miles

0

Escape route of Rudolf Vrba and Alfred Wetzler, 7-25 April 1944

Oswiecim

Birkenau

Buna-Monowitz

Auschwitz

EAST UPPER SILESIA

POLAND

River Vistula

River Sola

Pisarowice

Porabka

Bielsko-Biala

fired on by a German patrol

Zywiec

River Vistula

Forest

Milowka

Zwardon

Skalite Sol Rajcza

Cadca

Beskid Mountains

SLOVAKIA

Zilina

Southward route of the two escapees
Railway from Poland to Slovakia
International borders, 1937
SS-run camps

0   kilometres   15

0   miles   10

© MARTIN GILBERT, 2003; for the HOLOCAUST MEMOIR DIGEST

Author: Samuel Pisar

Title: *Of Blood and Hope*

Publishing details: Little, Brown and Company, Boston. 1980. 311 pages.
Library of Congress #80-10696.
ISBN #0-316-70901-8.
Pre-war, Holocaust, and immediate post-war experiences make up just over one-third of the book; the following two-thirds describes his post-war life from his emigration from Europe through the 1970s. For the purpose of the *Digest*, this summary focuses on the first five chapters.

Focus:

A young boy from Bialystok, Poland, survives Soviet occupation, Auschwitz, and several slave labour camps, and becomes a noted international lawyer.

Features:

Foreword: Prologue written by the Author, pages 15–23.
Photographs: Photographs of family and friends, pages 45–50, 117–21, 165–7, 212–15, 251–3, 299, and back cover.
Afterword: Epilogue written by the Author, pages 303–11.

Contents: (by topic, with page numbers)

Pre-war Jewish home and community life

(27–8) Pre-war life in Bialystok, a "commercial crossroads" and: "… the same vibrant center of Jewish cultural life it had been for almost three centuries."
(28–32) Family concerns: "My mother wanted us to leave Europe while there was still time," but: "My father did not want to hear about leaving Poland. The prospect of becoming a refugee in some foreign land went against his grain."

The coming of war

(34) Bialystok becomes part of the Soviet Union until the German invasion on 22 June 1941; members of the Jewish community open their homes to Jewish refugees: "I did not mind giving up my bedroom to a family of Jewish refugees from Warsaw who had fled east before the Nazi bestiality."
(177–80) 1 September 1939 to 22 June 1941, under Soviet rule: "The Russians were occupiers, but we had known them as such before. It is true that they were communists now, and that made one apprehensive, but the revolution that had established Soviet power had its roots in cities like Bialystok." After the German invasion: "More even than the Russians' early defeat, it was the way their zeal evaporated that astonished me. I saw my Soviet teachers and other Soviet officials behave in a manner that signaled a profound loss of faith in their cause."

Creation of the ghetto

(35–6) After a reign of terror, eviction to: "… a designated slum section of the city."
(36–40) He becomes Bar Mitzvah in the ghetto: "… today our Wailing Wall is right here."

Daily life in the ghetto

(41–2) "We had been living for months in an atmosphere of absolute terror. All around me people had talked about death and I knew perfectly well what it meant. But for my mother, still so young, for my little sister, and for me to have to die without having really lived seemed inconceivable."

Deportation

(41, 51–5) At the liquidation of the ghetto, his mother considers him: "'If you're dressed in short pants, they'll let you go with Frieda and me. If you wear your long pants, we'll probably be separated. You will go with the men.'" From Bialystok, they are taken by train, with the men in the front wagons, and the women and children in the rear wagons; at Treblinka, the rear cars are unhooked, the train proceeds to Majdanek.

Death camps

(53, 59) "Then the train stopped. I … saw we were at a huge crossing with multiple railway lines going off in different directions. I looked for the station, as we were obviously near a large city, but could see nothing, only a field and thick forest in the distance. Several wooden signs marked the place. Painted on them was the word 'Treblinka'. … Some time would pass before I learned … that the women and children whose cars had been unhooked from our train at Treblinka were taken straight into the ovens."

Slave labour camps and factories

(60) Volunteering as a tailor, a buttonhole maker, he leaves Majdanek: "The next day our entire contingent – the others all bona fide tailors – was piled into trucks, and after two days of intermittent driving and stopping, was unloaded in a place called Blizin." (Blizyn).

(61–3) At Blizyn he finds his friend Ben. The High Holidays at camp: "On this Yom Kippur the fasting came easier than the atonement."

(66–7) The slave labour camp distinction within the Nazi system: "… we knew that if we died it would be from hunger, dysentery, or typhus, or as a penalty for some conscious or unintentional infraction of the rules. They wanted to get some work out of us before we gave up the ghost and made room for another shipment of deportees."

(82–4) Early winter 1944, building the camp of Kaufering: "Many men died from exposure, hunger, and punishment while putting up the barracks and workshops, but at least the blueprints did not call for the construction of a furnace."

(86–8) Taken from Dachau to Leonberg near Stuttgart, to work in a "major underground aircraft plant" deep within Engelberg, the "Mountain of Angels": "… my comrades and I had been promoted to the status of slave laborers, at the heart of the Nazis' military industrial complex. Our work was important to the war effort."

(246–8) The business relationship between I. G. Farben and the SS and the use of slave labour: "The indigenous workforces in wartime Germany were disastrously reduced by manpower requirements on the military front. Logic and efficiency dictated the solution: new giant factories would be built near concentration camps."

Auschwitz-Birkenau

(67) Auschwitz: "… its shifting population of 200,000 to 300,000 persons was the remnant of an already stringent elimination process."

(69–71, 79–80) Rules for survival : "How to make the most of my chances of putting off being sucked into the deadly funnel? The first rule is absolute submission. … We did everything possible, in short, to make ourselves invisible. … the second rule: never admit the least sign of infirmity. … the weakest, and often the bravest and the best, go first."

(74–5) The power of the mind: "Strange, how an organism that can go beyond the limits of physical endurance will often give up under a blow against the mind. In this world without mirrors, with nothing that could give us even a faint reflection of ourselves, we were psychologically vulnerable to others' estimation of our physical state."

(76–7) Work where extra food might be available: his, collecting garbage, and "Canada" which cleaned the incoming train cars.

(80) Fall 1944, the three friends, Niko, Ben, and Samuel, are taken with a group of prisoners to slave labour camps in Germany: "… we were aware that to leave Auschwitz by the same gate through which we had entered was little short of miraculous."

(217–8) A Russian prisoner of war is hanged for trying to escape, dies with faith in Stalin.

Death marches

(91–2) Six of them escape from the death march from Kaufering en route to Dachau.

Concentration camps

(55–9) The train from Bialystok comes to Majdanek. He learns to eat: "'Son, you listen. Do you want to eat or do you want to croak? … eat. Or else give it to me.' I forced the stuff down my throat. … I didn't even begin to realize what his words would mean to me later, what it is like to be crazed by hunger, when a helping of lukewarm liquid in a rusty container makes the emaciated body tremble in anticipation."

(81–2) Transferred for several weeks to Sachsenhausen: "… a major concentration camp reserved largely for German dissidents." Fall 1944.

(85–6) From Kaufering, he is taken to Dachau: "… an immense installation filled for the most part with German common criminals, political prisoners, religious dissidents, and homosexuals, as well as some foreign nationals. … Everything ran with the efficiency of clockwork, possibly because there were so many Germans on both sides of the wall."

Witness to mass murder

(71–2) At the gas chambers in Birkenau (Auschwitz II): "In three minutes it is all over."

(77–9) In Birkenau, the children and adolescents are coaxed out with an announcement of: "… a supplementary ration of white bread and milk. … For several days the miracle continued. … The fifth or sixth day was the last. The children lined up. … Instead, there was a blast of whistles … a platoon of SS men … the children were thrown into trucks. Some were taken to the 'clinic' for medical experiments; the others went directly to the gas chambers."

Resistance, ghetto revolts, individual acts of courage and defiance

(39) His father resists: "While road-testing the cars in his charge, he would occasionally spirit from the ghetto children whose parents wanted to give them to non-Jewish peasant families in the hope that this would offer them a better chance to survive."

(40) Jewish resistance during the destruction of the Bialystok ghetto: "Unarmed, their resistance was as heroic as it was futile."

Specific escapes

(52–3) A few men jump off the train between Bialystok and Treblinka: "When I stuck my head out again I saw that many of the escapees from other cars had been mowed down."

(56–8, 60) He is selected to leave Majdanek with a group of tailors, then taken to Blizyn. "The irresistible logic of my explanation – that whenever tailors are needed, buttonhole makers are needed too – must have impressed the SS officer, because he waved me to one side, the side of life. … Joseph becomes an interpreter of dreams and wins his life. He has invented his buttonhole machine."

(72–4) In Birkenau (Auschwitz II): "One day I found myself among the condemned." Yet by luck: "… other groups were placed ahead of us. They had priority …" and he survives. He is selected again, this time, he finds a pail and scrub brush in the room where his group is being held: "I go over one section, then another, scrubbing and drying vigorously as hard as I can, like a good worker performing an assigned task. Slowly I inch my way toward the exit. … Carrying the pail, with the brush and rag inside, I walk slowly to the door, then out into the open. … With slow, measured steps I walk toward the other barracks and lose myself in the anonymity of the camp."

(90–1) He forsakes his "Gerhardt" identity to join the Jewish line in Kaufering: "… the non-Jewish column … was mowed down by the SS guards."

In hiding, including Hidden Children

(88–90) Leonberg to Kaufering as an Aryan: "I shed the biblical name my parents had given me, which until then had been a passport to the crematorium, and baptized myself 'Gerhardt'."

Liberation

(92–3) Liberated in an abandoned barn near Penzing: "… a huge tank was coming toward the barn. … I looked for the hateful swastika, but there wasn't one. … In an instant, the realization flooded me: I was looking at the insignia of the United States Army. … I was in front of the tank, waving my arms. The hatch opened. A big black man climbed out, swearing unintelligibly at me. Recalling the only English I knew, those words my mother had sighed while dreaming of our deliverance, I fell at the black man's feet, threw my arms around his legs and yelled at the top of my lungs: 'God Bless America!'"

(97–8) The war ends: "… for us this was not the happy ending. It was the beginning of something unknown, disturbing."

(99–105) "We thrived in the middle of chaos and destruction." From Penzing, to Landsberg, to prison, the result of: "… a kind of postwar juvenile delinquency."

(105–7) United Nations Relief and Rehabilitation Administration help them: "… our free-wheeling days were over."

(108–12) Uncle Leo and Aunt Barbara Sauvage from Paris convince the two boys to come to Paris: "For your mother's sake."

(112–14) Coming into France: "'What's your nationality?' 'Well, I was born in Poland, so I was Polish, then the Russians came, so I was Russian, then the Germans came and took me to Germany but they sure as hell didn't make me into a German …' 'The only identity card he has is the number on his arm.'"

(114–16) Uncles Nachman and Lazar Suchowolski in Australia prevail on the boys to emigrate there: "Without regret, I was abandoning the psychotic and suicidal continent of Europe, forever."

Stories of individuals, including family members

(28, 40–3) Hela Pisar and 8-year-old Freida, prior to deportation, Bialystok: "Mother and Frieda were being marched the other way. My eyes were glued to the two frail shapes as they moved off in the distance. With one hand my sister held on to my mother, with the other she clutched her favorite doll. They too looked over their shoulders. Then they disappeared from sight."

(28, 123–6, 141) Uncle Nachman welcomes him to Australia: "… it was thought better for me to stay with Uncle Nachman and Aunt Rachel, who had two children; they would give me a sense of family." Uncle Nachman dies in his arms, a heart attack at age 48: "… he had seen the fulfillment of his mission, the success of a personal Marshall Plan for what was left of his Europe – me."

(28, 126–30, 272–4) Uncle Lazar, from Bialystok, to Paris, to Melbourne, retires in Israel, retells the story of Masada to the next generation, Samuel's children. He: "… wanted to insure that these children also would be nourished by the ethic of their forefathers."

(33–4) Henry Kissinger: "He and his family were able to take the last boat before the night closed in on my family and me. His father had guessed right; mine had guessed wrong."

(36–8, 60–3, 194–6, 243–4) Ben, at his Bar Mitzvah: "… was the first to congratulate me on becoming a man in the eyes of God." Reunited at Blizyn, they are determined to see each other survive. Visits him in France, in 1970: "'How are you, Mula? All right?'" And at a later visit: "'Mula, you're doing all right. You have a real home.'"

(38–9, 43) Death of his father, David: "One morning my father kissed us goodbye, and we never saw him again. He was caught in his clandestine activities, tortured by the Gestapo, and executed." Post-war search for grave, photo of marker, page 48.

(41, 124–5) Uncle Nachman's friend Dr Kniazeff offers refuge at his hospital for the last night in the Bialystok ghetto; his memory, a hope that Uncle Nachman: "… had been useful, even from afar."

(54–5) His impression of Prime Minister Golda Meir at their first meeting, fall 1972: "… she seemed to carry the entire tragedy of the Jewish people on her frail, hunched shoulders … just like my grandmother. The reincarnation of the grandmothers without number that I saw deposited by those trains at the doors of the gas chambers."

(67–8) Family friend Heniek rebuffs him in Birkenau (Auschwitz II), teaches him survival lesson: "Every human tie implying dependency or sentiment threatened to bring on complications that, at any moment, could mean the difference between life and death."

(68–9, 84–5, 158–62) "The wild Dutchman" Niko from Rotterdam becomes their protector and brother, beginning in Auschwitz. At Kaufering he becomes an Oberkapo: "… tough in words when the SS were close by, and mild in deed when they were out of sight." In 1957, while living in Paris, Sam finds Niko in Amsterdam. Nathan Waterman dies of a heart attack at age 48: "He was marvelously fashioned for times of disaster."

(83, 89) Bela from Budapest in Kaufering: "By making her lot a little easier, I deprived her of a chance to fend for herself."

(93, 176, 218) "The black American soldier who, near Dachau, pulled me to safety from the machine guns that were barking around us had come to save freedom in Europe. Twenty years later his son was sent to Vietnam, also to defend freedom, only to return a broken man, his life stained forever by a dirty war."

(98–9) Ben tries to return to Bialystok after the war, refugees: "… gave him a firsthand account of what had become of the town – the entire Jewish population massacred, the Soviet Army in tight, iron-handed control – and had persuaded him not to go farther."

(99) "Warsaw Moshe", a fighter in the ghetto revolt continues fighting after the war ends.

(110, 126–7) Stachelberg, desperate for help, appeals to Aunt Barbara. The uncles bring him to Australia.

(130, 136, 295–7) Ben joins Sam in Melbourne, marries Bialystok girl Bebka Mandel; Ben dies from a heart attack, at the age of 48.

(199–200) His children at the time of the book's publication (1979): Helaina: "… is about to graduate from the University of California"; Antony: "… is at my Landsberg age"; Alexandra: "… is of the age when I entered Majdanek"; Leah: "… is the same age as Freida was when the bombs began to fall."

Post-war life and career

(43–4) In 1961, travelling on a United States diplomatic passport, he returns to Bialystok: "To cross the threshold of that home, to give in, even for a moment, to the pain that I had so carefully kept under control year after year, was more than I could face."

(123–6) Enroute to Australia, his Uncle Nachman meets him in Singapore: "… he had a right to his full hour of the kind of grieving that, with me, had been parceled out in spasms."

(126–7, 130–1) Adjusting to a civilized life with Uncle Nachman and Aunt Rachel: "I appreciate now the tact and determination they used in a mission they considered sacred – to rescue the son of David and Hela from the dehumanized heritage that otherwise would strangle his life."

(127–9, 134–8) Schooling: "My mind soaked up knowledge like a dehydrated sponge. … Physically I had escaped, I was breathing, but Hitler had programmed my mental and moral destruction from his grave. The struggle for survival was going on once more, survival through study. It had to be waged with the same determination, the same fury."

(132–4) With Ben, he becomes a Zionist at the time of Israel's War of Independence: "As for ourselves, we decided that continuing the moral and intellectual rehabilitation we had begun, the undoing of Hitler's destructive work, even on the infinitesimal scale of two individuals, was perhaps the only meaningful form of vengeance."

(152–8) Meets and marries Norma Weingarten, completes a PhD in juridicial science from Harvard, and after the birth of daughter Helaina, accepts a position with UNESCO in Paris.

(188–190) Germany pays reparations to survivors. #B-1713 submits his claim: "Expiation was impossible, repentance was all that could be asked."

(197–200) His fifteen-year marriage to Norma ends; he faces fear of breaking up family and home: "I was afraid because this time the mayhem would be voluntary, not the violence applied by a vicious enemy." He and Judith Blinken are married in 1971.

(200–11) Summer 1971, he participates as an American delegate at the Dartmouth Conference, held in Kiev. He speaks out against Soviet anti-Semitism and leads the delegation to Babi Yar: "As Yevtushenko has written, there was no monument at Babi Yar, no plaque, nothing to tell of the infamous mass grave under the newly planted birch trees."

Personal reflections

(62) "My mother had given me life a second time on the night we were parted. This second birth had been much more painful for her than the first. My life, I felt, was no longer entirely my own. That part of her, of all the others, that was within me would have to live on too."

(65–6) His comparison to Solzhenitsyn's description of the Soviet gulag: "His gulag, horrible though it was, was not, like my camp, a place of extermination. Nothing can equal life in the shadow of a continuously active gas chamber. … I feel an obligation, to the memory of those who agonized and perished in the Nazi death factories, to make sure that the historical record is not blurred, that the vocabulary of the Holocaust is not deprived of its unique value as a warning for the future."

(69) In Auschwitz: "I cannot share my anguish with any of my fellow sufferers. And yet their anguish is the same as mine."

(87) "A human being faced with the harshness of nature will somehow manage to survive even against seemingly impossible odds. But when hardship is placed in his way by the deliberate act of his fellows, the solution to the problem often is beyond human reach. Even at its cruelest, nature is kinder than man touched by evil."

(128) "The English language … became for me a marvelously unencumbered vehicle to the world of knowledge, a vehicle that did not carry with it, as did all the other languages I already knew, the emotional baggage, the fears and terrors I carried from my violent past."

(143) "The real world is not as calm and comfortable as it appears from here; nor does my life belong entirely to me. It remains rooted forever in the tragedies of the past and it is from these tragedies that it must draw its meaning and direction."

(196) Ben to Sam, summer 1970: "'We may not have to live in the past, but the past lives in us. The most important thing about you is your past.'"

(217) Of the German people, today: "It was not for me to remind them of their past. In my mind, the only benefit of doubt I was able to give them was that, while my mother put me in long pants to keep me out of their ovens, some of the German mothers put their sons in short pants to keep them out of the SS."

(229) "… the intense intellectual and highly personal vision I have of Europe. It is both the source of our civilization and the matrix of our destruction."

(248–9) "Most contemporary political leaders, despite the vast armies they command, are powerless; by and large they fail miserably in their efforts to govern. Either ignorant of or insensitive to the new and real problems of the world, they merely respond to momentary shifts of public opinion and the whims of the media."

(293) "One of the most salient lessons I have brought out of the jungle that waited for me at the end of my cattle-train journey from home is that a human being has a surprising, an infinite, capacity to endure and to invent, even in the most unimaginable conditions, provided he has the will. Neither hunger nor pain, neither horror nor fear has ever shaken me in this belief."

Places mentioned – in Europe: (page first mentioned)

Athens (124), Auschwitz Main Camp/Auschwitz I (33), Babi Yar mass murder site (Kiev) (207), Berlin (81), Bialystok (27), Birkenau/Brzezinka/Auschwitz II (66), Blizyn slave labour camp (60), Brussels/Bruxelles (110), Budapest (82), Canada/Kanada (Auschwitz II) (77), Dachau concentration camp (85), Engelberg slave labour camp (86), Kaufering slave labour camp (82), Kiev/Kyiv (200), Landsberg Displaced Persons camp (100), Leonberg slave labour camp (86), Lithuania (34), London, England (116), Majdanek concentration camp (54), Munich/München (85), Naples/Napoli (124), Paris (37), Penzing (92), Rotterdam (68), Sachsenhausen concentration camp (Oranienburg) (81), Sorbonne (Paris) (37), Strasbourg (114), Stuttgart (86), Treblinka death camp (53), Warsaw/Warszawa/Warschau (34)

Places mentioned – outside Europe: (page first mentioned)

Australia (28), Bangkok (124), Beverly Hills (152), Boston (39), Cairo (124), Cambridge (Massachussetts) (155), Chicago (97), Cleveland (39), Delhi (124), Georgetown (District of Columbia) (172), Haifa (106), Israel (53), Jerusalem (38), Johannesburg (106), Leningrad/St Petersburg (200), Los Angeles (152), Melbourne (38), New York City (39), Palestine (106), Singapore (124), Southampton (115), Tehran (123), Tel Aviv (54), United States of America (28), Yonkers (New York) (199)

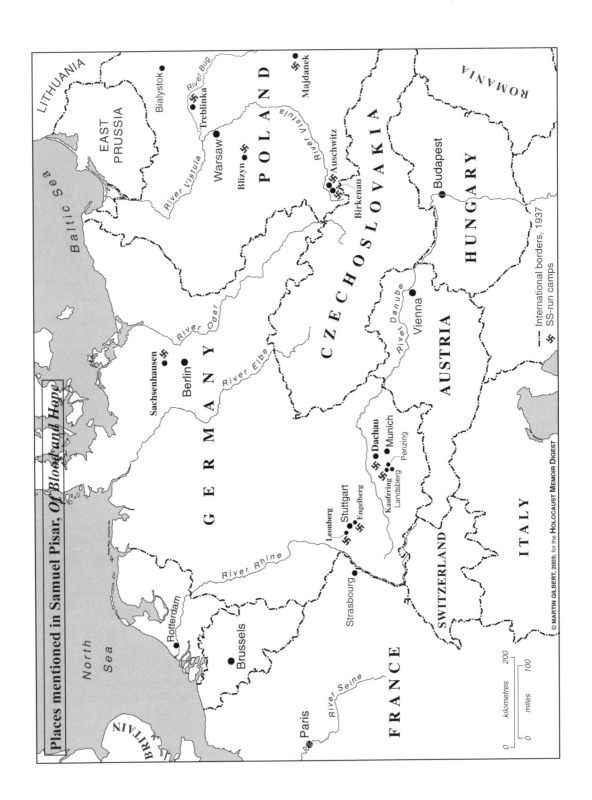

Places mentioned in Samuel Pisar, *Of Blood and Hope*

LITHUANIA

EAST PRUSSIA

Baltic Sea

North Sea

BRITAIN

• Bialystok

River Bug

⚜ Treblinka

River Vistula

• Warsaw

Blizyn •⚜

P O L A N D

River Vistula

Majdanek ⚜

⚜ Auschwitz

⚜ Birkenau

• Sachsenhausen

• Berlin

River Oder

River Elbe

G E R M A N Y

C Z E C H O S L O V A K I A

River Danube

• Vienna

Budapest •

H U N G A R Y

ROMANIA

AUSTRIA

Leonberg ⚜

• Stuttgart

⚜ Engelberg

⚜ Dachau

• Munich

⚜ Kaufering

Landsberg

Penzing

River Rhine

• Strasbourg

Rotterdam •

• Brussels

F R A N C E

SWITZERLAND

I T A L Y

River Seine

• Paris

- · - International borders, 1937
⚜ SS-run camps

0 ___ 200 kilometres
0 ___ 100 miles

© MARTIN GILBERT, 2003; for the HOLOCAUST MEMOIR DIGEST

Author: Bertha Ferderber-Salz

Title: *And the Sun Kept Shining …*

Publishing details: Holocaust Library, New York. 1980. 233 pages.
Library of Congress #80-81684.

Focus:

A woman survives in Poland and reclaims her two young daughters from hiding; the events take place between September 1939 and 22 October 1946.

Features:

Foreword: Written by Menachem Z. Rosensaft, pages 7–10.
Photographs: Family photographs.
Documents: The "Aryan" birth certificates of her daughters, page 182.
Maps: Map of the Cracow region, page 235.
Afterword: Conclusion written by the Author, page 233.

Contents: (by topic, with page numbers)

Pre-war Jewish home and community life

(201) Her grandparents in Rzeszow: "They had both died at a ripe old age, my grandfather at the age of ninety-six and my grandmother at ninety-seven, after having been happily married for seventy-seven years."
(204–5) Life in Kolbuszowa revolved around the water pump.
(214–17) The history of the pearl necklace heirloom: "Once our mother said to us, 'The pearls are not very valuable in money terms, but in our family they serve as a guarantee of the continuity of the generations.'"
(219–20) Memories of her home, 36 Starowisla Street, Cracow, a glimpse of life before.

The coming of war

(19–24) September 1939, Cracow is bombed, the family flees eastward, to Lvov: "The Germans would not get as far as Lvov, surely." First night in Bochnia, then on to Pilzno to friends where they rest, then to Rzeszow: "After a week of wandering we arrived in Lancut. … The Germans had already arrived."
(25–7) In Lancut: "The Nazi plague had spread to every side and there was no point in attempting to flee from it." They decide to return to Cracow; they obtain false documents and travel for five days and nights on the train.

Life under German occupation

(27–9) "My husband returned to his place of employment; a Nazi commissar had already taken over there." Salaries are cut, food prices go up, refugees crowd in, the Jewish suburb of Podgorze is searched: "Only the devil himself could have thought up deeds such as theirs."
(37–40) Forced labour, 1939–40: "My husband had to report each day for work … even though

he received no salary. He was also required to clear the snow and ice from the streets on alternate days. Since he could not be in two places at once I went in his stead to do forced labor, cleaning Cracow's main street, together with other Jews."

(46–8) Health care and hope: "Having no alternative, I wrote down the names of medicines for easing pain. … I knew that the medicines I had written down would not harm them, even if they did not help."

(103–4) Refugees flood into Cracow at the beginning of the war: "There was not a single Jewish house in the city that did not take in a refugee family. … At the end of 1940 it was the turn of many of Cracow's Jews to begin wandering. …"

(105, 108–11) Life as refugees in Grodzisko Dolne (called Grodzisk in the memoir): "The first words my younger daughter learned to say were 'Germans' and 'hide'."

(112–13) The blindness, the indifference of a nation, the Germans.

Creation of the ghetto

(30–2) The Cracow ghetto, established in the Jewish suburb of Podgorze, the end of 1940: "Before the war 3,000 people had lived there, and now they wanted to crowd in four times as many. Everyone knew what this decree meant: epidemics, hunger, poverty, and in addition a high wall all round, like the walls around old Jewish cemeteries, symbolizing the situation of the Jews who were being buried alive."

(32) Summer 1942: "They announced that … ghettos would be allowed to exist in five large cities: Warsaw, Cracow, Lvov, Radom, and Bochnia."

(41–2) They move into the ghetto, but she and her sister move with their five children to the village of Grodzisko; her husband and his parents remain in the ghetto.

Daily life in the ghetto

(67–8) March 1943, surviving the liquidation of the "little ghetto" in Cracow, she finds work preparing the houses for their new Polish occupants: "We had been given the task of erasing every trace of the Jewish children who had lived their miserable lives in these houses."

Deportation

(31) "Suddenly there was a new concept in the ghetto: 'resettlement' (deportation). … The deportations continued from the first to the eighth of June, 1942." (from Cracow to Belzec)

(34, 36) 28 October 1942 deportation from the Cracow ghetto (to Belzec), among those who are killed, the poet Mordechai Gebirtig, whose "… poems of the ghetto survived and reached freedom", and the painter Abraham Neiman, whose "… paintings were burned along with the ghetto …".

(54–7) August 1942, deportations from Grodzisko to Belzec: "When the bitter day came and all the Jews were ordered to assemble in the marketplace, we knew what it meant."

(58–9) Cousin Lola's 10 October 1942 letter, Lubaczow: "'On one of the hot summer days a transport arrived from Cracow and Wieliczka. There were eighty people crammed together in each carriage, and they begged for a little water for the children. Since I live near the railway station I see the convoys of miserable people, and my heart bursts with pity. I heard their pleas, took a bucket of water and managed to reach the carriages. Of course the Gestapo saw me. I knew that was the end but wasn't at all afraid.'"

(132–3) From Plaszow to Auschwitz by train, end of November 1944.

Death camps

(40, 57) To the peasant in Grodzisko Dolne who had promised to help them: "'You took our money but did not give us refuge. At least go after the convoy and find out where they are being taken.' ... A week later he returned with the information that all the convoys were being taken to Belzec." Her sister, brother-in-law, and one of their sons are taken in the convoy.

(57–60) August 1942, area convoys taken to Belzec; 10 October letter from cousin Lola in Lubaczow, reprinted in full.

(92) Her view of the purpose of all of the various camps: "... all the camps had one aim and one alone: to put us to death in a variety of ways."

Slave labour camps and factories

(31) "Workshops were established in the ghetto, where we performed manual labor for our oppressors. Jews sought ways of becoming useful and necessary in order to save their lives."

(33, 36) Plaszow under construction, 1942.

(68–9) Her niece Sabina already at Plaszow, then: "One day the order came through: the ghetto was to be liquidated, and all the Jews were to be transferred to the Plaszow camp. The order also included a statement to the effect that old people and children would be taken elsewhere."

(72, 86–7) March 1943, arrival at Plaszow; smuggling of extra food for her husband and niece Sabina.

(80–1, 131) Camp Commandant Amnon Goeth's torments and tortures in Plaszow; his excesses, his greed.

(83–5) No longer being sent out of the camp to work, she still finds a way to maintain contact with the outside.

(94, 96) May 1944, selection at Plaszow of 1,600 by Dr Blanke from Auschwitz, among them, her husband.

(118–19) Labouring in the sewing workshop, Plaszow: "There were eight of us. ... Each day we had to sew sixty-four items – that is, every one of us had to produce eight pairs of pants."

(127–30, 132) Torturers add to hunger, cold, Plaszow, 1944: "'Finish it up,' he bellowed. ... More than twenty women from our group went without food that day, and that girl almost died from overeating."

Auschwitz-Birkenau

(133–6) Entrance to Birkenau (Auschwitz II): "When we entered the block we found hundreds of women there, their heads shaven, staring at one another. We were all unrecognizable. We looked terrible, even more ghastly than death itself."

(137–40) November, December 1944, in Birkenau (Auschwitz II), hunger and cold: "Auschwitz had deprived me of fear and of the will to continue the fight."

Death marches

(140–1) The nine-day train journey, Auschwitz to Bergen-Belsen, December 1944.

Concentration camps

(141) Entrance to Bergen-Belsen: "Immediately upon our arrival we were given rusty bowls and spoons. Each of us tore off a strip of cloth from her dress, passed it through the handle of the bowl and hung this priceless jewel around her neck. We had learned to appreciate the value of eating utensils."

(142) "When we reached Bergen-Belsen, at the end of December, the camp was full to overflowing. Until there was room for us in the blocks, we were accommodated in tents outside the camp. ... One night the wind blew the tents away. ... Many among us did not live to enter that 'paradise' called Bergen-Belsen. ..."

(145–7) Forced labour at Bergen-Belsen: sorting the stolen property, "Each time we touched these objects we felt as if their owners' souls were fluttering beneath our fingers, bewailing their bitter fate." Hauling carts of garbage: "... considered a good place to work, as from time to time one could find among the garbage a piece of potato peel, which the women ate hungrily."

(148–50, 154) Beatings and tortures, Bergen-Belsen: "We waited for the fateful shot, but none came; they were not going to waste precious ammunition on us."

(151–3) Delivery of her "last bequest": two potatoes. Lying with the sick and dying: "... the transition from life to death was almost imperceptible and unimportant there." Bergen-Belsen, spring 1945.

(155–6, 160–1) "... our emaciated bodies like fleeting shadows on the walls." Gaining strength, "organizing" food and clothes, and "hygiene", Bergen-Belsen.

(158–9) "'Are children born in this hell?'" Bergen-Belsen, winter 1945.

Witness to mass murder

(37–8) Refugees from the area move into Cracow during the winter of 1939–40, live in schools and synagogues. One spring night they are taken away: "I ran to the synagogue and found it deserted. Clothing, utensils, and rags lay on the floor. It looked as if the people had not even had time to pack their belongings properly. In the dead of night they had been taken into the unknown."

(72–3) Liquidation of the ghetto in Cracow, March 1943: "As we walked to work we would encounter wagons piled high with corpses. We realized the liquidation of the ghetto was continuing. The victims, whose blood flowed onto the road, were being taken to a mass grave at the new cemetery near the Plaszow camp."

(95) The patients in the camp infirmary are all killed except: "My husband and the other survivor had been the only ones not suffering from an infectious disease, and for that reason had been left behind."

(96–8) Children in Plaszow coaxed out by deception, taken by truck to Auschwitz with those who had not passed the selection, 13 May 1944.

(99–102) The "eternal flame" at Plaszow, which "kindled human bodies": "It was situated at the foot of a hill on the outskirts of the camp, and Jews who had been caught on the 'Aryan' side and Polish resistance members were taken there and burned."

(131) Plaszow, autumn 1944: "Only a few thousand people were left in the camp, the rest having been taken to the various sites of destruction. We continued taking bodies out of the mass graves and burning them."

(132) Plaszow liquidated, those remaining are loaded onto a train. She is told later: "The first carriages went to Stutthof, near Danzig. The train reached the seashore, and the people were put on ships, which were sunk in mid-ocean." The last carriage goes to Auschwitz.

(137) In Birkenau (Auschwitz II): "We were forbidden to be outside when the people were being taken to the incinerators from the nearby blocks. Only yesterday the block beside us had been full of gypsies; today it was empty."

(143) In Bergen-Belsen: "It was clear to us that this was where we were to end our lives. Our

murderers had condemned us to a slow death, without using ovens or poisonous gasses. They did in fact achieve their aim, for hundreds of dying women occupied the wooden bunks in each block."

(148) Hauling garbage, Bergen-Belsen, spring 1945: "On our way to the mill pit we passed the crematorium. This was the first time I ever saw the entire building; before I had seen only the smoke."

(149) Death by running, Bergen-Belsen, spring 1945: "... they would take groups of people out of the camp and make them run across plowed fields for days on end until most of them collapsed from exhaustion and sank into the muddy ground. Only a handful survived this immense effort and returned to the camp."

Resistance, ghetto revolts, individual acts of courage and defiance

(31) Resistance in Cracow: "But our heroic youth began as well to organize an underground resistance movement."

(33–6) Leaders Gusta Drenger and Dolek Liebeskind organized the Cracow underground; the rabbis' blessing: "We must ask God to give us the strength to die bravely so that the generations to come can be proud of us."

(43–5) Ten-year-old daughter Rachel saves the family's sacred books from the book-burning, Grodzisko.

(49–50) Summer 1941, Grodzisko, she learns important information: "All I wanted was to get away from my house as quickly as possible and run to the forest so I could pass on the information to the partisans."

(75–6) A "beggar" in the cellar of the building where the girls are being hidden worked for the Resistance.

(87) Resistance by workmanship defects, Plaszow: "I decided to wage my own personal war against our oppressors and to undermine their war effort. ... Not one pair of pants left my workbench without a serious defect made by me in some hidden part."

(91) "My husband worked gladly and devotedly for the resistance, and it was his task to supply the organization with paper and printing services for the underground news sheet that was published in the ghetto."

(93–4) She finds a way to make matza in the slave labour camp of Plaszow, March 1944: "As a result there were Jews in that hell who ate unleavened bread, the symbol of our emergence from slavery to freedom, on Passover."

(131) Yom Kippur: Kol Nidre in Plaszow, 1944: "We had threaded the needles of the sewing machines and placed cloth underneath them, so that everything would be ready if we had to jump to our places if surprised at our prayers."

(135) Auschwitz "efficiency" compromised by revolt: "through an act of sabotage".

(143–4) Spiritual resistance to their fate: January 1945, Bergen-Belsen, a Hungarian woman remembers Shabbat: "'It is our duty to praise God at all times and in every place. God hears our prayers, even when they are said from the deepest pit. And even if He does not come to our aid, there are other Jews in the world for whom we should request a good week.'"

Partisan activity

(48–50) In the woods they meet two partisans: "Our encounter with the partisans had encouraged us. We had seen for ourselves that there were people fighting our oppressors, trying to destroy them with every weapon they had." She is able to pass on helpful information to them.

Specific escapes

(51–3) Summer 1941, arrested for sending food parcels to her husband in Cracow: "'Don't you know that you violated German law by sending the parcels?'" She is freed after interrogation at Gestapo headquarters in Jaroslaw.

(117) Released from the prison in Plaszow: "A senior officer entered, and I explained to him that we were being held for a minor offence. We had to get up early the next morning in order to work. … To my immense surprise he listened to what I had to say and released us."

In hiding, including Hidden Children

(54–6, 60–1) August 1942, hiding with a peasant to avoid deportation, Grodzisko: "The peasant remained firm; he was not going to risk execution to save us. In the end he agreed to a compromise: he was prepared to conceal one of us and one alone for a few days in his neighbor's attic. There were five of us."

(62–3) Disguised as a sick Pole she returns to the ghetto. Mrs Lublin retrieves her niece from her hiding place in Lezajsk.

(61, 69) Nephew Romek hidden with the Polish carpenter, the Lublins; her girls taken out of the ghetto by Polish protectors, before ghetto liquidation.

(69) Before they are moved to Plaszow, she sends her daughters into hiding: "I do not know from where I drew the strength – maybe because of the one thought that kept going through my mind: We have nothing to lose."

(73–8) Children's life in hiding with Poles; she tries to protect them, although she is in the Plaszow camp; sees them from a distance, summer 1943: "For a moment our eyes met. How can I put into words what went through my mind during those seconds."

(78–9) Her friends Rushka and Halina help her to reconcile giving up her daughters to save them: "'Your daughters need you. Some sixth sense tells me that they will survive, and they are going to need you so much after the years of suffering and fear.'"

(107) Children robbed of their childhood: "… the fact that I had to leave them when their lives were in constant danger tortures me still today."

(178–80) She finds her daughters after the war. At night the younger one kneels down in prayer: "Their rescuer stood in the doorway, a smile of satisfaction on her face. 'You see,' she said to the kneeling child, 'because you asked the Virgin Mary to help you every night your mother has been saved and has come back to you.'"

(183–8) Her difficulties to retrieve the children from their Polish rescuers: "'The children have to be educated among their own people, with their family.'"

(199) Reb Moshe's daughter in a Christian orphanage, protected from her past she grew up: "… without knowing that she was Jewish." Grodzisko.

Righteous Gentiles

(54, 60, 64–6) "Our benefactor, the teacher Sigmund Szeliga, was different from the others and acted without asking for payment. … When I met him again after the war, he still spoke with deep regret of the failure of his plan to save us."

(61) Mrs Lublin from Cracow: "That good woman was a support to us throughout the war. In our darkest hours she was our salvation."

Liberation

(15–18, 165–6) Liberated at Bergen-Belsen, May 1945: "In the camp there were almost sixty thousand people struggling with death. Our liberators could do little to help us, for how could they breathe life into living skeletons?"

(162–4) A block supervisor taken prisoner by an English soldier, Bergen-Belsen: "'I'm taking her round the camp, collecting evidence from survivors.' I told him everything I knew about her, about the torments, humiliations, and distress we had suffered from her."

(167–8) With a Canadian Jewish soldier's help, she contacts her brother in New York: "A week later he brought me a reply from my brother in New York. The rumor about the letter that had arrived from overseas spread like wildfire through the camp. There was a great commotion, as it was the first letter ever to reach our closed and enclosed community."

(168–78) August 1945, she decides to return to find her children. She and her niece Sabina make the perilous four-week journey to Cracow to retrieve the children.

(189–95, 200–8) After finding the children: "For weeks and months I wandered the length and breadth of the Cracow region in search of my relatives. I found no sign of life, and nearly all trace of the dead had been wiped out too."

(196–8) In Lezajsk she overhears a discussion on the murder of nine Jews who had returned: "The customers in the inn were divided into two camps, one of which claimed that the right thing had been done. … The other group maintained that … they should have been informed that they had better leave, and only afterwards, if they had insisted on remaining, should they have been killed."

(209–11) She takes out birth certificates for the children: "I wanted the children to revert to their previous identities, with their original surnames, leaving their false identities behind with their foreign names."

(221–4) Her three-week return from Cracow to Bergen-Belsen, spring 1946.

Displaced Persons camps

(170) Used for safe passage on her journey from Bergen-Belsen to Cracow.

(225–6) March to June 1946, in Bergen-Belsen and Zeilsheim: "New life had been breathed into the walking skeletons I had left behind me when I went to Poland, and a vital Jewish community had been established."

Stories of individuals, including family members

(39–40, 56–7) Her sister Feiga contemplates suicide when forced to leave their hiding place: "'Our fate has been sealed. We go to meet our death without fear or dread. Our suffering is coming to an end. But you, my poor sister, are going into the unknown.'" She and her husband and one son die in Belzec.

(61, 69, 82–4, 178) Nephew Romek hidden with a Polish carpenter, survives surgery, his secret identity intact, finds her at Bergen-Belsen.

(60) Cousin Lola in Lubaczow reports in a letter: "She wrote that the son of my oldest sister, a young man of twenty-two, had jumped off the train taking them to Belzec, together with a relative of ours from Grodzisko. They hid in her house and then went to the forest, hoping to join the partisans, but were caught and shot."

(70) "I looked back for the last time at the ghetto as it emptied. I saw a little boy of about three walking along a deserted alley, crying and calling for his mother. A murderer in SS uniform silenced him forever with one shot from his pistol. Later I met the child's mother in the camp but did not dare to look into her eyes. Her sobs echo in my ears to this day."

(70–1) Neighbour's daughter taken out of hospital, carried to Plaszow, liberated at Bergen-Belsen.

(89–90, 178) Cousin Abraham, 13 years old, hides as a member of the Hitler Youth, is liberated by the Russians, finds her at Bergen-Belsen after the war.

(87, 90–2, 95–7, 134–5) May 1944, her husband is deported to Auschwitz; in the ghetto he had worked for the Resistance: "… the ability to continue the struggle had left him." His death in Birkenau (Auschwitz II) is confirmed: "They had been taken straight to the gas chambers."

(106) Reb Tuvia survives an attack by "two murderers": "He regained his strength and by the irony of fate was as healthy as he had always been when he was killed in the gas chambers of Belzec."

(114–17) Recollections of those who found creative outlets for their pain: Olga the dancer, Mira the puppeteer, Steffa the artist, Plaszow.

(118–26) Memorable characters in Plaszow: the workers in the sewing workshop; Gisa and Benek in the camp; Gusta and her husband; Mekhlovitz, who finds his place.

(157) Her sister-in-law survives to liberation: "… but could not take the liberation itself." She dies two weeks later.

(197) Nineteen-year-old Simon returns to Grodzisko, she is told he: "'… hid in the surrounding forests and returned to the village immediately after the liberation. His parents' "heirs" shot him, fearing that he would demand what they had stolen.'"

(210–11) Rabbi Menashe Levertov, rabbi of the remaining Jews of Cracow helps her: "Each time I felt despair getting the better of me, I hurried to the rabbi's house to hear some encouraging words."

(212–13) Two weddings in Cracow 1946: "My heart bled at the thought that I would have to take the place of mothers, aunts, sisters, relatives, and friends at the marriage of two people who were the sole survivors of large families."

Post-war life and career

(228–33) From Bergen-Belsen to Paris, and on to her brother in America, on the *Isle de France*, arriving in New York on 22 October 1946: "How could we adapt to being among people whose flesh had not been scorched by the fires of hell?"

Personal reflections

(18) "Maybe it was the ancient precept 'And you shall tell it to your children' that impelled me to tell the world what the Nazi beasts of prey did to us. Perhaps this is the price that those of us who survived the fires of hell are required to pay."

(9) From Menachem Z. Rosensaft's Foreword: "It is generally forgotten by these so-called 'experts' on the Holocaust that the survivors are the only ones who can discuss the experience from a personal, authentic perspective. It is their words which must form the basis for any historical understanding of the event."

Places mentioned – in Europe: (page first mentioned)

Akra (173), Auschwitz Main Camp/Auschwitz I (16), Belsen/Bergen-Belsen concentration camp (15), Belzec death camp (40), Berlin (174), Bochnia (20), Cracow/Krakow/Krakau (19), Dabrowa (190), Danzig/Gdansk (132), Debica (190), Frankfurt-on-Main (188), Görlitz/Zgorzelec (185), Grodzisko Dolne (41), Helmstedt (223), Jaroslaw (51), Jaslo (101), Jaworow (201), Kolbuszowa (203), Lancut (22), Le Havre (229), Leipzig (223), Lezajsk (60), Lodz/

Litzmanstadt (28), Lubaczow (57), Lublin (30), Lvov/Lemberg/Lwow/Lviv (19), Magdeburg (174), Mielec (191), Montelupich Prison (Cracow) (35), Nowy-Sacz (70), Oswiecim/Auschwitz town (44), Paris (228), Pilzno (21), Plaszow slave labour camp (33), Podgorze (Cracow) (27), Potsdam (174), Przemysl (42), Przeworsk (200), Radom (32), Rawa-Ruska (201), Reinharz (170), Rozwadow (193), Rzeszow (22), Smolensk (90), Stalowa-Wola (193), Stutthof/Sztutowo concentration camp (132), Tarnopol (65), Tarnow (21), Wannsee (174), Warsaw/Warszawa/Warschau (32), Wieliczka (58), Zeilsheim Displaced Persons camp (225)

Places mentioned – outside Europe: (page first mentioned)

New York City (232)

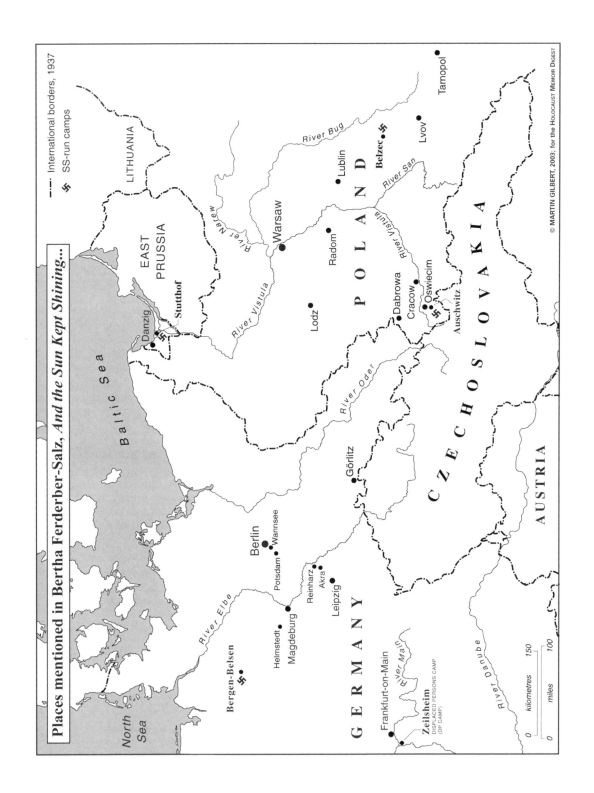

Places mentioned in Bertha Ferderber-Salz, *And the Sun Kept Shining...*

International borders, 1937

卐 SS-run camps

© MARTIN GILBERT, 2003; for the HOLOCAUST MEMOIR DIGEST

Baltic Sea

North Sea

LITHUANIA

EAST PRUSSIA

Danzig
Stutthof 卐

River Narew

River Vistula

Warsaw

River Bug

Lublin

Belzec 卐

Tarnopol

Lvov

River San

P O L A N D

Lodz

Radom

Dabrowa

Cracow

Oswiecim

Auschwitz 卐

River Oder

C Z E C H O S L O V A K I A

AUSTRIA

Görlitz

Berlin
Wannsee

Potsdam

Reinharz

Akra

Leipzig

Helmstedt

Magdeburg

River Elbe

Bergen-Belsen 卐

G E R M A N Y

Frankfurt-on-Main

River Main

Zeilsheim
DISPLACED PERSONS CAMP
(DP CAMP)

River Danube

0   150
kilometres
0   100
miles

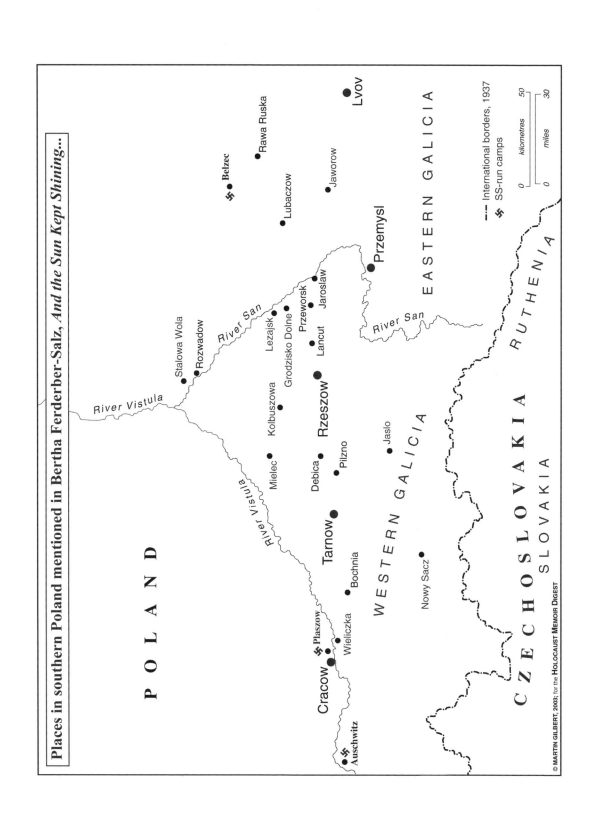

Places in southern Poland mentioned in Bertha Ferderber-Salz, *And the Sun Kept Shining...*

POLAND

EASTERN GALICIA

WESTERN GALICIA

RUTHENIA

CZECHOSLOVAKIA

SLOVAKIA

Lvov

Rawa Ruska

Belzec

Lubaczow

Jaworow

Przemysl

River San

River San

Stalowa Wola

Rozwadow

River Vistula

Lezajsk

Grodzisko Dolne

Przeworsk

Jaroslaw

Lancut

Rzeszow

Mielec

Debica

Pilzno

Jaslo

Kolbuszowa

Tarnow

Bochnia

Nowy Sacz

River Vistula

Plaszow

Wieliczka

Cracow

Auschwitz

International borders, 1937

SS-run camps

0   kilometres   50

0   miles   30

© MARTIN GILBERT, 2003; for the HOLOCAUST MEMOIR DIGEST

Author: Nechama Tec

Title: *Dry Tears, The Story of a Lost Childhood*

Publishing details: Oxford University Press, 200 Madison Avenue, New York, New York 10016. 1982. 216 pages.

ISBN #0-19-503500-3.

Originally published by Wildcat Publishing Company, Westport, CT, 1982.

Focus:

A young girl survives in hiding in Poland with her older sister and parents; the events take place between September 1939 and early 1945.

Features:

Afterword: Author's Acknowledgements.

Epilogue: Written by the Author, on immediate post-war events leading to their decision to leave Poland; also some historical perspective on Russian/Polish tensions, pages 217–42.

Contents: (by topic, with page numbers)

Pre-war Jewish home and community life

(44–6) Pre-war Lublin, a city of 200,000, of whom 40,000 were Jews. Nechama's father, Roman Bawnik was raised to become a rabbi: "Eventually there was an outright confrontation between him and his teachers, which brought his religious instruction to an end." He became an atheist; her mother, Estera Hachamoff: "… was an 'instinctive' Jew, who behaved in a religious way naturally and without thought. Observing the various rituals was second nature to her, and she was sincere about them."

(47–8) The attempt to assimilate, by moving to a predominantly Christian part of town, by speaking in Polish, not Yiddish: "Furthermore, instead of calling me by my Hebrew name Nechama, they gave me the Polish name Hela, with Helka as the diminutive."

(49–50) Pre-school memories of market days with her mother; her parents' emphasis on learning: "Education, they believed, was an individual's most valuable and durable commodity, to be obtained at any cost. … They enrolled us in an excellent and expensive private school, owned and run by Jews, and attended exclusively by students from affluent Jewish families. Its entire atmosphere, however, suggested an attempt to de-emphasize anything of religious or particular Jewish significance."

(50–3) The courtship and marriage of her parents Roman Bawnik and Estera Hachamoff; her father's successful business ventures: "He had gained the reputation of being a man people could trust."

(53–4) Her mother's parents: "In accordance with Jewish customs of those days, their marriage had been arranged by the respective parents, who considered the young pair a suitable match. How either of them felt did not matter, and indeed they met for the first time under the 'hupa', the wedding canopy, during the wedding ceremony. According to the story that came down to us, when my grandmother's veil was lifted and she first set eyes on her bridegroom, she fainted."

(54–6) Her mother's siblings: two older sisters, younger brother Josef, and younger sister

Zelda, all were married except Zelda: "My grandparents' favorite was their only son, Josef. … They allowed him to follow his inclinations and finish a secular high school, something they denied all four girls. … Happily for my sister and me, my father took a different view of daughters."

(56–7) Her father, orphaned at a young age: "My father had two younger siblings to whom he was devoted and for whom he felt responsible – a sister Ella, and a brother Gershon. Gershon worked in my father's candle factory …" Ella married Szymon: "a 'professional' socialist, and a journalist of sorts. … My father supported him and his family with a steady allowance, for which Szymon refused to be grateful. … Fortunately my father expected no gratitude. 'You give because of the pleasure it gives you,' he said. 'Don't ever expect anything in return.'"

Pre-war anti-Semitism

(46) On anti-Semitic attacks on Jewish owned businesses: "Neither Jews nor Poles dared enter a store surrounded by an anti-Semitic mob. As a rule, at such times the police managed to be out of sight. … I grew up with the idea that Jews were despised, and that they suffered only because of their Jewishness."

(106–7) The Pole Stanislaw's view of his son-in-law Tosiek: "It wasn't just that Tosiek was socially unworthy of Marta, it was because his mother had been born Jewish. She had been orphaned as a little girl and the nuns who adopted her brought her up as a Catholic. At sixteen they married her to Tosiek's father. Although she had been a devout Catholic for almost sixty years, to Stanislaw she was nothing but a 'plain Jewess'."

(121–2, 129–30) The Homars' anti-Semitism and view of Jews: "My father tried to explain that the Homars, like most Poles, took anti-Semitism for granted. … He believed that the Homars hated an abstraction, the stereotype of the Jew, but not actual people like us, who happened to be Jewish. … We were not 'typically Jewish', we did not conform to the image that phrase evoked for them. It did not matter that they had perhaps never encountered anyone who did conform to the image. … They simply treated us as an exception, which allowed them to keep their anti-Semitism intact."

The coming of war

(1–3) "Shortly after the occupation of Lublin in 1939 Jewish children had been barred from attending school and private instruction was prohibited. As with all such Nazi directives, disobedience if discovered met with severe punishment, even death." Nechama's parents arrange for a tutor to teach her and her older sister.

(4–6) Jewish prisoners of war, who had been part of the Polish army, were interned in a slave labour camp in Lublin: "Their visits added joy to our otherwise dreary existence. Perhaps inevitably, one of them fell in love with my sister who, though not yet fifteen, was mature, intelligent, and very pretty."

(58–9) Rumours of impending war, and then the reality, early September 1939: "The rumors kept multiplying, and according to the radio we would defeat the Germans. … when the Germans arrived, I was angry. I felt as if someone had lied to me; I felt betrayed." Nechama is 8 years old, her sister, 12.

(59–60) The influx of Jewish refugees to Lublin from German border areas: "These refugees had been thrown out of their homes on no provocation and without warning, and they spoke of many who had been killed before they could get away. Most of our Jewish acquaintances remained stubbornly skeptical, even about these first-hand accounts."

Life under German occupation

(6–8) Her father Roman works at the chemical factory he had previously owned, which had been taken over by the Germans; her mother Estera works as a housekeeper for a Nazi official.

(9) The murder of those in hospitals and orphanages: "When there were no more Jewish orphanages, and when most of the hospital patients had perished, the Nazis turned to the rest of the Jewish population."

(12) Remnants of the Lublin Jewish community raided during the night: "In accordance with the established practice, those who were ill or were for any reason too weak to move were murdered on the spot. The rest were divided into two groups … the larger one was made up of the wounded who had managed to stay upright, women with children, older men, and women, and a few young men. They were destined for deportation, no one knew where. The second group consisted of healthy-looking individuals, more of them men than women and very few of them children. This group was moved to the new ghetto, a worker's settlement called Majdan Tatarski."

(60–1) Her mother sustains a beating at their candle factory: "For the first time I saw for myself what the Nazis were capable of doing."

(63–6) "One Nazi restriction followed another, and soon our part of the city was declared 'Judenrein', which meant that Jews could neither live in nor visit this section of Lublin. The order specified that not more than one room should be allotted to a Jewish family." They move closer to the old city; Jews are subjected to a curfew; they must sew a yellow star on their clothes, and Jewish men must remove their hats and bow to Germans.

(89) On Jews trying to pass as Christians: "In those days Jews looked frightened. They walked cautiously, without self-confidence. Most of them desperately tried to become invisible. Ironically, those very efforts made them more conspicuous."

(110–15) Nechama's sister comes with Wojtek to bring Nechama to rejoin the family; they go by train through the night from Otwock to Kielce: "I kept looking at my sister and squeezing her hand, not yet convinced that this was really happening. We did not talk, knowing that an unguarded remark might arouse suspicion. I welcomed this enforced silence." Spring 1943, she is 11 years old.

(148–50) Shopping on the Kielce black market: "Little attention was paid to the illegality or danger it entailed, because life under the Nazis was dangerous whether or not one engaged in illegal activities. So the black market was thriving." Nechama takes over the shopping from Stefa: "Unlike Stefa, I thoroughly enjoyed selecting and bargaining. To me, the whole business of shopping at the market was a challenge and an adventure."

(165–9) November 1943, their financial picture grim: "But we could not ask the Homars, who had taken us in because they did not want to starve, to eat less." They decide to begin a business baking bread for Nechama to sell on the black market: "Only then did it occur to me that none of my buying experience had really prepared me for the role of seller."

(180–4) She takes the black market baked-goods business "wholesale" by selling to "stores": "Without exception they were all black-market operations, carried out in private homes and selling a wide variety of goods. … I suggested to my parents that I could sell them Tadek's vodka as well as the rolls, and so increase our earnings without much extra effort."

(187–91) German raids on their apartment: "No matter how many precautions we took, the possibility of sudden disaster was a constant, hovering presence."

Creation of the ghetto

(17–19) "The new ghetto, Majdan Tatarski, was located on the outskirts of Lublin close to Majdanek. … The Nazis offered their usual assurances that the survivors would live undisturbed if they abided by the rules."

Daily life in the ghetto

(21–3) She goes to stay in the Majdan Tatarski ghetto with her tutor Hela, nicknamed "Czuczka" and has the companionship of a few other children, summer 1942: "We knew that we lived in a dangerous and unstable world, but we preferred not to talk about it. Did we think that the danger would go away if nobody mentioned it? Or was the situation simply too frightening for discussion?"

Deportation

(8) 1939 Lublin, Nechama's mother works as a housekeeper for a Nazi: "As she served meals she learned from conversations at the table that what the Germans called 'deportations' were often executions – that groups of Jews who were rounded up in raids were taken no farther than a nearby forest, where they were shot."

Slave labour camps and factories

(142–3) "Once, in town, a Polish friend and I saw a small group of Jewish workers from a local factory walking along in the middle of the road, surrounded by German soldiers with machine guns. … They looked exhausted, depressed, depleted of energy, almost of life itself. … If dead people could walk, I would expect them to walk that way."

(198–9) "As the killing of some civilians continued, so did the rounding up of others for deportation to Germany as cheap labor. By now the Nazis' standards for qualified workers had grown far less exacting, and my age and size were no longer a protection." She survives a raid while hiding in a hay loft with Polish children, summer 1944.

Witness to mass murder

(27–30) Fearing an "Aktion" in the ghetto of Majdan Tatarski, her mother comes to bring her back to the factory. Nechama pleads with her to wait until the next day so she can say goodbye to her friends, but that night the "Aktion" begins and they barely find a place to hide: "At last Mother's pleas were heard, and I found myself squeezed into a cramped cellar where I almost had to sit on someone's head. There was no place for my mother, so she left me there. I learned later that only at the last minute did she find shelter." After the raid: "Almost all of those I cared about were gone; there would be no point in looking for them." She says goodbye to Czuczka and Stach.

(195–8) Summer 1944, the Nazis retaliate for partisan and Polish underground attacks: "They acted with particular speed and fury after the death of one of their comrades, executing ten or more innocent Poles for every slain Nazi. … They were very precise. Whatever ratio they decided upon – ten Poles, or twenty, for one Nazi killed – it had to be met." During a raid, she finds refuge in the home of a young woman: "Her whisper was followed almost immediately by a shot. Then there was another, and another after that, and more until I stopped counting." Nechama hurries home: "On the sidewalk close to the houses, almost in a straight line, lay the bodies of the victims just as they had fallen."

Specific escapes

(10–12) Forewarned of a deportation, the family moves to their chemical factory: "The German commissioner received us with courtesy and kindness. ... 'You will work here and I will legalize your stay. From now on this will be your home.'"

(13–14) Uncle Josef escapes from the deportation train: "He explained that he had jumped off the moving train not so much to save himself, but to die breathing fresh air."

(14–17) Uncle Josef is discovered in their factory hiding place, taken to Majdanek, but Nechama's father Roman: "... persisted, and finally, after considerable financial sacrifice, a miracle was performed. Josef was released from Majdanek."

(138–40) On a mission to buy cooking oil in Kielce before the 8 p.m. curfew, she is accosted by a man: "He wore a uniform and was perhaps a German soldier." She succeeds in breaking free.

(160–2) Searching for Partisans and Poles working for the underground, the Germans raid their apartment, but do not find her parents in their hiding place.

In hiding, including Hidden Children

(33) Her father's decision to hide, 1942: "He emphasized that passivity could mean disaster. He had been convinced almost from the start that the Germans were bent on our destruction. He felt that the only way we could survive was to hide our identity by passing as Poles. He was preparing for this eventuality, not just for the four of us but for Josef and Czuczka as well."

(34–6) "In order to go into hiding, my parents therefore had to find a Polish family willing to provide them with the necessary cover. My father and mother would have to become in effect invisible by living with such a family. ... Because of our appearance, and because our Polish was flawless, we could lead relatively normal lives. But because we were both young, my sister fifteen and I eleven, we too would have to live with a Polish family." 1942.

(40, 69–71) Bolek arranges for Polish identification. Nechama becomes "Pelagia Pawlowska" a fictitious person, for the journey to Warsaw. Once there: "... my sister and I exchanged our false birth certificates for new ones, which were duplicates of real documents. ... I became Christina and she Danuta Bloch. The diminutive of Christina was Krysia, of Danuta was Danka, and from then on everybody had to address us by these names. ... This rule was followed by every Jew who had Polish identification papers."

(41–3) The train journey from Lublin to Warsaw, her sister went ahead, acting as the fiancée of their Polish guide. The parents decide not to leave Nechama, she travels next to her mother who is dressed in mourning, her father in a different train compartment.

(67–9) Coming into Warsaw, hoping to hide among the crowds, November 1942: "Already eleven, I knew that I had to appear calm by substituting numbness for this fear." Arriving from the train to the platform, they are met by Nazis searching for Jews: "The use of flashlights increased as they kept illuminating the eyes. Jews had sad eyes. We knew that Jews could be recognized by the sadness of their eyes. It was well known."

(71–4) With new identities, names, fictitious family, and familiarity with Catholicism, the family leave Bolek to live with Jan and Magda on the outskirts of Warsaw: "Of the four of us only my father officially lived in the apartment, and he served as our contact with the outside world."

(77–9) Antek, the son of the Poles who were hiding the Rubins, suggests of one of his sisters: "... that for payment, Marta and her husband Tosiek would be willing to have my sister and me live with them," and their children Jurek, 6, and Ania, 4. "My parents saw this as the best opportunity that had yet presented itself, and the arrangements were completed."

(92–3) Nechama's parents join her sister in Kielce with Wojtek and his family. Nechama remains with Marta and Tosiek until arrangements can be made to bring her. Her father leaves her: "'Remember,' he whispered. 'Never tell anyone where we went. And never, never, admit to anyone that you are Jewish. No matter how hard it is, you must guard these secrets. You must be strong.'"

(94–8) Alone with Marta and the children, she is consumed by her hunger, her fear, her nightmares to which Tosiek offers some protection: "Although I felt immense gratitude to Tosiek and felt a need to confide in him, I knew that I must not monopolize his time. I stayed discreetly in the background and did not speak to him about my fears or my longing for my family, or about Marta's mistreatment. … I was convinced that if she knew. … she would throw me out …"

(108–9) "An extra layer of secretiveness, combined with a fear of discovery, became part of my being. All my life revolved around hiding; hiding thoughts, hiding feelings, hiding my activities, hiding information. Sometimes I felt like a sort of fearful automaton, always on the alert, always dreading that something fatal might be revealed."

(115) A respite from the hiding, Nechama is returned to her family, now hiding in Kielce: "It was good to feel like a child again, to 'be' a child, loved, protected, and not to have to talk about anything serious or upsetting. I was particularly grateful that no one asked me about my life in Otwock. The memory of the humiliation and despair I had suffered there stayed with me for years. I could not talk about Otwock then, or at any other time. The scars were too deep."

(116–20, 124–6) She describes their two-room apartment, its amenities, and their situation: "In Kielce, my parents did not officially exist. … My sister and I … passed as Poles and were free to come and go, while my parents never left the house even at night. … Of the two of them, my mother had an easier time … she could more easily find work within the house, and thus fill most of her time. … His becoming involved helped him bear his enforced confinement to the two rooms."

(136–8) The visits from the neighbours Mr and Mrs Koziarz: "When they did come, my sister or I, whose existence was official and acknowledged, would retire to the second room so that if my father had one of his seizures, the cough could be attributed to one of us."

(141–5, 169) In her friendships with neighbourhood children, she learns to accept their anti-Semitism so as to not arouse suspicion: "It was as if in certain circumstances I lost track of who I really was and began to see myself as a Pole. I became a double person, one private and one public. When I was away from my family I became so engrossed in my public self that I did not have to act the part; I actually felt like the person I was supposed to be."

(145–7) She helps with the hay harvest to bring in some money: "When the work ended at last and payday came, the old man took one look at me and mumbled, 'You are too little. I shall pay you half.' I protested. My friends stood up for me, telling him what a good worker I was, but all in vain. His answer was, 'Half or nothing.'"

(150–5) Tadek's bootlegging business takes over the apartment, so they move to an apartment not far, and set about making a hiding place for her parents: "They cut an opening in the floor just large enough to let one adult through at a time, and dug a hole that would accommodate a total of three." In order to have warning of a German raid, they acquire a dog: "whom we called Czarus, Polish for 'charming'."

(199–203) Ziutka and Tadek, "financially independent" from the Bawniks due to the bootleg vodka business, concoct a plan of an imminent German raid to force them to leave: "In effect my father was trying to convey to Ziutka the idea that by getting rid of us now she would not free herself from danger, but on the contrary would surely invite disaster. Ziutka was shrewd enough to understand the message. She may even have realized that my father saw through her scheme."

Righteous Gentiles

(11, 32, 62, 163, 233) The German commissioner of her father's chemical factory helps the family move into the factory, legitimizes their being there, takes their valuables for safe-keeping: "'I will do all I can to protect you.'" Later when asked to, he returns the valuables: "along with a warm letter expressing his delight that we were alive, and asking us to turn to him for help again if we needed to."

(21) Fifty Jewish girls come to the factory to work and live: "They were young, between fifteen and twenty years of age. They came from the ghetto, and all of them had lost their families." Although not mentioned specifically in the memoir, this could not have happened without the approval of the German commissioner.

(31) "The mother superior from the convent adjoining our factory was also ready to accept me as one of her charges. This was both generous and courageous of her, because if she took in a Jewish child she ran the risk of the death penalty." Her offer was not taken.

(38–40, 231) Former employee Mr Pys: "… had agreed to our taking refuge in his home if events forced us to leave the factory." After a short stay with the Pys family, her parents and sister plan to leave Lublin for Warsaw: "They felt that it would be too dangerous for me to go with them, arguing that if they were killed on the way at least I would survive. … It was understood that if they were killed the Pys family would be stuck with me. … In fact, it was to their credit that they agreed, no matter how reluctantly, to go along with this arrangement."

(122–3) The business arrangement between the Homars and Nechama's family, Kielce: "The Homars' needs were modest, but even so the combined salaries of all the working members of the family could not cover their expenses. … To provide shelter for Jews who in turn would support them seemed a perfect solution to their financial problems. … By helping us they were shielding themselves from hunger and economic uncertainty. In a sense we were only a means to an important end, a means that could be justified only by this end. In return for their protection, we had to feed the entire family and pay the rent."

(170–4) Magda, her protector and friend in the Kielce blackmarket, November 1943, guides her during a raid: "She gave me one significant look and yelled, 'Run after me.' … Soon Magda and I were in a courtyard. A door opened, someone pulled us in, we were safe."

(175–8) Christmas 1943, the relationship with the Homars deepens: "In our day-to-day contact they never took advantage of us, they never behaved cruelly or even inconsiderately, but treated us instead with respect and kindness. … Considering our close quarters and the dangerous times, this was a real blessing."

(192–3) Summer 1944, Stefa Homar survives a beating at Gestapo headquarters but does not betray them: "Because of her mild self-effacing manner we had thought of her as a coward. Her resistance and presence of mind seemed out of character. In adversity she had drawn upon unsuspected resources of courage and had saved us all."

Liberation

(208–9) Early 1945: "The Germans themselves were aware that their time was running out, and this very knowledge propelled them into increasingly vicious retaliation. More and more their behavior was like that of a wounded wild beast, which strikes out before it dies with all its fury and fading strength. We could not help but conclude that although time brought us closer to our liberation, it also brought us closer to disaster."

(209–11) Bombs and artillery fire force them all to seek safety in a community shelter, they come out when they hear Russian spoken: "We came out into a free world. All was silent. There was no wild excitement. There was nothing and I felt nothing except exhaustion. We looked at one another in disbelief. Was this the end?"

(213–15) With liberation, the mood in the house changes: "The Homars wanted us to leave Kielce as Poles, without revealing our true identity. They did not want anyone to know that they had helped a Jewish family to survive. … We were upset because they themselves failed to reassure us that they were glad we were alive and felt gratified by the part they played in our rescue."

(215–16) Leaving the Homars: "Hugging Waldek, I felt a tremendously deep sadness that dissolved all the misunderstandings and tensions. After all, we had gone through a great deal together. A wave of genuine love and affection swept us into one embrace after another. …" They return to Lublin, a city and a home in ruins.

(217) "With liberation, my struggle for survival ended only to be replaced by other less concrete, less tangible kinds of struggle that had to do with personal losses, Jewish identity, and the seeming indifference of others to our survival."

(218–20) Returning to Lublin, to the chemical factory her father once owned, the janitor Jan and his wife Genia welcome them in: "When I began to look around it dawned on me that I was seeing familiar objects. The table was covered with our tablecloth, the silver was ours. I continued to recognize more and more items. … As I stretched out next to my sister, I became aware of the familiarity of the comforters and linens. … So many of our belongings switched masters, becoming a part of someone else's lives; objects have no loyalty. It was as if my finding them so well-adjusted to the new owners mocked my claim to them. Their settled presence made me an intruder."

(223) "Before the war Lublin had a Jewish population of forty thousand. … In the end, the estimated figure for Jewish survivors in Lublin did not exceed one hundred and fifty." This number of "Lublin" survivors included those from adjacent towns: "Among them were only two intact families. Now we became the third."

Displaced Persons camps

(236–41) By the end of 1945, they decide to leave Poland: "Like most others my sister and I ended up in one of those DP camps. After a while my parents reached Germany as well."

Stories of individuals, including family members

(1–3, 39) Hela Trachtenberg, 30, from Warsaw, returns to Lublin to tutor Nechama and her sister. Called "Czuczka": "Often I would think before I acted. How would Czuczka look at it? … I knew she would urge me to be good, just and decent. Invariably, thinking about her helped me make the right decision." She is murdered at the ghetto's liquidation.

(7–8, 20, 53) News of the loss of her mother's parents in a little town, Miedzyrzec, beyond Lublin: "At first we heard that they had both been shot during a raid. Later someone brought the news that they had been seen in a concentration camp. Only one thing was certain: we never saw them again."

(9–10) Her father's sister Aunt Ella taken with her husband and three children during a raid: "We never saw my Aunt Ella and her family again, and we never knew how they perished."

(10, 41) "In another raid my easygoing Uncle Josef, my mother's brother, lost his wife and their two sons." Josef is killed while hiding in the factory warehouse at the final liquidation.

(19–20) Her mother's sister Zelda is brought by truck into Lublin, then is deported by train to a camp other than Majdanek. She escapes from the train, hides with Polish peasants, and declines offer to hide with the family: "She refused, believing that she had a better chance to survive in the countryside. After that we had no further communication with her."

(24–5) The collaborator Graier and his mistress Golda: "Ill-matched as they seemed, Graier and Golda were the best-known, best-fed, and best-dressed couple in Majdan Tatarski." He is forced to marry the 17-year-old Mina: "As Graier's wife, Mina was relieved from work and free to concentrate on clothes and amusement. … We understood why she had obeyed a Nazi order, but we could not forgive her for being happy about it. She was no longer one of us. She had become one of them."

(25–7, 37) Their neighbour in the ghetto Stach, gardener, close in friendship to Czuczka, included Nechama in their friendship: "I learned that during the last raid his wife, who was eight months pregnant, had been beaten to death by a Nazi right in front of his eyes." He is deported from the ghetto, Autumn 1942.

(33–4, 163–4) Distant cousin Bolek: "Before the war Bolek had been a marginal character, moving from one occupation to another, living mostly on dreams and borrowed money. … The war, which brought drastic and terrible changes for so many of those we knew, wrought a marvelous change for Bolek. He became a success." His end: "… caught between two hostile German factions. Those who arrested him had taken advantage of his chief protector's temporary absence. Terrifying him into committing suicide … would spare them from reprisals from the other faction."

(36) Her father's former business partner Moshe: "… who had lost his fighting spirit." He wanted to believe the Germans who: "promised the Jews tranquility and peace if they volunteered for deportation to the East."

(60, 223, 225) Father's brother Gershon Bawnik, crossed into Russia with the intention of returning to bring his family, unable to return: "He would survive in Russia, while the wife and son he had left behind would perish." This Aunt Sylvia's brother Mietek was to be their only surviving relative after the war; he had survived fighting with a Polish partisan group.

(74–5) Father's former business partner Mr Lerner, hiding in Warsaw with his daughter and her husband, with Poles, warned that the Gestapo were coming: "Mr Lerner was a proud man, determined never to be taken alive, and for just such an eventuality as this one he always carried poison with him. He swallowed it. But the Gestapo never came. They were looking for someone else in a different building, and had entered this one by mistake."

(76, 184) Roman Bawnik from his daughter's perspective, Warsaw, November 1942: "I wondered, often, if he had any doubts. If so, he was careful not to show them. On the contrary, he tried to give us courage by insisting that eventually we would overcome our difficulties and all would be well. He wanted us to believe him, and we did. He wanted us to lean on him, and we did. And as he was giving us support, he also kept us informed about his efforts to find a solution for our problems."

(76–7, 91) The Rubin family, brewery owners in Lublin, the father: "… had had the misfortune of being ill at the time of a Nazi raid. He was taken out of bed and shot. Mrs Rubin and her three sons came to Warsaw …" Zygmunt, in his late 20s and Pawel, 24, "could both easily pass for Christians." Stefan, 21 and Mrs Rubin who, "had what was considered a 'typically Jewish look'," in hiding with a Polish family in nearby Otwock. Zygmunt, betrayed.

(80–2, 85–8) Marta and Tosiek, with whom Nechama and her sister were hiding in Otwock: "She conveyed the impression of an intelligent woman who was also cold and unapproachable. … In no time we discovered that he had an easygoing cheerful disposition and seemed always ready with a joke. … With Tosiek home, even Marta was less disagreeable."

(81, 84–5) Marta's parents, Stanislaw and Maria, with whom the Rubins were hiding in Otwock: "Stanislaw was selfish and wholly self-centered. He focused his whole attention on his own suffering and on growing poppies to relieve it. … Yet his self-absorption and his grumpiness were oddly inoffensive. … Totally unlike Stanislaw, she never complained. Her moods showed no variations. Her entire person spelled moderation. Because of this she was a colorless person and she did not appeal to me at all."

(83–4, 98–100) Stefan Rubin and his mother, in hiding in Otwock: "What Stefan lacked in looks he made up for with a sparkling personality. Despite the conditions he now lived under he never lost his sense of humor. … It was obvious that neither his wit nor his intelligence came from Mrs Rubin, who was quiet, limited, and dull."

(89–90) Marta and Antek's younger sister Ziutka: "… who lived with her husband Tadek and his family in the city of Kielce." Tadek's 19-year-old brother Wojtek came to visit: "he knew from his sister-in-law Ziutka how Stanislaw and Maria had improved their economic situation by protecting Jews. Wojtek and his family barely managed to survive on the wages the Germans paid him; he had come to find out if he and his family could also profit from such an arrangement." Nechama's sister returns with him to Kielce to determine whether it is a good situation for the parents who are still in Warsaw.

(100–3) Pawel Rubin visits his mother and brother in hiding: "Pawel was as conceited as he was handsome, and constantly patronizing Stefan. It was this patronizing attitude that infuriated Stefan the most." Pawel is caught in a roundup of Poles needed for labour: "It was no longer possible to doubt that Pawel had perished. … Although it was no secret that Stefan had loved Zygmunt and had little affection for Pawel, he now mourned more intensely than he had for Zygmunt."

(103–6) The aunt, who with her niece share the other half of the house with Marta and Tosiek: "The aunt kept house and the niece worked in a canteen for German officers, with whom she was on the most friendly terms." The aunt reveals to Nechama that they are mother and daughter and that they are Jewish: "There was something appealing in her approach and her whole manner and I was in such need of comfort that I had an impulse to throw my arms around her and cry. Yet some inner power prevented me from doing so. I remembered my father's injunction never to admit that I was Jewish. …"

(123–4) The Homar family: Helena, her widowed daughter-in-law Stefa, and Stefa's three children, 16-year-old Basia, 19-year-old Wojtek, and Tadek, who is married to Zuitka, Marta's sister. Tadek and Zuitka have two children Jadwiga and Waldek. Nechama's family of four brings the total to twelve people, in two rooms.

(126–7) When Stefa, "now in her mid-fifties", had lost her husband in an accident in 1939, she had moved her family from Warsaw to Kielce: "She was a kind well-meaning person who tried to be helpful, even though her help was clumsy and inefficient. I never heard her express a single independent opinion."

(127–9, 185–7) "Helena, Stefa's mother-in-law, was at least eighty, and to me, she looked one hundred or more. … She was fiercely independent and refused to let herself be supported by the family or us. … She worked as a professional beggar." Her short illness and death: "True to herself, on her deathbed as in life, she hated any kind of pretense. … She died simply, without fuss, just as she had lived. Even Czarus, our watch dog, seemed heartbroken."

(130–4, 204–8) Stefa's son Tadek: "… even though Tadek resented his job and all that was connected with it, he did not try to find different and better employment. … He sometimes spoke about his dreams of financial success, but he never tried to make them come true." Tadek's wife: "Ziutka was almost wholly absorbed in her own needs, and for her family she did as little as possible." Together: "Tadek and Ziutka had a stormy marriage, in which violence was mixed with love. … In our poor neighborhood violence was an accepted pattern, and unless the man was a total pushover, his dominance over his wife had to be periodically reestablished by beatings."

(134–5, 155–6, 178–9) The children Jadwiga, 2-years-old, and Waldek, 8 months: "… she was lively, undisciplined, and extremely jealous of her baby brother. … His affection was for me like a soothing medication and to dispel a gloomy mood all I had to do was pick him up. His responsiveness made me forget all my troubles."

(157–60) Nechama's sister works in a club for German officers; Nechama walks her home at night: "Only then did we feel free to complain about our difficult life. We never did so with our parents because we wanted to protect them from pain and worry." Her sister's friend from Lublin stops writing: "We knew from what he had written that he was among the small handful of prisoners in Lublin still left alive. With time we understood that he too must have perished. We never found out how."

(212) A Polish Jewish soldier with the Russian liberators enquires about his parents who used to live in the house, Kielce: "Who could give him an answer? With a gentle disbelief, my father asked, 'Don't you know what happened to Jews?' … He nodded in distress, accepting the knowledge, and yet kept repeating as if to himself, 'Where are my parents? Where are they?' No one could help him."

(233–5) After the war, Stefa Homar and her daughter Basia visit them in Lublin on their offer to provide a bridal trousseau for Basia; the relationship is strained: "As I watched them depart I was filled with a strange mixture of regret, guilt, and relief. … We were not invited to the wedding, and we never saw the Homars again."

Post-war life and career

(241–2) Her father died at age 62, her mother remarried and lived in Israel, her sister lives with her family in Israel.

(back cover) She became a Sociology Professor, University of Connecticut, Stamford, Connecticut, and noted Holocaust scholar.

Personal reflections

(48) On pre-war Lublin: "Because of its location, most of the tenants in our apartment house were Christians, and yet the only neighbors we knew were Jews. Our Christian neighbors, both adults and children, were complete strangers to me. I never wondered why this was so, nor was I ever upset by it. Indeed only later did I realize that although I lived in the Christian section of the city, I had never succeeded in entering the Christian world."

(175) "'Fear,' my father had said, 'is a luxury we cannot afford. We must be cautious, but we

must not be fearful.' And as we followed his precepts we tried hard to give to our lives some semblance of normality. We tried desperately not to indulge in gloomy thoughts. We tried to plan ahead, pretending and believing that life would continue to move along relatively uneventfully until the end of the war."

(203) "I never complained to either parent about my burdens, and I was glad that they never told me how sorry they felt for me. If they had done so, I might have begun to feel sorry for myself. Keeping our true feelings to ourselves, never revealing to each other that we all knew how desperate our situation really was – all this helped us to endure."

(225) Survivors, speaking of their experiences, 1945: "None of us was able to speak specifically of our own wartime experiences. None of us asked for elaborations or details from the others. Later I realized that if, as it rarely happened, one of us felt like saying more, more than just identifying the mode of survival, such information had to be volunteered by the speaker. It was never requested by the listener. Somehow, automatically, without discussion, we learned not to probe into each other's wartime past. … stirring up memories of what happened during the war can hurt too much, and we must each choose our own time to endure this necessary pain."

Places mentioned – in Europe: (page first mentioned)

Berlin (241), Germany (102), Hungary (76), Kielce (89), Kovel/Kowel (60), Lodz/Litzmanstadt (239), Lublin (1), Majdan Tatarski ghetto (12), Majdanek concentration camp (16), Miedzyrzec Podlaski (53), Naleczow (53), Otwock (77), Poland (44), Warsaw/Warszawa/Warschau (1)

Places mentioned – outside Europe: (page first mentioned)

Connecticut (242), Israel (242), Russia (60)

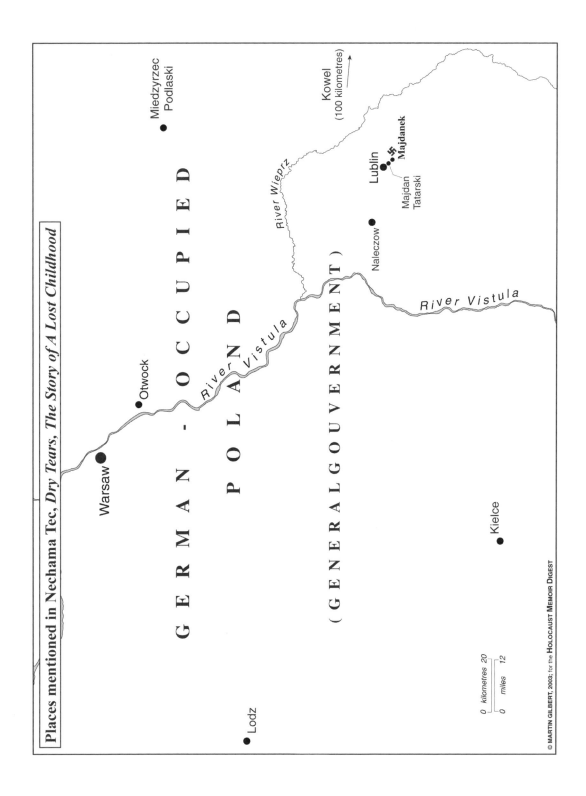

Places mentioned in Nechama Tec, *Dry Tears, The Story of A Lost Childhood*

Miedzyrzec Podlaski

Kowel (100 kilometres)

River Wieprz

Lublin
Majdanek
Majdan Tatarski

Naleczow

G E R M A N - O C C U P I E D

P O L A N D

(G E N E R A L G O U V E R N M E N T)

River Vistula

River Vistula

Otwock

Warsaw

Lodz

Kielce

0 kilometres 20
0 miles 12

Author: Dr Salim Diamand

Title: *Dottore! Internment in Italy, 1940–1945*

Publishing details: Mosaic Press, P.O. Box 1032, Oakville, Ontario L6J 5E9. 1987. 159 pages. ISBN #0-88962-369-4.

Published by The Mosaic Press Eyewitness Series, which "… is devoted to personal, eyewitness, first-hand accounts, analyses, memoirs of significant historical events."

Focus:

A Polish Jew comes to Italy before the war to complete his medical training, spends the war in Italian internment camps and in hiding in the countryside, and after the war becomes a camp doctor in Italian refugee camps until he emigrates to Canada; the events described take place between 18 June 1940 and 6 December 1950.

Features:

Foreword: Introduction written by the Author, pages 9–10.

Photographs: Photographs of friends and inmates in Ferramonti and Eboli, of friends in post-war Naples, and of staff at Camp Rivoli and Trani, as well as a contemporary photograph of the author, pages 69–98, and back page.

Documents: Certificate from and design of, Ferramonti internment camp, pages 69, 79.

Maps: Map of Italy, front cover.

Contents: (by topic, with page numbers)

Pre-war anti-Semitism

(11–13) Polish quota system for Jews to receive an education forces him to go to Reims, France in 1933, and then to Italy. He goes to Pisa in 1934, Genoa, 1935, and Naples from September 1936 to June 1939, for medical school and training.

The coming of war

(11, 14–15) Arrested 18 June 1940 in Naples, taken to the Poggiorele jail for eight days, and then by train to the town of Eboli. In September, taken by truck to Ferramonti.

(29–32) The air battle over the Adriatic Sea forces the camp to move from Corropoli to Civitella del Tronto, 1943.

(33–4) He is permitted to expand his medical ministrations to help sick people in outlying areas.

(107–11) Captured by the Germans, he carries mail and food for them, feigns a sprained ankle and is spared the work detail which is bombed, killing all, Christmas 1943.

Life under German occupation

(25–7) The train journey from Ferramonti to Corropoli: "I thought of escape."

(34–8) Encounter with the Germans: "'I wish to apologize for the shooting this morning.'"

Death camps

(148) After the war, he receives "… a Polish newspaper that contained a long article about

Treblinka. I translated it into Italian and it was published in a left-wing journal, 'La Voce'. It may have been the first article of its kind to be published in Italy."

Slave labour camps and factories

(41–4) Taken by truck to a former brick factory, now slave labour camp, near Castelfrentano.
(45–8) As an interpreter, and a doctor at Castelfrentano.
(119) An Austrian Corporal suggests he "… can find work with the Todt Organization" thinking him to be "… fleeing the Americans at Naples. … I learned later that Todt was a construction company that employed slave labour throughout Europe."

Death marches

(49-52) Taken from Castelfrentano northward by forced march to the village of Tollo.

Concentration camps

(15-20) Life in Ferramonti: "Italy's largest concentration camp, built to house 2,000 inmates."
(21-3) His medical credentials qualify him to be transferred from Ferramonti to Corropoli, to become a doctor at a camp for British prisoners of war, October 1942.

Partisan activity

(33) Cryptic messages on the BBC news broadcasts: "'Please stand by for further recipes.'"
(38-9) Caught between the British Eighth Army and the Germans, with: "… rumour of Partisan activity in our district."
(53-7, 128-30) Count Luigi "head of the Partisan groups in the district" and his guide Mario help him escape from the Germans at Tollo and find places to hide. Later, they escort groups across the lines to the British side, at the Caporosso Cemetery, spring 1944.
(125-6) The Lazarovichs and Signora D'Allesandro help him to get identification papers and to cross to the British side.

Specific escapes

(52-5) Escapes from forced march at the village of Tollo, with the help of Partisans.

In hiding, including Hidden Children

(59-68) In hiding from the Germans, he moves around, treating the sick and wounded, being paid with food and shelter, Tollo region.
(103-5) Hiding in caves: "Our constant concern was to avoid contact with the Germans."

Liberation

(130-4) Escapes to Canadian soldiers of the British Eighth Army at Caporosso, taken to Casoli and Foggia, and on to Bari to the Carbonara refugee camp.
(135) The thought of returning to Bolechow: "The Jewish Brigade soldiers ended my innocence. … I knew now that to go to Poland was to visit a graveyard."
(137-47) Trying to find work in Naples, he develops "… a small medical practice".
(148-9) 3 May 1944, he is: "… appointed as a Medical Officer of Health for the City of Naples … to restore an adequate level of public health to the city after the War." He is able to complete his training in pediatrics.

Displaced Persons camps

(133–5) Transported to the Carbonara refugee camp run by the United Nations Relief and Rehabilitation Administration. For Passover 1944, the Jewish Brigade: "... organized a massive Seder. Thousands of people – refugees, Jewish soldiers from the American, British and Polish armies – sat down to a festive meal celebrating the Exodus from Egypt. ... It was a sad reminder of family that had vanished."

(151–7) August 1946, he becomes Camp Doctor in United Nations Relief and Rehabilitation Administration refugee camps, Cremona, Rivoli, Trani, and while based in Bagnoli in Ancona province, he works in three small transit camps of Senigallia, Fermo, and Jesi, moving on as each camp closes when refugees emigrate to Palestine/Israel, United States, Canada, Australia, and South America.

Stories of individuals, including family members

(27–9) Dr Habibi: "... a man of astonishing competance, energy, and charisma ..." his predecessor in Corropoli.

(99–101, 127–8) He diagnoses gangrene in Mario's father, who is operated on in Chieti by his classmate Giovanni Tampoia.

(113–20) The Tomaso Di Bartolomeo family welcome and include him: "I admired Tomaso for his endless resourcefulness and his iron will to survive."

(121–2, 124) Friend Jacobson from Ferramonti gives him advice in Chieti, February 1944.

(122–4) Marek and Etta Lazarovich, from Ferramonti, to the Partisans, to being interpreters for the Gestapo.

(132–3) "Volksdeutsche" Marchinek becomes a Pole again. In Casoli with the British Eighth Army, Dr Diamand recognizes Marchinek, a former guard at Castelfrentano: "This unfortunate fellow was a Pole, whom the Nazis declared to be a German and had conscripted into the Army. Now he was a prisoner." Dr Diamand intercedes: "By the end of the day they removed him from the German prisoner group and sent him to the Polish Corps of the 8th Army. Marchinek was now a Pole again!"

(138–9) Matteo Scarfuri of Boiano and the fate of his three sons.

(138, 152, 156) Romanian Giacomo Eisenberg converts to Catholicism: "... he had not been bothered in any way as a foreigner or a Jew."

Post-war life and career

(157–9) In 1950, he decides to emigrate, accepts a position in hospital in New Westminster, British Columbia, Canada; arrives 6 December 1950 in St John's, Newfoundland, with his friend Annie.

Personal reflections

(10) "Throughout my years of confinement in various camps during the war years in Italy, I never found racism in Italians ... I never found any Italians who approached me, as a Jew, with the idea of exterminating my race."

(138) "I questioned why I and the others had been rounded up, placed in camps, or lived in hiding, while others were almost untouched. I can only explain it as the total arbitrariness of unrestricted authority which allows rulers to act on whim."

Places mentioned – in Europe: (page first mentioned)

Abruzzi (27), Ancona (157), Appenine Mountains (27), Bagnoli Displaced Persons camp (156), Bari (133), Boiano (138), Bolechow (11), Calabria (15), Caporosso (129), Carbonara Displaced Persons camp (134), Casoli (131), Cassino (50), Castelfrentano (42), Catania (14), Chieti (48), Civitella del Tronto (31), Corropoli prison camp (22), Cosenza (15), Cracow/Krakow/Krakau (19), Cremona Displaced Persons camp (152), Eboli internment camp (14), Fermo Displaced Persons camp (157), Ferramonti internment camp (15), Fiume/Rijeka (30), Foggia (133), Forcella (Naples) (148), France (12), Galicia (11), Genoa/Genova (13), Germany (13), Greece (17), Grugliasco (154), Italy (13), Jesi Displaced Persons camp (157), Latvia (124), Milan/Milano/Mailand (51), Minervino Murge (127), Naples/Napoli (11), Paris (151), Pergola (115), Pisa (13), Pisticci internment camp (18), Poggiorele Jail (Naples) (14), Poland (12), Potenza (26), Pozzuoli (152), Reims/Rheims (12), Rivoli Displaced Persons camp (153), Rome/Roma (16), Saarbrücken (45), Salerno (32), Senigallia Displaced Persons camp (157), Sicily (32), Switzerland (122), Tarsia (15), Teramo (27), Teschen/Cieszyn/CeskiTesin (47), Tollo (51), Trani Displaced Persons camp (154), Treblinka death camp (148), Trieste (30), Turin/Torino (154), Vatican City (Rome) (125), Vesuvius (152), Vienna/Wien (12), Villamagna (66), Yugoslavia (52)

Places mentioned – outside Europe: (page first mentioned)

Australia (152), California (153), Canada (130), Chile (156), Hollywood (158), Israel (155), Japan (47), Lebanon (28), Libya (27), New Westminster (British Columbia) (159), New York City (158), Palestine (20), St John's (Newfoundland) (159), Tripoli (53), Tunisia (32), United States of America (14)

Places mentioned in Dr. Salim Diamand,
Dottore! Internment in Italy, 1940-1945

Treblinka

HOLLAND

GERMANY

POLAND

BELGIUM

Cracow

Bolechow

CZECHOSLOVAKIA

Teschen

EASTERN
GALICIA

Reims

Saarbrücken

Paris

Vienna

FRANCE

SWITZERLAND

AUSTRIA

HUNGARY

ROMANIA

Trieste

Fiume

Turin

Milan

I

Genoa

YUGOSLAVIA

BULGARIA

Pisa

T

Ligurian
Sea

Ancona

A

Adriatic Sea

CORSICA

Rome

L

ALBANIA

Naples

Bari

Y

GREECE

Aegean
Sea

SARDINIA

*Tyrrhenian
Sea*

CALABRIA

*Ionian
Sea*

M

e

d

i

t

SICILY

Catania

e

r

r

a

ALGERIA

n

e

MALTA

TUNISIA

a

n

—·— International borders, 1937

S

e

a

0   kilometres   300

0   miles   200

© MARTIN GILBERT, 2003; for the HOLOCAUST MEMOIR DIGEST

Tripoli

LIBYA

Places in Italy mentioned in Dr. Salim Diamand,
Dottore! Internment in Italy, 1940-1945

△ Internment camps
▲ Displaced Persons camps
(DP camps)

Author: Ingrid Kisliuk

Title: *Unveiled Shadows, The Witness of a Child*

Publishing details: Nanomir Press, P.O. Box 600577, Newton, Massachussets 02460-0005. 1998. 223 pages.
ISBN #0-9663440-0-6.

Focus:

A young Viennese girl survives in hiding in Belgium with her parents; the events take place between early 1938 and 7 May 1945.

Features:

Foreword:	Introduction written by the Author, pages xi–xiii.
	Preface written by the Author, pages ix–x.
	Author's Acknowledgements, pages vii–viii.
Photographs:	Family photographs, also photographs of Belgian war memorials.
Documents:	Postcards from the train, reproduced, transcribed, translated, pages 193–214.
Afterword:	Epilogue written by the Author, pages 189–92.
	Commentary written by daughter Claudette Beit-Aharon, pages 225–8.
	Commentary written by daughter Michelle Kisliuk, pages 229–33.
Footnotes:	pages 215–21.
Bibliography:	pages 222–3.

Contents: (by topic, with page numbers)

Pre-war Jewish home and community life

(2, 6–10) Family and life in Vienna: parents, Helene Kohn and Saly Scheer, brother Ernst, 19, sister Herta, 17, author Inge, aged 8, 1938.

(12–13, 15) Grandfather's funeral and family religious traditions: "Although everyone in the family had a very strong Jewish identity, we were not particularly pious. We observed dietary laws on major holidays only, and attended religious services solely then."

(29–34) Summer 1938, in the Anderlecht district of Brussels: "… a Jewish agency set up to provide help and social services for Jews fleeing Nazi persecution. … financial assistance was the principal purpose of the Jewish community in founding 'Le Comité des Refugiés'."

(34) Refugees passing through: "Besides my parents and my siblings, my Aunt Pepi and my cousin, Brussels harbored for a short time various friends and relatives, some of whom I had heard of but had never met."

(35, 37) Intermarriage within the family: "Whatever the disagreement and lack of affinity, they were family. On the other hand, since quarrels are often common in families and had occurred in the past in ours, the occasional discord may have provided an appearance of normalcy."

(42–6, 50–4) Her involvement in Yiddish theater in Belgium in 1938, organized by the Comité des Refugiés: "The organization provided the Brussels refugee community with most of its social life. The program was especially extensive for children." Her own stage career brings her into contact with Molly Picon.

(43–5) Her ambivalence toward her use of Yiddish in the theater in Belgium: "Regrettably, among many German-speaking Jews, Yiddish was not regarded as a real language. It was thought of as an adulterated, deformed low German, the jargon of backward Jews from Eastern Europe. … Yiddish seemed much more accepted in Belgium, but I felt ill at ease in that language."

(47–50, 60–1) Schooling and friendships for pre-war refugees in Brussels; the difference between them and the local community: "… the victim feels shame for having been the object of persecution, so that even then, under our seeming childish unconcern, lurked the sadness at being strangers, at having had to flee."

Pre-war anti-Semitism

(1–4) With the *Anschluss*, in Vienna: "From our apartment windows on Tabor Strasse, in Leopoldstadt, a district inhabited by a large Jewish population, I saw many spectacles that frightened me. Standing next to my moaning mother, my being anguished increased by her lament, I saw young Jews being assaulted."

(5–6) They witness Hitler's arrival in Vienna from their window: "When the motorcade appeared with Hitler standing in a convertible, his arm raised in his Nazi salute, the masses went into a frenzy. … Indeed, the view of the street overflowing with people screaming their approval and devotion to this man Hitler, was at once terrifying and riveting."

(9) "My mother and Aunt Pepi occasionally accompanied my father on his travels as a representative for Singer sewing machines. … Also, anti-Semitism was rampant in Austria, and my mother's gentile appearance diffused some of the hostility that my father met in his business dealings."

(16–17, 19–20) Preparations to leave Vienna: "My mother was bagging objects that she planned to give away when I noticed her including a small doll, one of my favorites. When I protested bitterly and asked for an explanation, her only answer was a very severe look. … I should understand that we were going to leave and could not bring toys along."

(19–21) Ernst and Herta leave Vienna first: "I remember only discussions of them leaving before us, and then their absence. Ernst was always taken for a gentile and would get into fights defending Jews from Nazi youths; he often came home bearing the marks of those fights. My parents feared for his safety and were relieved at his departure, although they then fretted about my siblings' dangerous flight as well as their illegal entry into another country."

(54–8) Father spends six months at a Belgian internment camp for refugees, Merksplas, 1938: "The law required provisional internment of refugees. When they had proof of future resettlement possibilities, they were set free."

The coming of war

(61–2) "With Belgium's entering the war, the greatest absurdity occurred when all Austrian and German men, being of enemy nationality whether Jewish refugees from Nazi persecution or not, had to report for internment." These people were taken to internment camps in southern France. However, "Many refugees who had to forfeit their nationality at the German or Austrian border were stateless and therefore were not called for internment. Usually to be a person without a country was considered a sad condition. This time it turned out to be a blessing for my family."

(65–7) Mother's Day, May 1940, Germany invades Holland and Belgium: "… people fled by the thousands, hoping to wait behind the Allied lines for the attacker to be stopped and thrown back."

(67–70) Caught up in the war as refugees: "But more significant for us was the 'normalcy' of our situation at this abnormal time. For now we shared the alarm of the general population with whom we participated in an enormous upheaval, fleeing a common enemy."

(72) As refugees returning to Brussels, summer 1940: "In many ways we were fortunate not to have reached France, for Vichy France blocked the return of the refugees of the 'exodus' and interned them in southern France. …"

(72–4) The return to Brussels on foot: "The helmets of the fallen soldiers hung from the crosses marking the burial place. We paused each time we passed a site identified by an Allied helmet; my mother would say 'nebich' … and I would echo her words." ("the poor thing")

Life under German occupation

(71–2) First impression of the German soldiers: "Wanting to win over the population, they were friendly and forthcoming. … Politely the soldiers requested shelter at the farm until their regiment was ordered to move on. The proprietors, charmed by their friendly demeanor and good looks were happy to comply with their request."

(74–6) Post-summer 1940: "For about a year and a half, the Jews of Belgium adjusted to the new political reality with the rest of the population. … Life took on a semblance of normalcy; people adapted and tried to ignore the widespread presence of German troops." Her classmates in fourth grade: "On the one hand we were 'Boches' because we came from German-speaking countries, on the other we were 'Smous' because we fled persecution. We laughed at being called Germans, but we only suppressed the hurt of the insulting expression for Jew."

(83–4) To mid-1941: "… Jews carried on with their lives as did the rest of the Belgian population. The primary everyday concern was to obtain proper food and clothing … I felt mostly boredom and loneliness and often the recurring feeling of foreboding."

(85–6, 139) Fall 1941: "One by one, decrees by the German occupier were put in place so that within several months, Jews found themselves totally isolated from the rest of the population."

Deportation

(10–11, 135–7, 193–214) Herta's letters from the train, and her "enigmatic" postcard from Auschwitz referring to her late grandmother; translated, reproduced, and transcribed at the end of the book.

(72) Her post-war discovery of the fate of those refugees from the May 1940, German bombing of Belgium, who succeeded in reaching France: they were interned in the camps of Gurs, Rivesaltes, Le Vernet, Les Milles, then deported to Drancy, and Auschwitz.

(92–3) Jews caught in daily roundups: "At the spur of the moment busy intersections in the city were cordoned off as the Germans went in search of Jews. They demanded identification, and those unlucky individuals caught in their trap were carted off to the Gestapo headquarters and from there to the assembly camp of Malines to be deported on the next convoy."

(102–4) Herta "… lured into believing that she might find some information as to the whereabouts of her husband", is captured, and is taken to Malines.

(169–70; Notes) Deportation information of her relatives that is listed in the Klarsfeld/ Steinberg book, *Mémorial de la Déportation des Juifs de Belgique*.

Transit camps

(87, 92–3) Young men summoned for obligatory work, among them, Herta's husband Srulek, and cousin Fred: "They were ordered to present themselves at Caserne Dossin, a former fort in the city of Malines, later used by the Belgians as army barracks. There the Jews would be assembled to be transported for work in countries to the east." June 1942.

(102–4) Herta is arrested and taken to Malines: "She was trapped with all the others who on that day had gathered at the assigned place in the hope of learning of their loved ones' whereabouts."

(173–7) Her post-war visit to Malines: "… Malines, a name associated with the dreaded camp where the trapped Jews were asssembled for deportation."

Slave labour camps and factories

(86, 190) June 1942, the German company Todt supervises "obligatory work" for Jewish young men in northern France. They worked along the English Channel coast, and were housed in three camps: Israel I, II, and III. Herta's husband Srulek was among them, later deported to Malines and Auschwitz.

(198, 209, 214) Srulek's postcard from the Auschwitz-area slave labour camp of Jawischowitz (misspelled as Fawischowitz in the memoir).

Auschwitz-Birkenau

(169–70) At a post-war conference, she discovers the fates of her relatives in the *Mémorial de la Déportation des Juifs de Belgique*: "The renewed feeling of sorrow was devastating as I found what I expected. Indeed, they were all there: my sister, her husband, my aunt, my two cousins. Listed as well were the dates and numbers of the transports that took them from the assembly camp of the old Caserne Dossin, the antechamber of death in Malines, to Auschwitz."

Concentration camps

(172–3) Her post-war visit to Breendonk: "… a former fort dating back to the middle ages that was transformed into a concentration camp by the German SS."

Resistance, ghetto revolts, individual acts of courage and defiance

(113) Signs forbidding entry of Jews to theaters: "… were displayed by law but ignored by patrons as well as managers and personnel. The Germans were our common enemy. The gentile Belgians did not fear them as we did, since they were not persecuted as long as they showed no overt opposition. But the Belgians disliked them intensely."

(133) Belgian resistance with ration cards: "It was in part a result of the refusal of the Belgian authorities to participate in the enemies' oppression of the Jews that people lucky enough to elude their persecution managed to survive."

(134–5) Their neighbour, a Belgian Resistance fighter, is captured by the Gestapo: "After Liberation, our neighbour returned, having survived the concentration camp. We then learned that our intuition had been correct. Indeed, the man was a Resistance fighter."

(161) Meeting soldiers of the Jewish Brigade of the Palestinian division of the British Army: "Everyone was filled with pride and gratitude at the sight of these young men."

(175) Description of the Memorial to the Jewish Martyrs and Freedom Fighters of Belgium. Photo, page 179.

(177) Description of the Memorial to the Jews who fought with the Belgian Resistance. Photo, page 182.

Specific escapes

(21, 23, 26–8) Recollections of the journey in 1938 from Austria through Germany and Holland to Belgium: "In short, the fleeing Jews were forced to leave all their possessions behind. At that moment, we were lucky to have escaped with our lives."

(23–5) Money hidden in her coat is discovered at German Customs: "After questioning my parents for what seemed an eternity, the officer may have been so annoyed at my outburst that he gave orders to let me go."

(97–100) Escaping a roundup by hiding in cupboards in their basement workshop: "Only my mother had any presence of mind; she decided our course of action, and our survival was the consequence of her decisions. … Her choice to put me in the safer cupboard, blocked from view by the large table, reminded me of the time she threw herself on top of me as we were machine-gunned by German aircraft during our second flight when we tried to escape the invading enemy."

In hiding, including Hidden Children

(82–3, 105–6) Psychological difficulties of hidden children: "… my parents' need for me to act as their spokesperson, which prevented them from hiding me apart from themselves in the terrible years that followed, preserved my sense of normalcy and equilibrium in adulthood. … my parents' need for me prevented my being psychologically damaged by separation, as were so many hidden children whose parents, for their children's safety, agreed to separate."

(90–2) "… my apprenticeship in hiding my true identity. … When confronted with a troublesome situation or question, I came up with explanations on the spur of the moment. … Little did I know then how much this instruction would be needed in the future during the continuous hiding of my identity."

(93, 96, 101) Hiding with other Jewish families in a clothing factory for German uniforms: "… given the product manufactured there, it was considered an unlikely place for the Germans to come searching for Jews."

(107–11, 171) Goes into hiding physically and mentally; moves with her parents to a Flemish area on the outskirts of Brussels, then to: "… build for myself the identity I longed for, yet one that was logical and believable to strangers … until I was totally entangled in a fictitious existence. … But all along there persisted inside the nagging guilt, the feeling of imprisonment in deception."

(111–14) The reality of their hiding: "Yet that constant fear was always present, that feeling of intense vulnerability, the sense of panic at the sight of a suspicious-looking black automobile. The fear of being followed and denounced by someone who suspected that we were Jews was continually with us."

(115–26) Her resistance to Catholicism at the convent school: "I was left to confront rituals I found objectionable and frightening."

(131–2) Her teaching job to young Henri in hiding: "Nevertheless, again I felt deceitful because I gave an appearance of maturity and capability, and yet I felt so deeply insecure."

(133–4) "Thanks to my father's versatility and talent to adapt to different types of work, my parents could pay rent for our attic rooms and could purchase the meager rations of food available with ration stamps."

(138–45) Friendships, neighbours, her fictional school, and fictional life: "… we gave the impression that our lives were no different from the rest of the population."

Righteous Gentiles

(74) Belgian Queen Mother Elisabeth: "She was to play an important role in saving Jewish children during the terrible years that lay ahead."

(170) Righteous Gentiles who hid Jewish children honoured at Hidden Child Conference, Brussels, 1995: "Thanks to their courage and generosity, the lives of five thousand Jewish children were saved."

Liberation

(145) News of Allied advances: "Soon convoys of German troops were rumbling in retreat through the city's streets."

(147–8) Brussels liberated 4 September 1944: "Posters in shop windows, and on kiosk walls shouted in huge bold colors and letters, 'On les a eus!' (We got them!)."

(148–50) "The fortunate Jews who had been lucky enough to elude the traps of the Nazis emerged from their hiding places. … Although we no longer feared being deported, we continued struggling for food, fuel, clothing, and shelter."

(150–2, 156–7) Returning to school: "The registrar inquired as to why I had not attended school all this time. … I was confronted with admitting a reality that I had constantly sought to evade and forget." Finally she finds a place in a business institute.

(152–6) German counter-offensive brings bombing raids, but in the spring: "Horribly emaciated, skeleton-like survivors of the death and concentration camps who had been liberated by the advancing Allied forces, arrived on the scene. … Words fail, adjectives are inadequate, they underrate the depth of the distress and sorrow of the experience."

(159–61) Post-war anti-Semitism: "I met a number of persons, during common occurrences, who kept blaming Jews for whatever difficulties they experienced. … At the time I wanted to merge with people who did not suffer. It took time for me to realize the futility of such attempts and the detriment to myself."

(162–5) 7 May 1945: The day the war ends, a day of jubilation, but her parents: "… remained frozen in sadness." Decades later she comprehends their loss.

Stories of individuals, including family members

(8, 21, 24–5, 29–31, 94–6, 169) Aunt Pepi Dermer and her son Fred flee with them to Brussels; Aunt Pepi caught in a roundup, taken to Malines, deported to the east (Auschwitz), 26 September 1942.

(19, 34) Aunt Franzi left Austria with her family in 1935. The family in Belgium hoped to join them in the United States.

(20–1, 31–2, 42, 59, 158) Her brother Ernst: "… never got over the hurt of having to flee"; arrives first in Brussels; leaves for South America in 1939, through France from Marseille to Bolivia and Argentina. They reconnect after the war.

(34–5, 38, 39, 97, 170) Cousin Max Glasz arrives from Czechoslovakia, deported to Malines and Auschwitz, 20 April 1943.

(35) Aunt Regin and her husband flee from Munich to London after the *Anschluss*.

(35, 97) Uncle Eduard, wife Mia, daughter Sonia flee from Vienna to Brussels; he, Jewish, survives on his own.

(62–3, 77–9, 164, 169–70) Israel Krygier, Herta's friend Srulek; they are married under difficult circumstances; he, deported 31 October 1942, Malines to Auschwitz; she, deported 24 October. Neither survived. Herta's death confirmed by father years later: "My father's expression was one of extreme surprise. At once I realized that he had totally forgotten that I had never been told."

(80–2, 94, 100–1) Anderlecht, Brussels neighbours Madame Gaby and Madame Yvonne, methods of survival; Madame Gaby's success in deception; her secret betrayed in the second raid.

(87–9, 169) Seventeen-year-old cousin Fred Dermer summoned to Malines, "delighted" at the "adventure". His mother Aunt Pepi "devastated" the family could not/would not help; deported on the first convoy, Malines to Auschwitz, 4 August 1942.

(114, 126–8. 172, 181, 184, 186) Friend Louise, in hiding with a Gentile couple, attending a convent school; remembered but not found at Hidden Child conference, 1995, Brussels.

(129–32) The Schönfeld/Sonnenfeld family in hiding who: "… also harbored overnight aquaintances."

(171–2) Edith Berger, childhood friend from Brussels recognizes her at 1995 Hidden Child conference, Brussels.

Post-war life and career

(167–8) Attends Hidden Child Conferences and returns to Belgium in 1995 to search out the places and people of her past.

(169–70) Finds the transport information and confirmation of the deaths of her family members, who had been sent from Malines to Auschwitz.

(175, 177) 25,257 Jews deported from Belgium, their names inscribed on walls in the Memorial to the Jewish Martyrs and Freedom Fighters of Belgium, in Anderlecht, Brussels.

(177–88) The journey to find the places and people of her wartime life in Belgium: "… the quest ended on a positive note."

(189–92) Confronts documents of the past from "the box": "During the interval between the first gathering of former hidden children in New York City (1991), and the journey back to the places of my childhood and the last conference in Brussels (1995), I have come full circle. … I owe it to them (loved ones) to make their stories known, to pass this history on to my children and grandchildren who deserve to know it, for it is our history."

Personal reflections

(20) "As I grew up, I always blamed my sense of isolation on having lacked the company of children my age. Decades later I understood that our not speaking of our inner lives was what made me feel isolated."

Places mentioned – in Europe: (page first mentioned)

Aachen (26), Anderlecht (Brussels) (107), Antwerp/Antwerpen (53), Auschwitz Main Camp/Auschwitz I (10), Austria (1), Belgium (12), Breendonk concentration camp (172), Brussels/Bruxelles (29), Cologne/Köln (26), Courtrai/Kortrijk (70), Czechoslovakia (34), Dachau concentration camp (2), Dilbeek (180), Dossin Camp (Malines) (87), Drancy transit camp (72), Flanders (70), France (72), Germany (23), Gurs internment camp (72), Halle (197), Holland (23), Hungary (10), Israel I/II/III slave labour camps (France) (190), Ixelles/Elsene (179), Jawischowitz/Jawiszowicz slave labour camp (191), Kassel (197), La Panne (67), Le Vernet internment camp (72), Leipzig (158), Leopoldstadt (Vienna) (4), Les Milles internment camp (72), Liège/Lüttich (195), Maastricht (26), Malines/Mechelen transit camp (87), Marseille (59), Merksplas internment camp (54), Munich/München (2), Nice

(59), Paris (72), Prague/Praha (35), Rivesaltes internment camp (72), Romania (143), St Gilles (Brussels) (133), Strasbourg (59), Vienna/Wien (1), Ypres (70)

Places mentioned – outside Europe: (page first mentioned)

Argentina (7), Bolivia (59), Cochabamba (Bolivia) (59), Great Britain (67), Jerusalem (167), La Paz (Bolivia) (59), Montreal (167), New York City (167), Ohio (33), Santa Cruz (Bolivia) (59), United States of America (15)

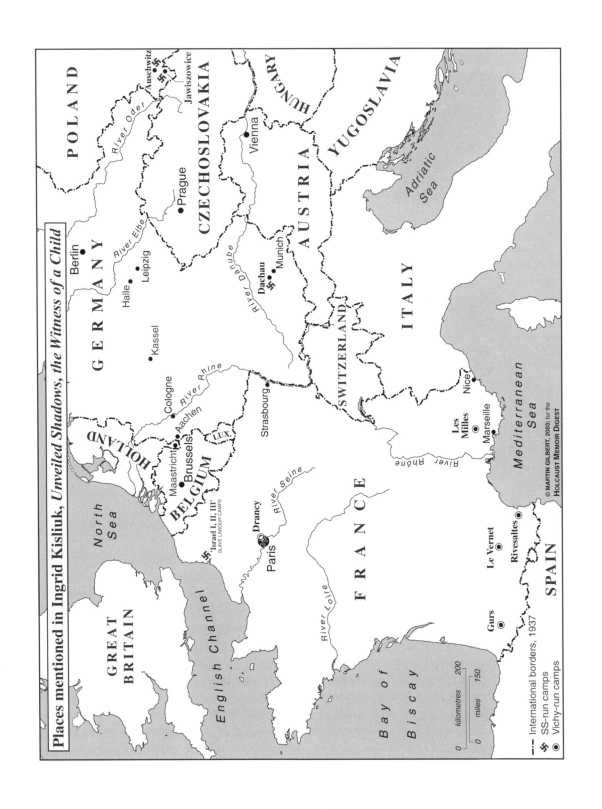

Places mentioned in Ingrid Kisliuk, *Unveiled Shadows, the Witness of a Child*

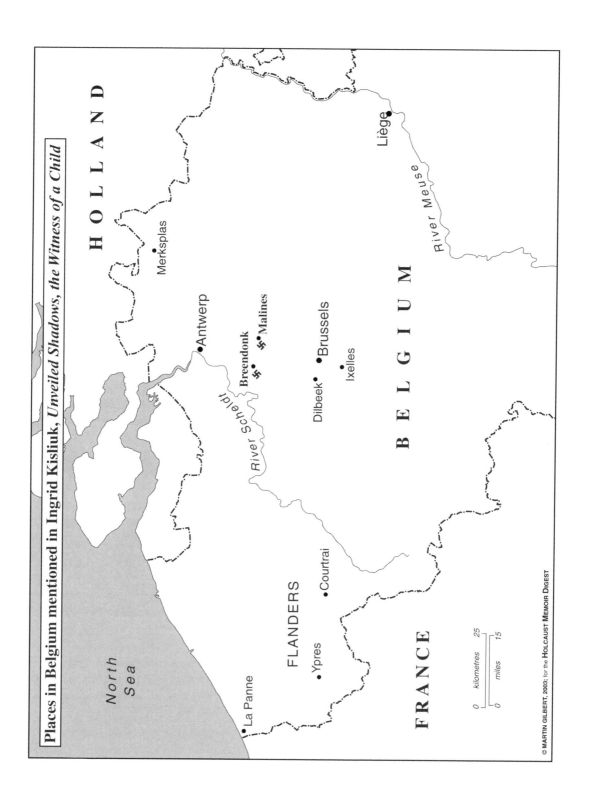

Places in Belgium mentioned in Ingrid Kisliuk, *Unveiled Shadows, the Witness of a Child*

HOLLAND

Merksplas

North Sea

Antwerp

River Scheldt

Breendonk

Malines

FLANDERS

La Panne

Ypres

Courtrai

Dilbeek

Brussels

Ixelles

BELGIUM

Liège

River Meuse

FRANCE

0 kilometres 25
0 miles 15

Author: Jack Klajman, with Ed Klajman

Title: *Out of the Ghetto*

Publishing details: Vallentine Mitchell & Co. Ltd., 47 Chase Side, London N14 5BP, England. 2000. 148 pages.
ISBN #0-85303-389-7.
The Library of Holocaust Testimonies

Focus:

A young Polish boy survives alone in Warsaw, comes to England after the war, and emigrates to Canada; the events in the book take place between 22 April 1931 and 1958.

Features:

Foreword: Introduction written by the Author, page ix.
The Library of Holocaust Testimonies, written by Sir Martin Gilbert, page vii. Biographical Note, page viii, and Editor's Note: Historical Background, by Series Editors, pages xi–xii.

Photographs: Photographs of pre-war and post-war family and friends, between pages 84 and 85.

Afterword: Epilogue written by the Author, including an update of fellow survivors, pages 149–54.

Contents: (by topic, with page numbers)

Pre-war Jewish home and community life

(1–3) The children in his family in Warsaw: in 1939, brother Getzel is 18, sister Brenda is 16, brother Menashe is 11, Jankiel (Jack) is 8, and little brother Eli is 6. "In our neighbourhood, if you were able to eat three meals a day you were considered well off."

(5–6) His widowed maternal grandmother had raised her three children alone, "She then bought a piece of land 20 miles outside of Warsaw where she ran a farm. …"

(30) Helping his mother at her sandal stall in the market in summers: "Working with her offered a fascinating education in the fundamentals of business, and in particular, how to treat customers properly."

Pre-war anti-Semitism

(61) "Groups of hooligans were often on the hunt for Jews, terrorizing us whenever the opportunity presented itself."

The coming of war

(3–4) The bombing of Warsaw, September 1939: "Our neighbourhood was a huge inferno, with flames leaping from many buildings." They flee to Uncle Chaim.

(6–8) The family finds temporary refuge in Uncle Jankiel's cellar. His brother Getzel returns home: "… the place had been totally obliterated; only the foundations remained."

(9–10) "On 27 September, the country surrendered. … People were in a state of shock and disbelief as September had been a month of nothing but death and destruction."

Life under German occupation

(10–11) 1 October 1939 the German Army marches into Warsaw: "The Nazis projected an image of invincibility. … Days after taking control, the Germans began a reign of tyranny against the Jews. …"

(15–16) He sells cigarettes to the farmers in the market who: "… were unable to leave their stalls so they would pay extra for delivered cigarettes."

Creation of the ghetto

(16–17) Warsaw Ghetto sealed, November 1940: "The situation was desperate before the walls were erected, but the conditions became even harsher by early 1941. Malnutrition was replaced by mass starvation."

Daily life in the ghetto

(17–21, 33–6) Smuggling from the Aryan side, initially with friend Sevek, then on his own: "This dangerous, hustling lifestyle quickly came to dominate my childhood."

(37–40) Survives typhus; May 1942, Brenda in hospital, Menashe in jail for smuggling food: "That put an extra strain on me. I now had two siblings to deliver food to – one in hospital and one in jail."

(41–4) Brenda sends the two young brothers to relative safety on the Aryan side. He reports to Brenda about Eli: "I told her how I kept close watch on him as he spent his day singing songs at the streetcar stand across the street from where I would kneel down and beg."

Deportation

(44–6) 22 July 1942, Warsaw deportations begin, to: "'resettlement in the East'".

Death camps

(45–6) The July 1942 deportations from the Warsaw Ghetto go to Treblinka: "The camps were nothing more than death factories." Both the destination and its purpose was unknown at the time.

(131–2) In Lublin, he sings the song "Treblinka" with Ludwig the accordian player: "It was a sad song that had been written about that death camp and had become somewhat of an anthem for the Jews of Warsaw."

Slave labour camps and factories

(61) He refers to the "enterprise zones" of the Brushmaker's Shop and Little Toebbens, which provided some employment for the remaining 40,000 Jews living in the ghetto at the end of 1942.

Witness to mass murder

(47) Of an escapee of Treblinka: "I recall being told a story by one of our leaders about a father who was given labour duty to stave off death for a few days. His job was to shove dead bodies into the ovens, including his own family."

(77–9) During the ghetto revolt Jack's bunker had been torched: "All that was left of my friends who chose not to come out was a jumble of bone fragments – barely recognizable body parts."

Resistance, ghetto revolts, individual acts of courage and defiance

(56–7) His friend Joe kills a Gestapo officer at the Umschlagplatz: "People talked about his courage for months after that incident."

(62–3) "… people in the ghetto finally realized death was certain to come sooner or later, and there was nothing to lose by resisting. … We just wanted to die with dignity." The Resistance begins to obtain and assemble weaponry.

(63–4) "From February to April 1943 the main activities of the ghetto focused on our hiding places."

(64–5) His involvement: "… my smuggling life got me in close enough contact with some of the Jewish Fighting Organization (JFO) that I had a sense of what was happening. … occasionally I was used as a messenger boy. I was sent from one section of the ghetto to another, delivering different weapons to various groups."

(69–71) 19 April, in a bunker: "That first day saw a clear Jewish victory. …" Although, "… our early success may have startled the Germans, but it wasn't going to deter them."

(80–1) "Although technically the uprising would last for another three weeks, to all intents and purposes it was over. … They could kill us but they could never take our accomplishments away from the history books."

(102–3) With the help of the "Jewish underground", he gets false identity papers: "I was finally able to document the existence of Janek Jankowski. … Those documents gave us a much-needed security blanket."

(124–5, 127) He describes how in August 1944, the Polish Resistance, led by the "Armia Krajowa" tried to liberate Warsaw from the Germans: "The Poles fought with Molotov cocktails, light machine guns and mortars. The Germans had heavy artillery at their disposal, and the manpower to go house-to-house and room-to-room in order to weed out the resistance. It was the closest the Poles ever came to knowing what it felt like for the Jews."

Specific escapes

(21–4) He survives encounter with German Major "Frankenstein": "He loved to hunt, but I suppose he must have become bored with animals and decided that shooting Jewish children was a more enjoyable pastime."

(25–6) Caught by the Gestapo as a smuggler: "With the cross around my neck I pretended I was a gentile child when they interrogated me. … they told me to tell my father to get a job so I wouldn't put myself at risk again."

(59) Friends Zenek and Pavel escape from the train to Treblinka: "They both jumped out of that moving train and luckily were unhurt. They got back to Warsaw, but stayed out of the ghetto. They were like us in that they spoke good Polish and could pass as Christian boys."

(71–6) Their underground bunker is discovered: "Rather than coming in after us, the Germans used the threat of fire to flush us out." His friend Sevek convinces him to leave: "'As bad as it is, give life a chance.'"

(82–6) He escapes from the ghetto through the sewers; escapes from the Pole whom he cannot pay.

In hiding, including Hidden Children

(46–7, 57) Friends Joe and Chawa hide 2-year-old daughter Schajadala with Gentile farmers, summer 1942: "I do not know what ever became of their daughter. I assume she married a Pole and lived the life of a gentile – never knowing her true heritage. … I thought that if I survived the war and they didn't I could find their daughter and pass on the truth of her past. But they refused to give me the information, fearing that if I was captured and tortured I might reveal the story."

(53–5) In hiding with Eli as Christians, sleeping in a nightwatchman's shed: "… he felt good about doing it – helping two boys he thought were Christian orphans."

(58–62) Hiding with Eli in Aryan Warsaw, fall 1942: "Even when begging and singing we didn't stay in one place for too long. It didn't matter if we were really successful there; we had to move around a lot so no one got too suspicious."

(89–93) Hiding as a Christian, living on the streets of Warsaw: "It was difficult living a lie all the time because I always had to keep my guard up. I had to think carefully before I said anything. All it took was one wrong word to slip out of my mouth. It was hard to stay so alert all the time."

(107–12) Life on the street with his friend Zbyszek: "'You're both Jews – rotten Jews, aren't you?'"

(113–18) Arrested by a German gendarme, he and Zbyszek are deposited in a Catholic orphanage: "I'm sure he knew we were Jewish, but for some reason he had saved us." After two weeks of daily showers and nurse inspections, his secret is discovered and the boys flee.

Righteous Gentiles

(19–20, 43, 50, 53) Mr and Mrs Slawcia provide food, lodging, and safety at their café in Praga: "They knew I was Jewish but always gave me strong support."

(93–101) Mrs Lodzia finds him, offers him help: "Looking into her eyes, I could tell she wasn't tricking me; she was different from everyone else. It seemed she really did care for me." She befriends him, includes him in her family: "After the terrible period that followed Eli's death, I finally had something to be happy about. Mrs Lodzia was nothing short of a guardian angel."

(119–22) Mrs Lodzia and her daughters Irka and Marysia welcome him back; help his friends give him a 13th birthday party: "… something I hadn't experienced since I was eight years old."

(151) Mrs Lodzia: "… was willing to risk her life, and her children's, in order to save me."

Liberation

(124–7) As the Russians advance, fall 1944, he travels with two friends to Malkinia to augment their food supply.

(128) "Liberation day finally arrived in the spring of 1945. … I was no longer a hunted animal."

(130–5) "I decided to leave. I had experienced a few weeks of unsuccessful searching in which I couldn't find a single surviving family member in Warsaw, so there was no reason to stay any longer." He travels to Lublin, Lodz, Sopot and to Straubing in the American zone of Bavaria.

(136–40) He comes to England, to Northampton and then to London with, "some one thousand" orphaned Jewish children: "It had been just a matter of months since I was struggling to survive under a cruel Nazi regime, and here I was a completely free young man who had his life in front of him. But there still was that emptiness, that sadness in my heart which I would be forced to endure the rest of my life."

(140–2) He emigrates to Canada in January 1948, to London, Ontario, where he apprentices to a furrier: "Life was better than I could have imagined and I was pleased that I had come to London."

Stories of individuals, including family members

(12–14) Brother Getzel flees to Russia, early 1940, finds work in Siberia: "When war broke out between the Soviet Union and Germany in June 1941, we lost contact with my brother and never heard from him again."

(17–18, 73–4, 151) Friend Sevek helps him begin his smuggling career; convinces him to leave the bunker; also emigrates to Canada.

(27–30) Death and funeral of father, spring 1941, at age 44: "My father's plight was typical of what happened to most adults in the ghetto. The only ones who had any chance to survive were the street-savvy, rough, tough deal-makers. … There was such a stark contrast between those smugglers and my father. My dad was just a kind-hearted, simple family man. He was doomed in the ghetto."

(31–2) Death of mother, summer 1941: "Like my father, she was brokenhearted, feeling totally helpless as she had to watch her children suffer while she couldn't do anything about it. It seemed she just lacked the will to live."

(47–9) Brother Menashe and sister Brenda taken to Treblinka in July 1942 "Aktion": "I knew I'd never see my lovely sister and dear brother again. There are no words to describe the pain I felt that night."

(51–2) With only the two of them left, he tries to take care of Eli: "'You are only ten years old. I am twelve. When you get to be my age, I'll let you smoke and drink, too,' I said facetiously as we both smiled. Then a look of concern came over his face. 'What if I don't make it to twelve?' he asked."

(59, 107–19, 149) Friend Zbyszek: "he became my closest friend"; hides in a Catholic orphanage with Jack, and is killed after liberation.

(59, 127–8, 149–50) Brothers Zenek and Pavel, part of his "family"; they fight in the "Armia Krajowa"; emigrate to Israel.

(87–9) Brother Eli betrayed: "I was told they approached the cellar with their guns drawn – as though Eli was some kind of dangerous gangster. … How could the people who witnessed the episode not feel sorry for the little boy and do something to help?"

(103, 123–4, 149–50) Friend Stasiek/Golec escapes a Polish labour brigade and hides with Mrs Lodzia; emigrates to Canada.

(104, 150) "Amchu Man" lived in a hole he'd dug in a field: "It was very similar to a grave." Jack shares food and conversation with him: "His Jewish appearance would probably have led to him being picked up within minutes of showing his face in public during the day."

(122) His friend "Frenchy" betrayed by his parents' German "friend".

Post-war life and career

(143–7) He builds a fur business in London, Canada from 1948 to 1959: "Then I went on the trip of my life and met the woman of my dreams."

(147–8) He and Sonia raise four children in Canada: "… I am pleased to say that because of my life here in Canada I will leave this earth a very happy man."

Personal reflections

(26) "… one day the Germans would be defeated and life would return to normal. Until then, our approach was to live for the moment, hoping to be around the next hour and the next day, and hoping that soon life would get better. You truly had to believe that. Survival is impossible without hope, even if it is false hope."

(53) "Have hope, we must have hope. Every day of survival is one more day of hope."

(89) "… somehow I found the motivation to survive. I decided that keeping the family name alive and telling the world what the Nazis had done to Eli and my family was enough incentive to keep living."

(128–9) "I was lucky to be alive and that – as I told myself many times during the war – life is to be cherished and each moment seized. I had fought so long and hard for survival that I couldn't let it go to waste."

Places mentioned – in Europe: (page first mentioned)

Bialystok (13), Brushmakers' Factory (Warsaw) (61), Cracow/Krakow/Krakau (135), Dachau concentration camp (104), Lodz/Litzmanstadt (132), London, England (136), Lublin (130), Malkinia/Malkin (125), Praga (Warsaw) (19), Prague/Praha (135), Saska Kepa (Warsaw) (89), Sopot/Zoppot (133), Straubing (135), Toebbens Factory (Warsaw) (61), Treblinka death camp (44), Umschlagplatz (Warsaw) (45), Warsaw Ghetto (16), Warsaw/Warszawa/Warschau (1)

Places mentioned – outside Europe: (page first mentioned)

Ashkelon (147), Berezniki (Molotovskaya Oblast) (13), Cyprus (134), Haifa (143), Halifax (Nova Scotia) (141), Israel (143), London (Ontario) (142), Montreal (141), Northampton (136), Palestine (134), Southampton (140), Tel Aviv (144), Toronto (141)

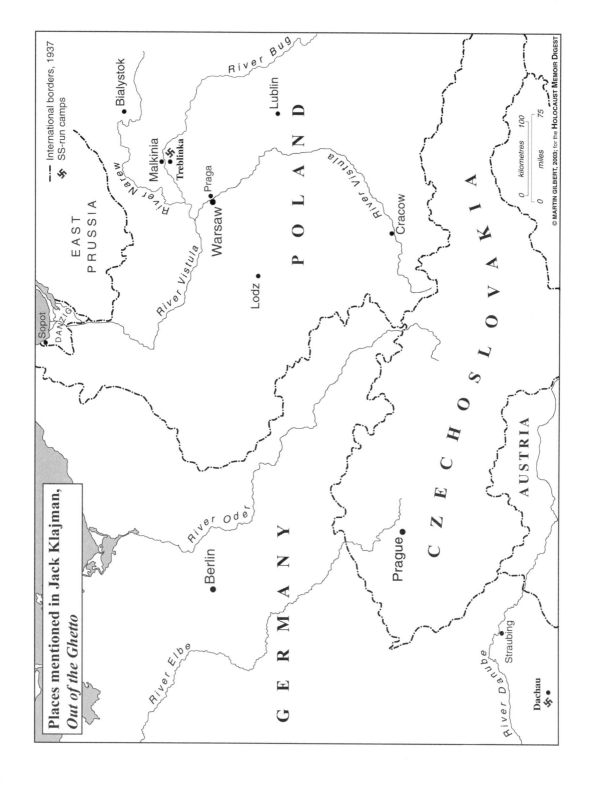

Places mentioned in Jack Klajman,
Out of the Ghetto

- - - International borders, 1937
卐 SS-run camps

EAST PRUSSIA

Bialystok •

River Bug

Malkinia •
卐 **Treblinka**

Lublin •

River Narew

Praga •

Warsaw •

P O L A N D

River Vistula

River Vistula

Cracow •

Lodz •

Sopot
DANZIG

River Oder

Berlin •

G E R M A N Y

River Elbe

C Z E C H O S L O V A K I A

Prague •

A U S T R I A

River Danube

Straubing •

卐 **Dachau** •

0   kilometres   100
0   miles   75

© MARTIN GILBERT, 2003; for the HOLOCAUST MEMOIR DIGEST

Study Guide

INTRODUCTION

This Study Guide accompanies the *Holocaust Memoir Digest*, and is intended to elaborate on aspects of the *Digest*.

The term "Holocaust", which has entered into common usage in the past few decades, comes from classical Greek and means "consumed by fire: a burnt offering". In Hebrew, which is both the language of prayer among Jews, and also the language of the State of Israel, the Holocaust is called "Shoah": "catastrophe", and in Yiddish, the traditional language of East European Jews, it is "Hurban": "destruction".

Since 1945, the Holocaust has come to refer to the planned, systematic murder of Jews who were living in European lands occupied or dominated by Germany during the Second World War. The war began with the German invasion of Poland on 1 September 1939. What had started as the random killing of Jews became, with the German invasion of the Soviet Union in June 1941, the mass murder of Jews on a daily basis. The surrender of Germany on 8 May 1945 brought the war in Europe to an end; six million Jewish men, women, and children had been killed.

From the first days of their liberation in 1945, many survivors felt the need to record their eyewitness accounts, to memorialize their destroyed families, to remember their pre-war way of life. The first such memoirs, written soon after the war, introduced the Holocaust to the public consciousness. In recent years, the passage of time and a growing interest in their experiences during that traumatic time have been the impetus for many other survivors to record their memories for posterity.

The will to live, to maintain hope, to survive and to rebuild – this gives the Holocaust its universality. Jews are known as the People of the Book, that book being the Bible, the narrative of their origins, laws, and early history. The need to write and record, to document, and to remember is an integral part of Jewish tradition. This makes the Holocaust a window into both the best and the worst of human behaviour. The Holocaust was not the only genocide of the twentieth century; it was almost certainly the most documented one.

Each survivor's experiences are unique; each memoir contains aspects of the Holocaust that add to our knowledge of that terrible time. The *Holocaust Memoir Digest*, by reviewing the published memoirs of Jews who survived the Holocaust, provides a guide and reference for the teaching, not only of the Holocaust, but also of recent history, human relations, the pattern of genocide, and the psychology of good and evil.

TOPICS

The entry for each memoir in the *Holocaust Memoir Digest* consists of the following six parts:

1. The **author, title**, and **publishing details**;
2. A one-sentence **focus** which sets the geographic area and time;
3. A list of **features** that are not part of the memoir itself but added to it;
4. The **contents** of the memoir, divided into 26 categories;
5. A list of **places** mentioned in the memoir, both in Europe and beyond;
6. A **map** or **maps** showing each place in Europe mentioned in that memoir.

The first two of the twenty-six categories are **Pre-war Jewish home and community life**, and **Pre-war anti-Semitism**. These describe what life was like throughout Europe for Jews, some of whose ancestors had lived in these countries for many hundreds of years. In **Pre-war Jewish home and community life**, survivors write about the culture, education, traditions, community structure, and the life Jews led as they struggled to grapple with changing twentieth-century values: Should they maintain family and religious traditions, or seek assimilation? Should they work toward a better economic situation where they lived, or would they find better opportunities elsewhere? Should they seek to fulfil their Zionist aspirations, or was carving out a life in the "desert" of Palestine too difficult?

One of the main factors that determined how pre-war European Jewish families faced these questions is that many of them lived amidst an all-pervasive **Pre-war anti-Semitism**, the second category of the *Digest*. They lived in a Christian world that was in many ways foreign to them or had alienated them.

The segregation and humiliation of Jews, legalized under the Nuremberg Laws of 1935, had begun in Germany when Hitler came to power in 1933. Hitler separated the Jews from the general population by making them into a scapegoat – by taking advantage of latent anti-Semitism and blaming Jews for Germany's ills. He then removed Jews from their positions in government, the law, universities, schools, and hospitals. German colleagues took over their positions; those who had been under them moved up the ladder. Jewish businesses were confiscated, or "sold" for a fraction of their worth to local people who were loyal to the Nazi Party.

By the time Jews had been physically isolated from the larger German community, those of Hitler's compatriots who had accepted his plan, and benefited from this exclusion of the Jews, were not particularly interested in helping the Jews when persecution intensified. This segregation and humiliation extended to Austria in March 1938, when it became part of the German Reich, and to the Sudetenland region of Czechoslovakia in October 1938.

The coming of war and **Life under German occupation** categories describe how the beginning of war in September 1939, the sudden violent imposition of Nazi rule, and the constant struggle for survival, affected the memoir writer. In each country that Germany conquered between September 1939 and June 1941 – Poland in September 1939, Denmark and Norway in April 1940, Holland, Belgium, France, and Luxembourg in May 1940, Yugoslavia and Greece in April 1941 – anti-Jewish legislation was put in place, often upheld by the local collaborationist regime. Jewish businesses and possessions were confiscated.

In Poland, from the first days of the German conquest, Jews were rounded up, beaten, and several thousand were murdered. Later the Jews were forcibly removed from their homes and crowded into ghettos.

Ghettos were established in Poland in many towns in which Jews were confined amid considerable hardship and privation. Some ghettos existed for only a short time. Others lasted up to four years. This is described in the two categories **Creation of the ghetto**, and **Daily life in the ghetto**. Having lost their property and livelihood, the only further value Jews represented to the Nazi occupier was in their labour. Thus the struggle by Jews for survival in the ghettos centred on trying to find food and obtain valid work permits, both of which were tightly controlled and restricted.

Those Jews deemed no longer "essential" by the Nazis were rounded up and removed from the ghettos. The category of **Deportation** describes the physical movement of Jews from their home towns or ghettos, in most cases to their deaths. Usually deportations took place by train, and were undertaken with deliberate deception, and promises that were recognized as false only when it was too late. The destination of the deportation trains was a tightly guarded secret. Only a few deportees returned.

Starting in June 1941, when Germany invaded the Soviet Union, four "commandos" of specially-trained SS killing squads, the *Einsatzgruppen*, rounded up Jews in hundreds of towns and villages, and took them by force to nearby ditches, ravines, and forests where they were shot. The largest of these **Mass murder sites** were located near cities which had large Jewish populations. These sites include Babi Yar outside Kiev, Rumbuli outside Riga, Ponar outside Vilnius, and the Ninth Fort outside Kaunas, at each of which tens of thousands of Jews were killed. Also included in this *Digest* category are smaller sites where thousands of Jews were murdered by shooting.

Transit camps: Drancy in France, Malines in Belgium, Westerbork in Holland, Fossoli in Italy, were among the principal transit camps where Jews were taken for short periods of time and then deported to an "unknown destination in the East" – in most cases, to their deaths. Other transit camps were to be found throughout Europe.

December 1941 saw the first systematic gassing of Jews. This took place in German-occupied Poland, near the village of Chelmno (in German "Kulmhof"), which became the first death camp. Belzec (pronounced Belzhets), Sobibor, and Treblinka were also **Death camps** in German-occupied Poland to which, with Chelmno, as many as two million Jews were deported and killed. A fifth death camp, Maly Trostenets, was situated near Minsk in German-occupied Byelorussia.

The only Jews who survived for more than a few days in the death camps were a small group of slave labourers forced to dispose of the bodies, usually in mass graves where the bodies were then burned. These labourers were also used to sort the clothing and belongings of the victims: material that was later redistributed among the SS, the German armed forces, and the German people. Almost none of the slave labourers in the death camps survived.

Many German factory owners took advantage of the plentiful labour supply and built factories and labour camps close to the ghettos and camps, as described in the category **Slave labour camps and factories**. Those Jews who were able to work had a better chance of survival, despite the harsh conditions in those camps which ensured a high turnover of labourers. Many memoir writers survived as slave labourers.

The deception practised by the SS in their killing operations depended on secrecy and the complete control of information. Northwest of Prague, the SS established a ghetto in the former Czechoslovak garrison town of **Theresienstadt (Terezin** in Czech). It was here that the Red Cross was shown what was "happening" to the Jews during a massive deception operation, complete with Jewish children at play. Much of the art, poetry, and music created by the Jews during the Holocaust came from those who were interned in Theresienstadt. Most of those who did not succumb to the privations in Theresienstadt were deported to Auschwitz and Maly Trostenets and killed.

While mass murder by shooting continued in the East throughout the last six months of 1941 and for all of 1942, experimental means were being investigated in German-occupied Poland to make killing more "efficient". What had begun at Chelmno with exhaust fumes was "perfected" at **Auschwitz-Birkenau**, where Zyklon B gas pellets were thrown into sealed "shower" rooms. The bodies were then burned in crematoria. This method of killing began in the summer of 1942. By the autumn of 1944, five crematoria were operating there.

Although the name "Auschwitz" has come to refer to the whole facility, it consisted of three large camps in close proximity. The original and Main Camp, with its single crematorium, was known as Auschwitz I. Birkenau, where four of the five crematoria were located, was known as Auschwitz II. Auschwitz also contained several satellite slave labour camps in the vicinity, the largest of which was attached to the Buna synthetic rubber and oil factory at the nearby town of Monowitz, and was known as Buna-Monowitz, or Auschwitz III. Descriptions of Buna-Monowitz and the other slave labour camps in the Auschwitz region are to be found in the *Digest* in the category of **Slave labour camps and factories**.

In January 1945, as Soviet forces approached the Auschwitz region, the SS evacuated the camp and the surrounding slave labour camps, and moved the surviving Jews westward, initially on foot. Those who were sent westward by rail were put in open railway wagons in mid-winter. Amid terrible brutality by their guards, many of the deportees were to "march" with little food, water, or shelter, until April. The toll from these **Death marches** was high.

When the Nazi Party came to power in Germany in 1933, it immediately established concentration camps for political prisoners. These camps were run by the SS. Dachau outside Munich and Sachsenhausen north of Berlin, date from this period. These concentration camps, located on German soil, were used for German political prisoners, opponents of the Nazi regime, writers, artists, teachers, religious leaders, pastors, priests, homosexuals, common criminals, and later, prisoners of war, particularly Russians. Towards the end of the war, tens of thousands of Jews on death marches were brought to these **Concentration camps** in Germany, among them Dachau, Bergen-Belsen, Buchenwald, and Mauthausen, and their many sub-camps.

Also included in the *Digest* category of **Concentration camps** is Majdanek, although this camp had many different aspects. Located in Poland near the city of Lublin, Majdanek initially served as a concentration camp for Russian prisoners of war who were held there in horrific conditions, and for Polish political prisoners. For the thousands of Jews who were taken to Majdanek and were later sent to Auschwitz, it was a transit camp. In addition, thousands of Jews from as close as Lublin and as far as Holland and Greece were brought to Majdanek and killed. After the defeat of the Warsaw Ghetto Revolt, the destruction of the Warsaw ghetto, and later the revolt in Bialystok, many thousands of survivors of those revolts were taken to Majdanek and murdered during the notorious "Harvest Festival" in November 1943.

One of the main reasons why survivors have written their memoirs of the Holocaust is to bear witness, to describe what they lived through, what they saw, and what the people whom they knew had witnessed. The category of **Witness to mass murder** makes it possible to begin to understand the scale of what happened.

As well as recording the details of the places to which Jews were taken, survivors also sought to chronicle the events and to write about the people who inspired them to continue, the people who helped them, and the ways they were able to evade death. The category **Resistance, ghetto revolts, individual acts of courage and defiance** includes acts of physical resistance, armed revolts, and also acts of "spiritual resistance": dignity in the face of inhumanity, the will to rise above the circumstances, the determination to live through the time of torment, the will to live.

Again and again, Jews fled to forests and outlying areas where they could fight the Nazi occupier. The category of **Partisan activity** refers to armed resistance against the German Army and German occupation, either by Jews, or by non-Jewish resistance fighters. Unfortunately, Jews who were able to escape to the forests and fight the Germans as Partisans, also had to fear some Polish and Russian Partisan groups who did not consider the Jews to be allies. One of the tragedies of the Holocaust is that some of those who were fighting the Nazi occupier were also fighting the Jews.

The category of **Specific escapes** refers to those few Jews who were able to escape from the deportation trains, or from those who would betray them, or from other situations of grave danger; or to find a brief respite from the constant terror.

In order to survive, many Jews went into hiding, as described in the category **In hiding, including Hidden Children**. This could involve a physical hiding place: often a cellar or an attic, a cupboard, or a cavity in a wall, or under the floor, or in a barn. For those who did not have "typically Jewish" features and were able to pass as Christians, it also involved a psychological hiding. In such cases, along with the false identity papers, a whole new persona and demeanour had to emerge. In the struggle to find safety, families were split up; children were often hidden separately from their parents. Of those children who survived, many lost their families; nearly all lost their childhood.

Many Jews were fortunate to receive kindness and help from non-Jews. Many of these **Righteous Gentiles**, as they have become known, risked, and some even lost their lives for helping Jews. Showing great humanity, they shared food, shelter, and risk. It is to their credit that thousands of Jews survived.

The category of **Liberation** denotes the time when Soviet, American, British, Canadian, and other Allied troops liberated the camps and the areas in which many Jews had been in hiding. For the Jews, liberation meant an end to their physical suffering, and the beginning of their quest to try to find family members, and to try to find a country that would give them safe haven. Many eventually made their way to Palestine (later Israel), many went to Britain, the United States, Canada, Australia, South Africa, and Argentina.

The category of **Displaced Persons camps**, describes the refugee camps where survivors lived after they had been liberated. These camps were also used as a base for those who travelled to find relatives. Most survivors began to rebuild their lives while in DP camps; some spent several years there while waiting to find a country that would take them.

The category of **Stories of individuals, including family members** identifies the lives and fate of individuals mentioned by the memoir writer, as well as the fate of family members if known. Each survivor identifies extended family, neighbours, friends, colleagues, and many of those individuals with whom he or she came into contact.

The category of **Post-war life and career** focuses not only on the achievements of the survivors after liberation, but on their search to explore their past. The final category of **Personal reflections** provides an understanding of how the survivors view the world, and gives the reader the opportunity to learn – through the survivors' own words – their philosophy, their psychology, their connection to religion, and what is important to them.

Because the borders of many countries in Europe have changed so much in the twentieth century, the names of **Places** also changed. For example, the capital of Slovakia is today Bratislava. When it was part of the Austro-Hungarian Empire, the Germans called it Pressburg, and the Hungarians knew it as Posony. The capital of Lithuania is today Vilnius. It was a part of Poland between the two world wars when Poles called it Wilno; to the Jews it was Vilna.

Many towns in the East had a Yiddish as well as a local name. Thus Brest-Litovsk was Brisk, and Vladimir Volynski was Ludmir. The *Digest* shows these various spellings of towns and cities. Also, by locating each place on **Maps**, specially prepared by the *Digest* for each memoir, we can follow the memoir writer's travels, experiences, and torments.

The following is a series of questions within each category, with a key indicating which memoirs address these particular issues.

Pre-war Jewish home and community life

How was a Jewish religious life observed?
On Both Sides of the Wall, Vladka Meed
Night, Elie Wiesel

In what ways was assimilation pursued?
Dry Tears, Nechama Tec
Unveiled Shadows, Ingrid Kisliuk

What were the discussions among members of the author's family about following Zionist dreams and moving to Palestine?
Night, Elie Wiesel
Of Blood and Hope, Samuel Pisar

Pre-war anti-Semitism

How did the annexation of Austria affect Jews living in those areas?
Unveiled Shadows, Ingrid Kisliuk

How did pre-war restrictions against Jews affect them?
Dottore! Internment in Italy, 1940–1945, Dr Salim Diamand

What was the prominence of local anti-Semitic gangs?
Dry Tears, Nechama Tec
Out of the Ghetto, Jack Klajman

The coming of war

What was it like to experience the bombing raids?
And the Sun Kept Shining …, Bertha Ferderber-Salz
Out of the Ghetto, Jack Klajman

What was the situation for Jewish refugees who had been driven out of their homes?
Of Blood and Hope, Samuel Pisar
And the Sun Kept Shining …, Bertha Ferderber-Salz
Dry Tears, Nechama Tec
Unveiled Shadows, Ingrid Kisliuk

What were the first encounters with the Germans like?
Night, Elie Wiesel
Dottore! Internment in Italy, 1940–1945, Dr Salim Diamand

Life under German occupation

How did life change for Jews under occupation?
Unveiled Shadows, Ingrid Kisliuk
Out of the Ghetto, Jack Klajman

How did the seeming politeness of the Germans gain the confidence of the Jews and dispel rumours?
Unveiled Shadows, Ingrid Kisliuk
Dottore! Internment in Italy, 1940–1945, Dr Salim Diamand

What was the evolving plight of Jews who were forced to flee?
And the Sun Kept Shining …, Bertha Ferderber-Salz
Dry Tears, Nechama Tec

Creation of the ghetto

How were the smaller ghettos established?
Night, Elie Wiesel
Dry Tears, Nechama Tec

How were the larger ghettos formed?
Of Blood and Hope, Samuel Pisar
And the Sun Kept Shining …, Bertha Ferderber-Salz
Out of the Ghetto, Jack Klajman

Daily life in the ghetto

What was life like in the smaller ghettos?
Dry Tears, Nechama Tec

What was the day-to-day existence in the larger ghettos?
On Both Sides of the Wall, Vladka Meed
Of Blood and Hope, Samuel Pisar
And the Sun Kept Shining …, Bertha Ferderber-Salz
Out of the Ghetto, Jack Klajman

Deportation

What were conditions like on the deportation trains?
I Cannot Forgive, Rudolf Vrba
And the Sun Kept Shining …, Bertha Ferderber-Salz

Which trains came to Treblinka?
On Both Sides of the Wall, Vladka Meed
Of Blood and Hope, Samuel Pisar
Out of the Ghetto, Jack Klajman

Which trains came to Auschwitz?
Night, Elie Wiesel
Unveiled Shadows, Ingrid Kisliuk

Mass murder sites

How did the killings take place, and where?
Night, Elie Wiesel
And the Sun Kept Shining ..., Bertha Ferderber-Salz

Transit camps

What were conditions in the transit camps?
I Cannot Forgive, Rudolf Vrba
Unveiled Shadows, Ingrid Kisliuk

Death camps

What was known about Chelmno and when?
On Both Sides of the Wall, Vladka Meed

What was known about Treblinka and when?
On Both Sides of the Wall, Vladka Meed
Of Blood and Hope, Samuel Pisar
Out of the Ghetto, Jack Klajman

What was known about Belzec and when?
And the Sun Kept Shining ..., Bertha Ferderber-Salz

Slave labour camps and factories

What was "life" like in Buna-Monowitz?
Night, Elie Wiesel
I Cannot Forgive, Rudolf Vrba

How were the Warsaw factories involved during the Uprising?
On Both Sides of the Wall, Vladka Meed
Out of the Ghetto, Jack Klajman

How were workers enslaved and then moved to different factories and camps?
Of Blood and Hope, Samuel Pisar
And the Sun Kept Shining ..., Bertha Ferderber-Salz

Theresienstadt/Terezin

No memoirs in this volume

Auschwitz-Birkenau

What was the routine upon entry into Auschwitz?
Night, Elie Wiesel
I Cannot Forgive, Rudolf Vrba

What was a "mussulman" and who became one?
I Cannot Forgive, Rudolf Vrba

How could the mind help or hinder survival?
I Cannot Forgive, Rudolf Vrba
Of Blood and Hope, Samuel Pisar
And the Sun Kept Shining …, Bertha Ferderber-Salz

How could relationships help or hinder survival?
I Cannot Forgive, Rudolf Vrba
Of Blood and Hope, Samuel Pisar

How did the author convey a sense of the number of people being killed in Auschwitz?
Night, Elie Wiesel
I Cannot Forgive, Rudolf Vrba
Of Blood and Hope, Samuel Pisar
And the Sun Kept Shining …, Bertha Ferderber-Salz
Unveiled Shadows, Ingrid Kisliuk

Death marches

How was the evacuation of Auschwitz carried out?
Night, Elie Wiesel

What were conditions on the death marches?
Night, Elie Wiesel
Of Blood and Hope, Samuel Pisar

Concentration camps

What were conditions like in these camps during the war?
I Cannot Forgive, Rudolf Vrba
Of Blood and Hope, Samuel Pisar
Dottore! Internment in Italy, 1940–1945, Dr Salim Diamand

What were conditions like for those who came in from death marches?
Night, Elie Wiesel
And the Sun Kept Shining …, Bertha Ferderber-Salz

Witness to mass murder

What were the early reports of mass murder?
On Both Sides of the Wall, Vladka Meed
Night, Elie Wiesel
And the Sun Kept Shining …, Bertha Ferderber-Salz

Which survivors saw mass murder at Auschwitz?
Night, Elie Wiesel
I Cannot Forgive, Rudolf Vrba
Of Blood and Hope, Samuel Pisar

What eyewitness accounts of mass murder were there in cities, slave labour camps, and other areas?
On Both Sides of the Wall, Vladka Meed
And the Sun Kept Shining …, Bertha Ferderber-Salz
Dry Tears, Nechama Tec
Out of the Ghetto, Jack Klajman

Resistance, ghetto revolts, individual acts of courage and defiance

What do we know about resistance in Warsaw and the Warsaw Ghetto Uprising?
On Both Sides of the Wall, Vladka Meed
Out of the Ghetto, Jack Klajman

What organized resistance was there at Auschwitz?
I Cannot Forgive, Rudolf Vrba

What could individuals do to resist?
Night, Elie Wiesel
Of Blood and Hope, Samuel Pisar
And the Sun Kept Shining …, Bertha Ferderber-Salz

Partisan activity

What were the successes in working with non-Jewish partisans?
On Both Sides of the Wall, Vladka Meed
And the Sun Kept Shining …, Bertha Ferderber-Salz
I Cannot Forgive, Rudolf Vrba

What were the betrayals, the hazards, of Jews forming or joining partisan units?
On Both Sides of the Wall, Vladka Meed

Specific escapes

What escapes from deportation trains were known?
On Both Sides of the Wall, Vladka Meed
Dry Tears, Nechama Tec
Out of the Ghetto, Jack Klajman

What were some examples of day-to-day escapes?
On Both Sides of the Wall, Vladka Meed
Of Blood and Hope, Samuel Pisar
And the Sun Kept Shining …, Bertha Ferderber-Salz
Dry Tears, Nechama Tec
Dottore! Internment in Italy, 1940–1945, Dr Salim Diamand
Out of the Ghetto, Jack Klajman

What were some examples of psychological escape?
Of Blood and Hope, Samuel Pisar

How was it possible to escape from Auschwitz?
  I Cannot Forgive, Rudolf Vrba

In hiding, including Hidden Children

What was involved in the hiding of children?
  On Both Sides of the Wall, Vladka Meed
  And the Sun Kept Shining …, Bertha Ferderber-Salz
  Dry Tears, Nechama Tec
  Out of the Ghetto, Jack Klajman

What was involved in taking on a new identity in order to survive?
  On Both Sides of the Wall, Vladka Meed
  I Cannot Forgive, Rudolf Vrba
  Of Blood and Hope, Samuel Pisar
  Dry Tears, Nechama Tec
  Unveiled Shadows, Ingrid Kisliuk

What was involved in finding a physical hiding place?
  On Both Sides of the Wall, Vladka Meed
  Dry Tears, Nechama Tec
  Unveiled Shadows, Ingrid Kisliuk
  Out of the Ghetto, Jack Klajman

Righteous Gentiles

What kinds of offers were made by non-Jews to help their Jewish friends?
  Night, Elie Wiesel

In what ways were Jews the beneficiaries of non-Jews who supplied assistance?
  On Both Sides of the Wall, Vladka Meed
  I Cannot Forgive, Rudolf Vrba
  And the Sun Kept Shining …, Bertha Ferderber-Salz
  Dry Tears, Nechama Tec
  Out of the Ghetto, Jack Klajman

Liberation

What did liberation feel like for the survivors?
  This question is addressed in every memoir.

What were the dangers involved in returning home?
  Night, Elie Wiesel
  Of Blood and Hope, Samuel Pisar
  And the Sun Kept Shining …, Bertha Ferderber-Salz
  Dry Tears, Nechama Tec
  Dottore! Internment in Italy, 1940–1945, Dr Salim Diamand

Displaced Persons camps

Who was able to benefit from the DP camps?
On Both Sides of the Wall, Vladka Meed
And the Sun Kept Shining …, Bertha Ferderber-Salz
Dry Tears, Nechama Tec

Who was able to be of assistance in the DP camps?
Dottore! Internment in Italy, 1940–1945, Dr Salim Diamand

Stories of individuals, including family members

What was the fate of parents, siblings, and extended family?
What was the fate of friends, and those met along the way?
This category is addressed in every memoir.

Post-war life and career

Which survivors were able to return home only after an absence of many years?
Of Blood and Hope, Samuel Pisar
Unveiled Shadows, Ingrid Kisliuk

How have survivors continued to seek justice for the perpetrators and the deniers of the Holocaust?
I Cannot Forgive, Rudolf Vrba

How have their experiences in the Holocaust inspired survivors to write and teach about the Holocaust?
On Both Sides of the Wall, Vladka Meed
I Cannot Forgive, Rudolf Vrba
Of Blood and Hope, Samuel Pisar
Dry Tears, Nechama Tec

How have survivors moved forward, despite their Holocaust experiences?
And the Sun Kept Shining …, Bertha Ferderber-Salz
Dottore! Internment in Italy, 1940–1945, Dr Salim Diamand
Unveiled Shadows, Ingrid Kisliuk
Out of the Ghetto, Jack Klajman

Personal reflections

Compare fear as described in Vladka Meed's *On Both Sides of the Wall* and Nechama Tec's *Dry Tears*.

Compare sharing inner feelings in Nechama Tec's *Dry Tears* and Ingrid Kisliuk's *Unveiled Shadows*.

Compare the struggle for survival, and hope, in Elie Wiesel's *Night*, Samuel Pisar's *Of Blood and Hope*, and Jack Klajman's *Out of the Ghetto*.

Compare the difficulty in revisiting their Holocaust memories in Nechama Tec's *Dry Tears* and Ingrid Kisliuk's *Unveiled Shadows*.

Compare evil and the capacity to endure in Samuel Pisar's *Of Blood and Hope* and Dr Salim Diamand's *Dottore! Internment in Italy, 1940–1945*.

Compare the responsibility of remembering in Rudolf Vrba's *I Cannot Forgive*, Samuel Pisar's *Of Blood and Hope*, and Bertha Ferderber-Salz's *And the Sun Kept Shining …* .

Compare the choices made by Samuel Pisar's mother Hela in *Of Blood and Hope*, and Bertha Ferderber-Salz for her daughters in *And the Sun Kept Shining …* .

GENERAL QUESTIONS

How did the following elements help the Germans to carry out their genocide?

Segregation
Restrictions
Confiscations
Control of information
Ruthlessness in dealing with those opposed to Nazism

What part did economics play in the Holocaust and in the German war effort, in terms of confiscated assets, and slave labour?

What is meant by "hunger", as experienced by the Jews?
What is meant by "fear"?
What is meant by "hope"?

In what ways can "courage" and "defiance" comprise very real resistance?

Why were some non-Jews willing to help, and for what reasons did they help?

To what extent has the reality of Auschwitz alerted us to the potential for evil in the world?

What is meant by "crimes against humanity" and why is it important to know what happened during the Holocaust?

GLOSSARY OF TERMS USED BY THE MEMOIR WRITERS

Compiled by Sir Martin Gilbert

Aktion (German: "action"): a raid on the ghetto, the roundup and arrest of Jews, often accompanied by mass slaughter.

Amcha (Hebrew: "a Jew", "the Jewish people"): "one of us", used as a form of code word between Jews to ascertain whether the person spoken to was Jewish.

American Jewish Joint Distribution Committee (*the Joint*): an organization set up in 1914 to help Jewish refugees in the Russian-Polish borderlands during the First World War, active to this day in Jewish welfare work worldwide.

Anschluss (German: "unification"): the union of Germany and Austria, forbidden by the Versailles Treaty of 1920, but secured by Hitler in March 1938.

Armia Krajowa (Polish: "Home Army"): Polish underground movement loyal to the Polish government in London.

Armia Ludowa (Polish: "People's Army"): Polish underground movement loyal to Moscow, and predominantly Communist.

Aryan side (*Warsaw*): the non-Jewish sections of Warsaw after the creation of the Warsaw Ghetto, which was surrounded by a high brick wall.

Aussiedlung (German: "resettlement"): a euphemism for deportation, usually to a death camp.

Bar-Mitzvah (Hebrew: "son of the covenant"): a Jewish boy's coming of age, on his 13th birthday, when he is able to assume religious obligations as an adult.

Block (also *bloc*): a barrack in a concentration camp usually designated with a number or a letter.

Boche (French: "a German", plural: *les Boches*): slang word for Germans.

Bund (Yiddish: "union"): the Jewish Social Revolutionary party, founded in Russia in 1898 as an association of Jewish workers worldwide, committed to world revolution and social equality.

Bunker: a hiding place, often in a cellar, or dug underneath a building.

Camps: places where Jews and other opponents of Nazism were confined, under strict guard. See also: *Concentration camps*, *Death camps* and *Slave labour camps*.

Canada (*Kanada*): a large hutted area at Auschwitz-Birkenau set aside for the sorting of the belongings of Jews deported to the camp from all over Europe. A vast storehouse of clothing and personal possessions.

Centos (Polish acronym): pre-war Polish Jewish welfare organization for orphans.

Concentration camps: camps where the Nazis incarcerated their opponents behind barbed wire and high walls; places of extreme brutality by the guards, who were often common criminals; places to which Jews were deported, and where murder was commonplace.

Crematorium/crematoria (*crematory*): places in concentration camps where the corpses of those who had died, or been murdered, were burned. Auschwitz had five, each one attached to a gas chamber where the murders took place.

Death camps: concentration camps in which almost all those deported there were murdered within a few hours, usually by gas.

Displaced Persons camp (*DP camp*): post-war camps in which survivors of the Holocaust were gathered, and awaited rehabilitation.

East (as in *"to the East"*, *"somewhere in the East"*): the "unknown destination" of almost all the deportation trains from mid-1942 to mid-1944. As a result of the escape of four Jews from Auschwitz in April and May 1944, the main "unknown destination" was revealed as Auschwitz-Birkenau, a death factory. Another long-kept secret destination "in the East" was the death camp at Maly Trostenets, near Minsk.

Folkschul (Yiddish: a Jewish "people's school"): usually a non-religious school.

Gestapo (*Geheime Staatspolizei*, of which "Gestapo" is an acronym): the much-feared German Secret State Police.

High Holy Days: The solemn festivals of the Jewish New Year, Rosh Hashana, and the Day of Atonement, Yom Kippur.

Hitler Youth (*"Hitlerjugend"*, *"HJ"*): the National Socialist youth movement, established as the "Adolf Hitler Boys' Storm Troops" in 1922, renamed Hitler Youth in 1926. By 1935 it comprised 60 per cent of German youth between the ages of 10 and 18. The Nazi ideology that the movement took was permeated with hatred of Jews. Many Hitler Youth members were later active in the Final Solution – the plan to wipe out all of Europe's Jews.

Hlinka Guard: Slovak militia named after the Slovak nationalist Andrej Hlinka (who died in 1938). When it was established in 1938, the militia acted against Jews, Czechs, socialists, and all opposition to Slovak independence. From 1941 its members were trained in SS camps in Germany. In 1942 it participated in the deportation of Slovak Jews to the death camps in German-occupied Poland. Its members wore black uniforms.

International Brigade: military formation made up largely of volunteers from all over the world who went to Spain between 1936 and 1939 to fight on the Republican side against the Franco nationalists. Several thousand Jews, including many from North America, joined the Brigade in the hope of playing an active part against fascism.

Internment camps: camps, mostly in German-dominated Western Europe, in which Jews were held before being sent to transit camps – and then to death camps.

Jewish Brigade: Jewish soldiers in the British Army, who in 1944 were given their own military formation and Star of David insignia within the British forces. After fighting against the Germans in Italy, many of them were active after the war in helping Jews to escape from Central and Eastern Europe and to make their way from Austria to Italy – and in due course to Palestine.

Jewish Co-ordinating Committee: a relief organization in the Warsaw ghetto. After the ghetto uprising it focused its efforts on helping those who had survived, including providing them with false papers. It also tried to help Jewish survivors of the Czestochowa ghetto after it had been destroyed.

Jewish Council ("Judenrat"): Jewish administrations established in the ghettos at German insistence. They were responsible for all aspects of Jewish internal life in the ghetto, including health and education. Some collaborated with the Germans, or were forced to do so; most resisted German demands, even taking a lead in helping Jewish resistance. Jewish Council members, including those who had collaborated, suffered the fate of all Jews in the ghetto. The head of the Jewish Council in Warsaw, Adam Czerniakow, committed suicide rather than hand over to the Germans the daily quota of Jews they had demanded for deportation to Treblinka.

Jewish Fighting Organization (JFO): see glossary entry for *ZOB*.

Joint, the: see glossary entry for *American Jewish Joint Distribution Committee*.

Kabala (also *Kabbalah*): a mystical Jewish system developed in the eleventh and twelfth centuries, which seeks to find an inner meaning to the scriptural writings.

Kapo: a supervisor of concentration camp or slave labour camp inmates, himself a prisoner. Often a common criminal. The word is believed to derive from the Italian word "capo" – "chief". Some kapos were cruel in the extreme; others could act fairly.

Kol Nidrei (Hebrew: "All Vows"): The opening prayer of the Day of Atonement. The phrase, based on the first two words of that prayer – which is mostly in Aramaic – has come to mean the whole evening service in synagogue at the opening of the Day of Atonement.

Kristallnacht (German: "night of broken glass"): the night of 9/10 November 1938, when hundreds of synagogues throughout Germany and Austria were destroyed, and many Jewish businesses and homes ransacked. Ninety-two Jews were also murdered that night, and tens of thousands of Jewish men sent to concentration camps.

Lagerführer (German): camp chief. If the head was a woman, then *"Lagerführerin"*.

Marshall Plan: United States aid package, introduced in 1947, to rebuild the war shattered economies of Europe. The Soviet Union rejected the plan and made all its Eastern European Communist satellites do likewise. Named after its founder, General George C. Marshall, Chief of Staff of the United States Army, 1939–45, and Secretary of State, 1947–49. In recognition of the success of his plan, Marshall was awarded the Nobel Peace Prize.

Masada: King Herod's palace and fortress overlooking the Dead Sea. In the final stages of the Jewish revolt against Rome (which lasted from 132 to 135) the surviving rebels held out against a Roman siege until the wall was breached. The Jews committed collective suicide to avoid capture.

Matza (Hebrew, plural *matzot*): unleavened bread, a thin, dry biscuit-type bread eaten by Jews during the eight days of Passover, in memory of the exodus from Egypt, when there had been no time to bake leavened bread.

Melina (Yiddish, a word mostly used in Poland and Lithuania): a hiding place, often in a cellar, or behind a cupboard.

Molotov Cocktail: a crude explosive device, usually a bottle filled with gasoline and ignited through a rag stuffed into the neck of the bottle. First used by the Finns in their defence against the Russians in the Russo–Finnish War (1939–40), and named by them derisively after the Soviet Foreign Minister at that time, Vyacheslav Molotov.

mussulman / muselmänner: an emaciated concentration camp prisoner who had given up the will to live, and was near death.

Nebich (Yiddish: "poor thing"): an unfortunate person.

Nyilas: Hungarian fascists who rampaged through Budapest in late 1944, murdering many thousands of Jews. Thousands more Jews were protected from the Nyilas gangs by the Swedish diplomat Raoul Wallenberg and his fellow diplomats in the city.

Oberkapo: a senior supervisor in a concentration camp (see *"kapo"*).

Palestine Mandate: The governance of Palestine, between the Mediterranean Sea and the River Jordan, granted to Britain by the League of Nations in 1922 as a Mandate. Britain relinquished the Mandate in 1948, when David Ben-Gurion declared a Jewish State (Israel). The West Bank and Gaza Strip areas of the Mandate were occupied in 1948 by Jordan and Egypt respectively, until occupied by Israel in 1967.

Papal Nuncio: the senior representative of the Pope and the Vatican in foreign capitals. The Papal Nuncio in Budapest – Angelo Rotta – was particularly active in trying to protect Jews.

Quisling: The surname of the head of the wartime Norwegian collaborationist regime in Norway – Vidkun Quisling. The word has become synonymous with treachery.

reparations: money paid by the German government, and by some German companies, in recognition of the personal suffering and material losses suffered by Jews during the Holocaust. The German government initiated this process in 1952, under the Luxembourg Agreement with the State of Israel.

resettlement: a deliberate and deceptive German euphemism for deportation, usually to a death camp. The German word was *"aussiedlung"*.

Rosh Hashana: the Jewish New Year, marking the start of the High Holy Days.

SS (*"Schutzstaffel"*, of which SS is an abbreviation): "Defence Squad", created in Munich in the 1920s to protect Nazi Party speakers from attacks by their opponents; from 1933, responsible for administering the concentration camps and slave labour camps, and with carrying out the racist policies of the Nazi regime. Following the German invasion of the Soviet Union in June 1941, SS mobile killing squads *"Einsatzgruppen"* murdered at least a million Jews. The SS was headed by Heinrich Himmler.

Selection (*selektsia*): the act of dividing Jews into two groups: those who were to be taken away and murdered, and those who were to return to the ghetto or concentration camp barracks – to work, and await yet another selection. Selections often took place during mass roll calls.

Shabbat (in Hebrew), *Shabbos* (in Yiddish): the Jewish Sabbath, beginning on Friday night at sundown. The Jewish day of rest.

Siberia: Eastern region of the Soviet Union, from the Ural mountains to the Pacific Ocean; the location of many Soviet labour camps and labour camp zones of the utmost severity.

Slave labour camps: SS-run camps, often attached to factories and factory zones, in which large numbers of Jews – and other captive peoples – worked amid extreme severity, and in which many died of the harsh conditions and brutality of the guards.

smous: a derogatory term for Jews (in Belgium).

Sonderkommando: Groups of Jewish prisoners forced by the Germans to work in and around the gas chambers disposing of the corpses. In almost every case the group selected were murdered within a few months, and replaced by others who were also subsequently murdered.

szmalcownicy: the Polish word for blackmailers, extortioners.

Todt Organization: a German organization, originally headed by a Nazi Party engineer, Fritz Todt (who died accidentally in 1942). The Todt Organization, which employed Jewish and non-Jewish slave labour, was responsible for the construction of projects of strategic importance, including the Siegfried Line defence in western Germany, railway facilities for the German Army on the Eastern Front, and the "West Wall" fortifications to protect against an Allied landing in northern France.

Torah: the Five Books of Moses (the Pentateuch).

Transit camps: camps to which Jews were taken, and then held until being deported to a death camp.

Umschlagplatz (German: "collection place"): a railway siding from which Jews were deported. In Warsaw, they were brought there on a regular basis from all over the ghetto and held until deported by train to Treblinka.

UNESCO (*United Nations Educational, Scientific and Cultural Organization*): established in 1946 to further "a universal respect for human rights, justice and the rule of law, without distinction of race, sex, language or religion", in accordance with the United Nations charter. Dedicated to the free flow of information, and the preservation of freedom of expression.

UNRRA (*United Nations Relief and Rehabilitation Administration*): set up in the aftermath of the Second World War to help refugees and Displaced Persons. Among its tasks was the distribution of food.

Ustachi: a fascist force in the wartime independent State of Croatia, responsible for the mass murder of Serbs and Jews.

Vichy: a town in central France, which, following the German defeat of France in June 1940, became the capital of the "Vichy" government, headed by Marshal Pétain, and subservient to Germany. Vichy's police, the *Millice*, were active in the roundup of Jews for deportation. The word "Vichy" became synonymous with collaboration.

Volksdeutsche (also known as "*ethnic Germans*"): German minorities living outside the German Reich, including the Sudeten Germans in Czechoslovakia and the Volga Germans in the Soviet Union. Some groups had lived many hundreds of miles from Germany for several centuries. Many became strong supporters of Nazism after the German Army occupied the regions in which they lived, and benefited considerably from the German occupation.

Yom Kippur: the Day of Atonement, the holiest twenty-four hours in the Jewish religious calendar, a time of prayer and fasting, and seeking forgiveness from God.

Wehrmacht: the German armed forces. In 1939 they consisted of 2,700,000 men, and in 1943 of more than 13 million. Separate from the armed forces of the SS (*Waffen SS*).

Yeshiva (plural, *yeshivot*): an institution of learning in which Jews pursue the study of the Torah. The word comes from the Hebrew verb "yashav", "to sit". The system of study is based on the keen debate of Biblical and rabbinical sources. Many famous *yeshivot* were destroyed during the Holocaust. Some were able to renew their existence after the war, mostly in the United States and Israel.

ZOB (Polish: *Zydowska Organizacja Bojowa "Jewish Fighting Organization"*): Established in Warsaw on 28 July 1942, when the mass deportations were taking place to Treblinka. Determined to offer armed resistance against the German occupation forces, its members organized two ghetto uprisings in Warsaw, the first in January 1943 and the second – the Warsaw Ghetto Revolt – in April 1943. In August 1944, many of its members who had survived the crushing of the ghetto revolt participated in the Polish Uprising in Warsaw.

Zachor (Hebrew "To remember"): a basic Jewish precept.

Zohar: The classical work of the *Kabala* (see glossary entry) containing a record of the divine mysteries said to have been granted to a second-century Jewish teacher, Rabbi Simeon ben Yohai, and his mystic circle. The word means "illumination" or "brightness".

Zytos (Polish, acronym): a Jewish relief agency in the Warsaw ghetto.

SS POSITIONS AND RANKS MENTIONED IN THE MEMOIRS

Reichsführer: the head of the SS (Heinrich Himmler)
Oberstgruppenführer: "Colonel-General"
Obergruppenführer: General
Gruppenführer: Lieutenant-General
Brigadeführer: Major-General
Oberführer: Brigadier
Standartenführer: Colonel
Obersturmbannführer: Lieutenant-Colonel
Sturmbannführer: Major
Haupsturmführer: Captain
Obersturmführer: Lieutenant (UK), First Lieutenant (USA)
Untersturmführer: Second Lieutenant
Oberscharführer: Sergeant-Major
Scharführer: Sergeant
Unterscharführer: Lance-Sergeant
Sturmmann/Rottenführer: Corporal
Obergrenadier: Lance-Corporal
Grenadier/Panzergrenadier: Private

REFERENCE WORKS CONSULTED

Danuta Czech, *Auschwitz Chronicle*, 1939–1945, I.B. Tauris, London and New York, 1990.

Martin Gilbert, *Atlas of the Holocaust*, 3rd edn (with gazeteer), Routledge, London and New York, 2002.

Martin Gilbert, *The Holocaust, A History of the Jews of Europe During the Second World War*, Henry Holt, New York, 1985.

Czeslaw Pilichowski, *Obozy hitlerowskie na ziemiach polskich 1939–1945: Infomator encyklopedyczny*, Glowna Komisja Badania Zbrodni Hitlerowskich w Polsce, Warsaw, 1979.

INDEX

Compiled by the editor

Study Guide Maps

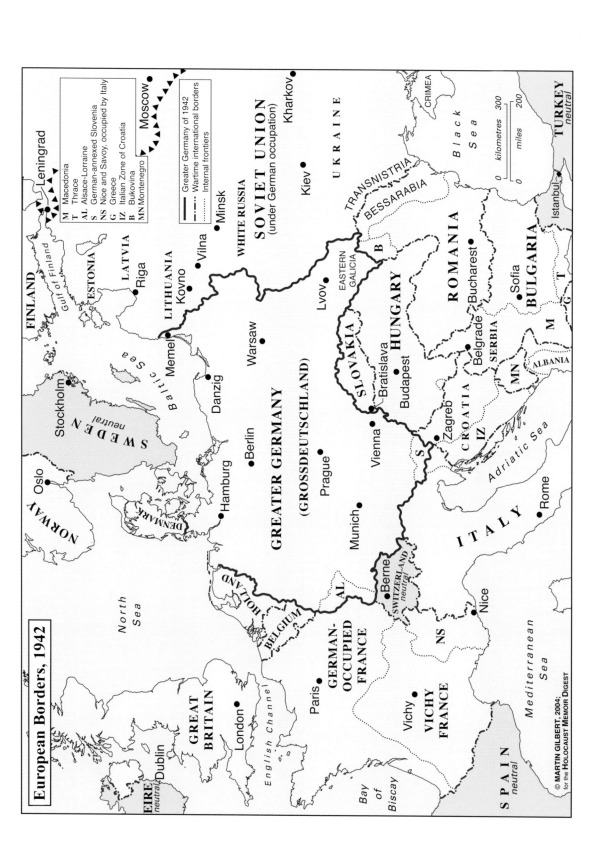

European Borders, 1942

Greater Germany of 1942
Wartime international borders
Internal frontiers

M   Macedonia
T   Thrace
AL Alsace-Lorraine
S   German-annexed Slovenia
NS Nice and Savoy, occupied by Italy
G   Greece
IZ Italian Zone of Croatia
B   Bukovina
MN Montenegro

NORWAY
Oslo

SWEDEN
neutral
Stockholm

FINLAND
Gulf of Finland
Leningrad

ESTONIA
Riga
LATVIA

LITHUANIA
Kovno
Vilna
Memel

Baltic Sea

WHITE RUSSIA
Minsk

Moscow

SOVIET UNION
(under German occupation)

Kharkov

Kiev

U K R A I N E

CRIMEA

Black Sea

TRANSNISTRIA
BESSARABIA

EASTERN
GALICIA
Lvov

B

ROMANIA
Bucharest

TURKEY
neutral

Istanbul

BULGARIA
Sofia

G
T

M

ALBANIA

MN

SERBIA
Belgrade

IZ

Zagreb

CROATIA

Adriatic Sea

HUNGARY
Budapest

SLOVAKIA
Bratislava

Vienna

S

ITALY

Rome

Nice

NS

Mediterranean Sea

SWITZERLAND
neutral
Berne

AL

GERMAN-
OCCUPIED
FRANCE

Paris

VICHY
FRANCE
Vichy

SPAIN
neutral

Bay
of
Biscay

English Channel

London

GREAT
BRITAIN

EIRE
neutral
Dublin

North
Sea

HOLLAND

BELGIUM

Munich

GREATER GERMANY
(GROSSDEUTSCHLAND)

Prague

Berlin

Hamburg

DENMARK

Danzig

Warsaw

kilometres   300
0
0   200
miles

© MARTIN GILBERT, 2004;
for the HOLOCAUST MEMOIR DIGEST

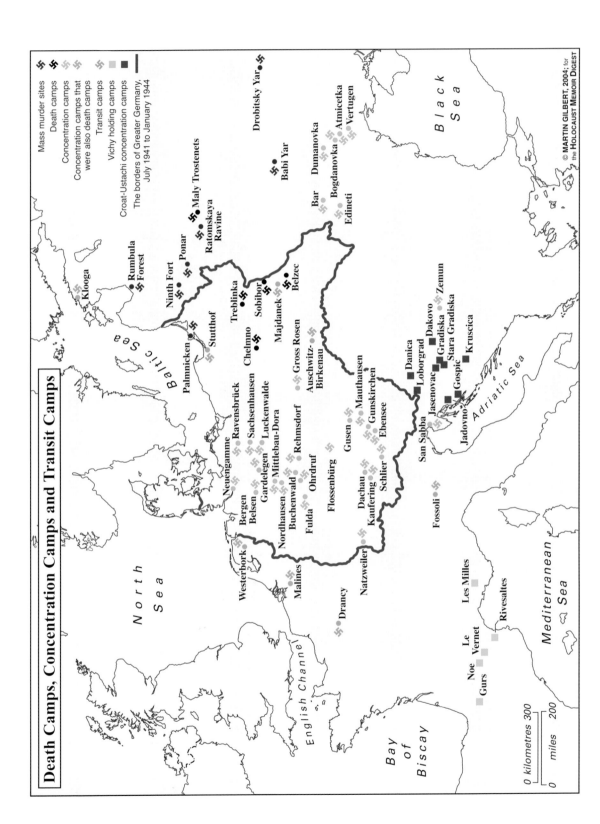

Death Camps, Concentration Camps and Transit Camps

Mass murder sites

Death camps

Concentration camps

Concentration camps that were also death camps

Transit camps

Vichy holding camps

Croat-Ustachi concentration camps

The borders of Greater Germany, July 1941 to January 1944

© MARTIN GILBERT, 2004; for the HOLOCAUST MEMOIR DIGEST

Drobitsky Yar

Maly Trostenets

Ratomskaya Ravine

Ponar

Babi Yar

Dumanovka

Bogdanovka Atmicetka

Vertugen

Edineti

Bar

Rumbula Forest

Klooga

Ninth Fort

Stutthof

Treblinka

Sobibor

Majdanek

Belzec

Palmnicken

Chelmno

Gross Rosen

Zemun

Dakovo

Gradiska

Stara Gradiska

Gospic Kruscica

Danica

Loborgrad

Jasenovac

Jadovno

San Sabba

Auschwitz-Birkenau

Mauthausen

Gunskirchen

Ebensee

Gusen

Neuengamme

Ravensbrück

Sachsenhausen

Luckenwalde

Mittlebau-Dora

Rehmsdorf

Gardelegen

Buchenwald

Ohrdruf

Flossenbürg

Fulda

Nordhausen

Bergen Belsen

Dachau

Kaufering

Schlier

Natzweiler

Westerbork

Malines

Drancy

Les Milles

Rivesaltes

Le Vernet

Noe

Gurs

Fossoli

Baltic Sea

North Sea

Black Sea

Adriatic Sea

Mediterranean Sea

English Channel

Bay of Biscay

0 kilometres 300

0 miles 200

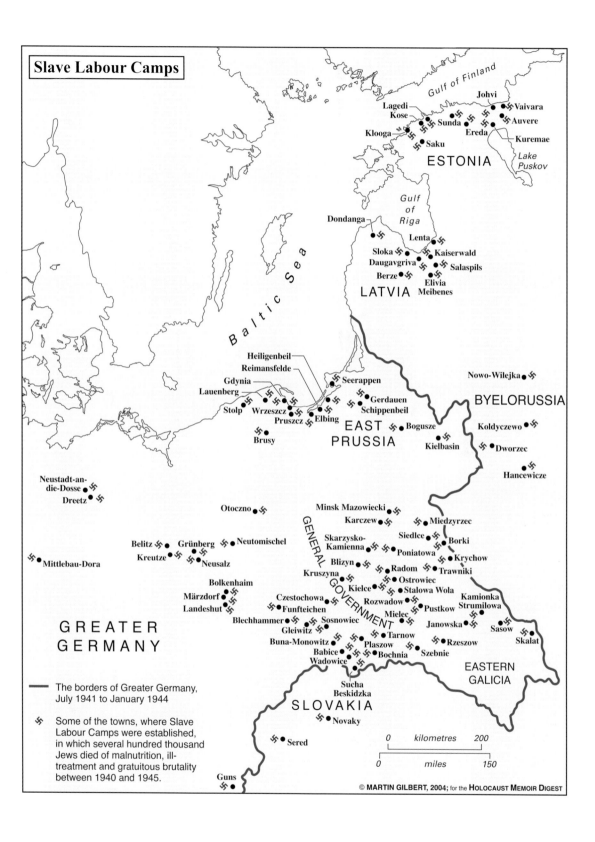

Slave Labour Camps

Gulf of Finland

Johvi

Lagedi ⌘
Kose ⌘ ⌘ Vaivara ⌘
⌘ Sunda ⌘ Auvere ⌘
Klooga ⌘ ⌘ Ereda ⌘
⌘ ⌘ Kuremae
⌘ Saku

ESTONIA

Lake Puskov

Gulf of Riga

Dondanga ⌘
⌘ Lenta ⌘
Sloka ⌘ ⌘ Kaiserwald ⌘
Daugavgriva ⌘ ⌘ Salaspils ⌘
Berze ⌘ ⌘ Elivia
⌘ Meibenes

LATVIA

B a l t i c   S e a

Nowo-Wilejka ⌘

BYELORUSSIA

Heiligenbeil ⌘
Reimansfelde ⌘ ⌘ Seerappen
Gdynia ⌘ ⌘ Gerdauen
Lauenberg ⌘ ⌘ ⌘ Schippenbeil
⌘ Koldyczewo ⌘
Stolp ⌘ Wrzeszcz ⌘ ⌘ Dworzec ⌘
⌘ Pruszcz ⌘ Elbing EAST ⌘ Bogusze
⌘ Brusy PRUSSIA ⌘ Kielbasin ⌘ Hancewicze ⌘

Neustadt-an-
die-Dosse ⌘ ⌘
Dreetz ⌘

Otoczno ⌘
Minsk Mazowiecki ⌘
Karczew ⌘ ⌘ Miedzyrzec ⌘
Belitz ⌘ Grünberg ⌘ Neutomischel Skarzysko- ⌘ Siedlce ⌘ ⌘ Borki
Kreutze ⌘ ⌘ Neusalz Kamienna ⌘ Poniatowa ⌘ Krychow ⌘
GENERAL Blizyn ⌘ Radom ⌘ ⌘ Trawniki
⌘ Mittlebau-Dora Kruszyna ⌘ ⌘ Ostrowiec ⌘
Bolkenheim ⌘ Kielce ⌘ Stalowa Wola Kamionka
Märzdorf ⌘ GOVERNMENT Rozwadow ⌘ ⌘ Pustkow Strumilowa ⌘
Landeshut ⌘ Czestochowa ⌘ Mielec ⌘ Janowska ⌘ Sasow ⌘
Blechhammer ⌘ Funfteichen ⌘ Sosnowiec ⌘ Rzeszow ⌘ Skalat ⌘
Gleiwitz ⌘ ⌘ Tarnow
Buna-Monowitz ⌘ Plaszow ⌘
Babice ⌘ ⌘ Bochnia Szebnie ⌘
Wadowice ⌘ EASTERN
GALICIA

GREATER
GERMANY

Sucha
Beskidzka

SLOVAKIA ⌘ Novaky

— The borders of Greater Germany,
July 1941 to January 1944

⌘ Some of the towns, where Slave
Labour Camps were established,
in which several hundred thousand
Jews died of malnutrition, ill-
treatment and gratuitous brutality
between 1940 and 1945.

⌘ Sered

Guns ⌘

| 0 | kilometres | 200 |

| 0 | miles | 150 |

© **MARTIN GILBERT**, 2004; for the HOLOCAUST MEMOIR DIGEST

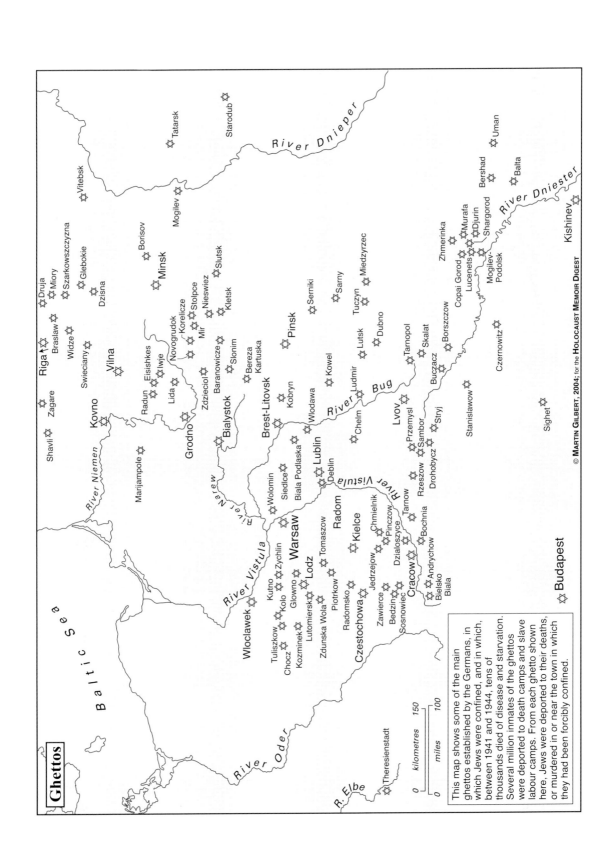

Ghettos

Baltic Sea

River Oder

R. Elbe

River Niemen

River Narew

River Vistula

River Bug

River Vistula

River Dnieper

River Dniester

Theresienstadt

Tatarsk

Starodub

Vitebsk

Mogilev

Uman

Bershad

Balta

Zhmerinka

Copai Gorod

Lucenets

Murafa

Djurin

Shargorod

Mogilev-Podolsk

Kishinev

Czernowitz

Sighet

Budapest

Druja

Miory

Szarkowszczyzna

Glebokie

Dzisna

Borisov

Minsk

Slutsk

Nieswiez

Kletsk

Semiki

Sarny

Tuczyn

Miedzyrzec

Riga

Braslaw

Widze

Swieciany

Vilna

Radun

Eisishkes

Iwje

Lida

Stolpce

Korelicze

Mir

Novogrudok

Zdzieciol

Slonim

Baranowicze

Bereza Kartuska

Pinsk

Kobryn

Kowel

Lutsk

Ludmir

Dubno

Tarnopol

Skalat

Buczacz

Borszczow

Stanislawow

Shavli

Zagare

Kovno

Grodno

Marijampole

Bialystok

Brest-Litovsk

Wlodawa

Chelm

Lublin

Deblin

Lvov

Przemysl

Sambor

Drohobycz

Stryj

Rzeszow

Siedlce

Biala Podlaska

Wolomin

Tomaszow

Chmielnik

Pinczow

Dzialoszyce

Bochnia

Andrychow

Bielsko

Biala

Cracow

Tarnow

Radom

Kielce

Jedrzejow

Zawierce

Bedzin

Sosnowiec

Czestochowa

Radomsko

Piotrkow

Zdunska Wola

Lutomiersk

Kozminek

Chocz

Kolo

Glowno

Lodz

Zychlin

Kutno

Tuliszkow

Wloclawek

Warsaw

Theresienstadt

© **Martin Gilbert, 2004; for the Holocaust Memoir Digest**

0   100   miles

0   150   kilometres

This map shows some of the main ghettos established by the Germans, in which Jews were confined, and in which, between 1941 and 1944, tens of thousands died of disease and starvation. Several million inmates of the ghettos were deported to death camps and slave labour camps. From each ghetto shown here, Jews were deported to their deaths, or murdered in or near the town in which they had been forcibly confined.

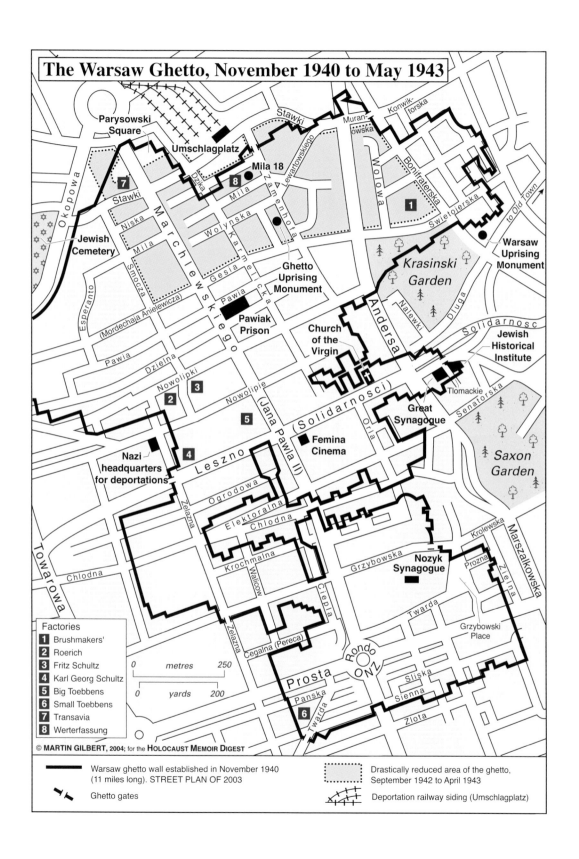

The Warsaw Ghetto, November 1940 to May 1943

Parysowski Square

Umschlagplatz

Mila 18

Stawki

Muranowska

Konwiktorska

Bonifraterska

Wolowa

Swietojerska

to Old Town

7

Stawki

Niska

Mila

Okopowa

Esperanto

Jewish Cemetery

Marchlewskiego

Wolynska

Karmel

Gesia

Smocza

(Mordechaja Anielewicza)

Pawia

Dzielna

Nowolipki

Nowolipie

8

Dzika

Zamenhofa

Lewartowskiego

1

Warsaw Uprising Monument

Ghetto Uprising Monument

Pawia

Pawiak Prison

3

2

Church of the Virgin

Krasinski Garden

Andersa

Nalewki

Dluga

Solidarnosc

Jewish Historical Institute

Tlomackie

Great Synagogue

Senatorska

Saxon Garden

(Jana Pawla II)

(Solidarnosci)

5

Femina Cinema

Orla

Nazi headquarters for deportations

4

Leszno

Ogrodowa

Elektoralna

Chlodna

Krochmalna

Walicow

Zelazna

Towarowa

Chlodna

Ciepla

Grzybowska

Nozyk Synagogue

Prozna

Zielna

Krolewska

Marszalkowska

Twarda

Grzybowski Place

Cegalna (Pereca)

Zelazna

Rondo ONZ

6

Prosta

Panska

Twarda

Sliska

Sienna

Zlota

Grzybowski Place

Factories

1	Brushmakers'
2	Roerich
3	Fritz Schultz
4	Karl Georg Schultz
5	Big Toebbens
6	Small Toebbens
7	Transavia
8	Werterfassung

0 metres 250

0 yards 200

© **MARTIN GILBERT**, 2004; for the HOLOCAUST MEMOIR DIGEST

Warsaw ghetto wall established in November 1940 (11 miles long). STREET PLAN OF 2003

Ghetto gates

Drastically reduced area of the ghetto, September 1942 to April 1943

Deportation railway siding (Umschlagplatz)

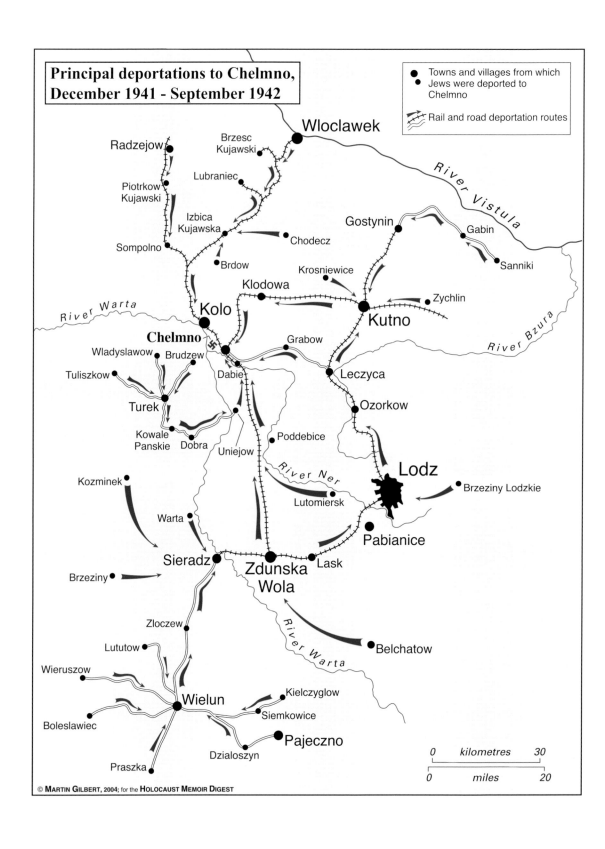

Principal deportations to Chelmno, December 1941 - September 1942

Towns and villages from which Jews were deported to Chelmno

Rail and road deportation routes

Wloclawek

Radzejow

Brzesc Kujawski

Lubraniec

Piotrkow Kujawski

Izbica Kujawska

Chodecz

Gostynin

Gabin

Sompolno

Brdow

Sanniki

River Vistula

Krosniewice

Klodowa

Zychlin

River Warta

Kolo

Kutno

Chelmno

Grabow

Wladyslawow

Brudzew

Dabie

Leczyca

River Bzura

Tuliszkow

Turek

Ozorkow

Kowale Panskie

Dobra

Uniejow

Poddebice

Lodz

Kozminek

Brzeziny Lodzkie

River Ner

Warta

Lutomiersk

Sieradz

Pabianice

Brzeziny

Zdunska Wola

Lask

Zloczew

River Warta

Belchatow

Lututow

Wieruszow

Wielun

Kielczyglow

Siemkowice

Boleslawiec

Pajeczno

Praszka

Dzialoszyn

0   kilometres   30

0   miles   20

© MARTIN GILBERT, 2004; for the HOLOCAUST MEMOIR DIGEST

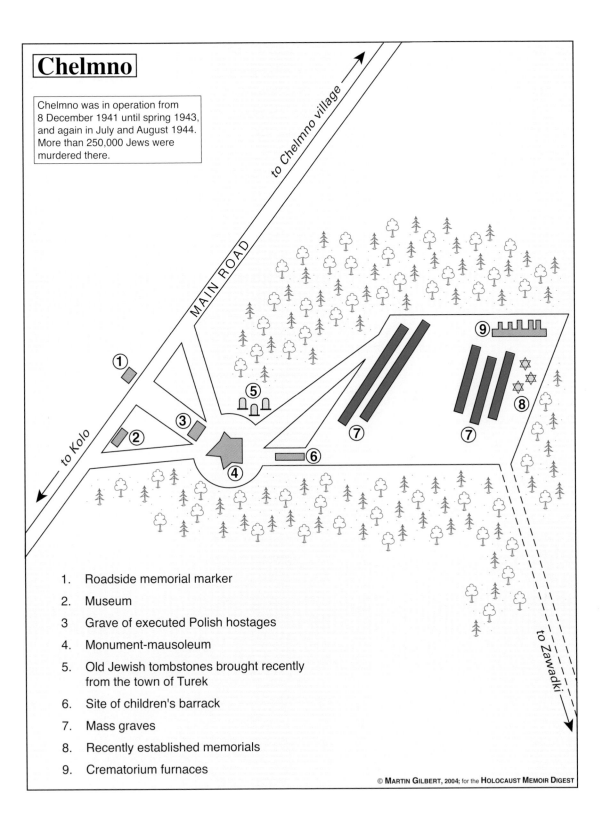

Chelmno

Chelmno was in operation from 8 December 1941 until spring 1943, and again in July and August 1944. More than 250,000 Jews were murdered there.

to Chelmno village

MAIN ROAD

to Kolo

to Zawadki

1. Roadside memorial marker

2. Museum

3 Grave of executed Polish hostages

4. Monument-mausoleum

5. Old Jewish tombstones brought recently from the town of Turek

6. Site of children's barrack

7. Mass graves

8. Recently established memorials

9. Crematorium furnaces

© Martin Gilbert, 2004; for the Holocaust Memoir Digest

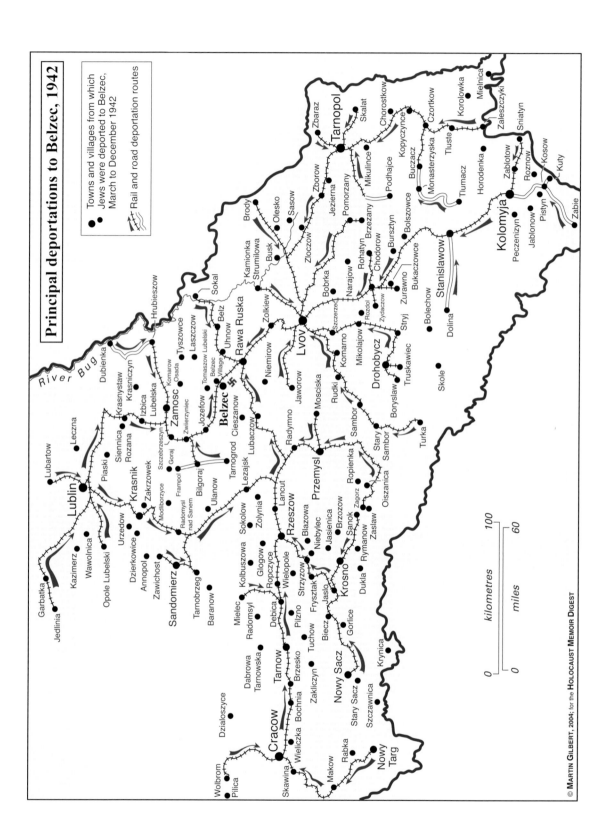

Principal deportations to Belzec, 1942

● Towns and villages from which Jews were deported to Belzec, March to December 1942

⟿ Rail and road deportation routes

River Bug

Garbatka
Jedlinia
Kazimerz
Wawolnica
Opole Lubelski
Dzierkowice
Annopol
Zawichost
Sandomierz
Tarnobrzeg
Baranow
Lubartow
Leczna
Lublin
Piaski
Siennica
Rozana
Krasnik
Zakrzowek
Modliborzyce
Radomysl nad Sanem
Urzedow
Krasnystaw
Izbica
Lubelska
Szczebrzeszyn
Zwierzyniec
Goraj
Frampol
Bilgoraj
Ulanow
Dubienka
Krasniczyn
Komarow Osada
Zamosc
Jozefow
Tarnogrod
Lezajsk
Lubaczow
Hrubieszow
Tyszowce
Laszczow
Tomaszow Lubelski
Belzec Village
Belzec
Cieszanow
Sokal
Belz
Uhnow
Rawa Ruska
Zolkiew
Niemirow
Jaworow
Mosciska
Radymno
Brody
Olesko
Sasow
Kamionka Strumilowa
Busk
Zloczow
Zborow
Zbaraz
Tarnopol
Skalat
Chorostkow
Czortkow
Korolowka
Mielnica
Zaleszczyki
Sniatyn
Zbarow
Jezierna
Pomorzany
Mikulince
Podhajce
Kopyczynce
Tluste
Monasterzyska
Buczacz
Tlumacz
Horodenka
Kolomyja
Zablotow
Roznow
Kosow
Kuty
Zabie
Pistyn
Jablonow
Peczenizyn
Brzezany
Rohatyn
Narajow
Bobrka
Lvov
Szczerzec
Rozdol
Zydaczow
Chodorow
Bursztyn
Bolszowce
Bukaczowce
Zurawno
Stryj
Bolechow
Dolina
Skole
Stanislawow
Mikolajow
Komarno
Drohobycz
Truskawiec
Boryslaw
Rudki
Sambor
Stary Sambor
Turka
Dzialoszyce
Wolbrom
Pilica
Wielopole
Skawina
Wieliczka
Bochnia
Zakliczyn
Dabrowa Tarnowska
Tarnow
Brzesko
Cracow
Makow
Rabka
Stary Sacz
Szczawnica
Nowy Sacz
Krynica
Gorlice
Biecz
Jaslo
Frysztak
Strzyzow
Pilzno
Debica
Tuchow
Radomysl
Mielec
Kolbuszowa
Glogow
Ropczyce
Sokolow
Zolynia
Lancut
Rzeszow
Blazowa
Niebylec
Jasienica
Krosno
Dukla
Rymanow
Sanok
Zaslaw
Zagorz
Brzozow
Ropienka
Oliszanica
Nowy Targ

0   100
kilometres
0   60
miles

© MARTIN GILBERT, 2004; for the HOLOCAUST MEMOIR DIGEST

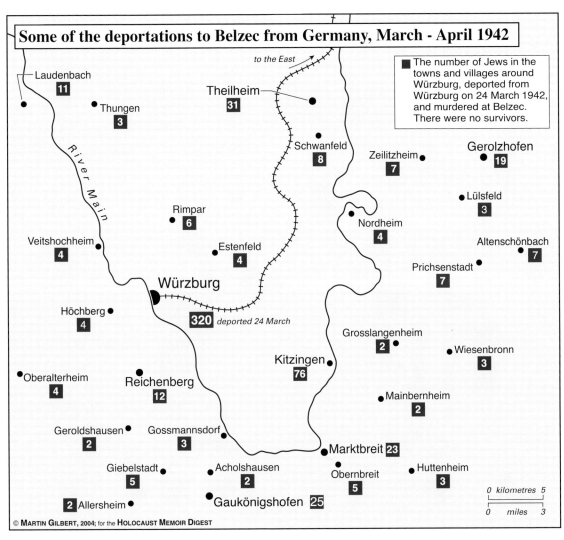

Some of the deportations to Belzec from Germany, March - April 1942

to the East

Laudenbach **11**

Thungen **3**

Theilheim **31**

Schwanfeld **8**

Zeilitzheim **7**

Gerolzhofen **19**

■ The number of Jews in the towns and villages around Würzburg, deported from Würzburg on 24 March 1942, and murdered at Belzec. There were no survivors.

River Main

Rimpar **6**

Nordheim **4**

Lülsfeld **3**

Veitshochheim **4**

Estenfeld **4**

Altenschönbach **7**

Prichsenstadt **7**

Würzburg

320 *deported 24 March*

Höchberg **4**

Grosslangenheim **2**

Wiesenbronn **3**

Oberalterheim **4**

Reichenberg **12**

Kitzingen **76**

Mainbernheim **2**

Geroldshausen **2**

Gossmannsdorf **3**

Marktbreit **23**

Giebelstadt **5**

Acholshausen **2**

Obernbreit **5**

Huttenheim **3**

2 Allersheim

Gaukönigshofen **25**

0 kilometres 5
0 miles 3

© MARTIN GILBERT, 2004; for the HOLOCAUST MEMOIR DIGEST

Dortmund

Julich

GREATER

● Some of the towns in Germany from which Jews were deported to Belzec in March and April 1942

⚡ Rail deportation routes from Germany to Belzec, March and April 1942

Piaski

Izbica Lubelska

Belzec

Bad Kissingen

Bamberg

Würzburg

see map above

Nuremburg

GERMANY

Augsburg

Lindau

SWITZERLAND
neutral

SLOVAKIA

0 kilometres 150
0 miles 0

© MARTIN GILBERT, 2004; for the HOLOCAUST MEMOIR DIGEST

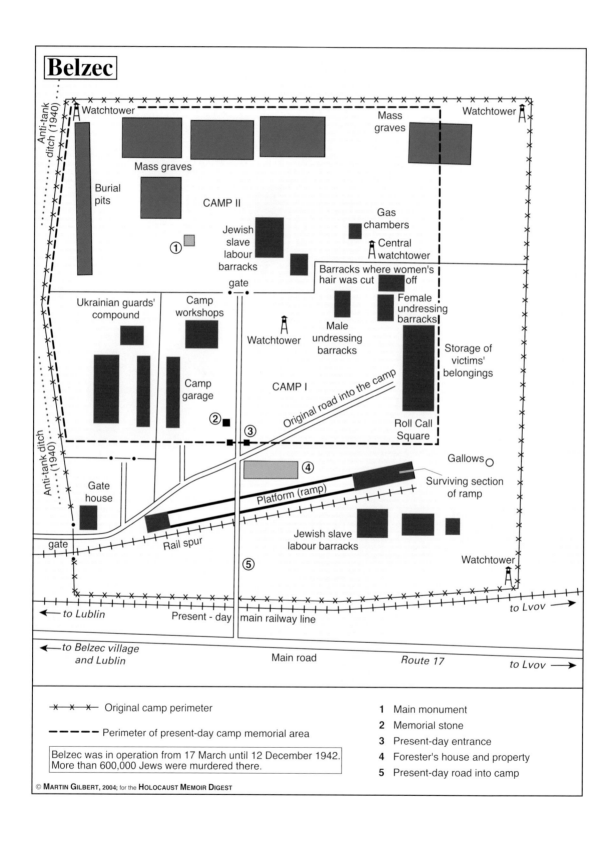

Belzec

Anti-tank ditch (1940)

Watchtower

Watchtower

Mass graves

Mass graves

Burial pits

CAMP II

①

Jewish slave labour barracks

Gas chambers

Central watchtower

Barracks where women's hair was cut off

gate

Ukrainian guards' compound

Camp workshops

Watchtower

Male undressing barracks

Female undressing barracks

Storage of victims' belongings

Camp garage

CAMP I

② ▪

③ ▪ ▪

Original road into the camp

Roll Call Square

Anti-tank ditch (1940)

Gate house

④

Platform (ramp)

Gallows ○

Surviving section of ramp

gate

Rail spur

Jewish slave labour barracks

Watchtower

⑤

← *to Lublin*   Present - day main railway line   *to Lvov* →

← *to Belzec village and Lublin*   Main road   *Route 17*   *to Lvov* →

—✕—✕—✕— Original camp perimeter

– – – – Perimeter of present-day camp memorial area

Belzec was in operation from 17 March until 12 December 1942. More than 600,000 Jews were murdered there.

© MARTIN GILBERT, 2004; for the HOLOCAUST MEMOIR DIGEST

1 Main monument
2 Memorial stone
3 Present-day entrance
4 Forester's house and property
5 Present-day road into camp

Principal deportations to Sobibor, 1942-1943

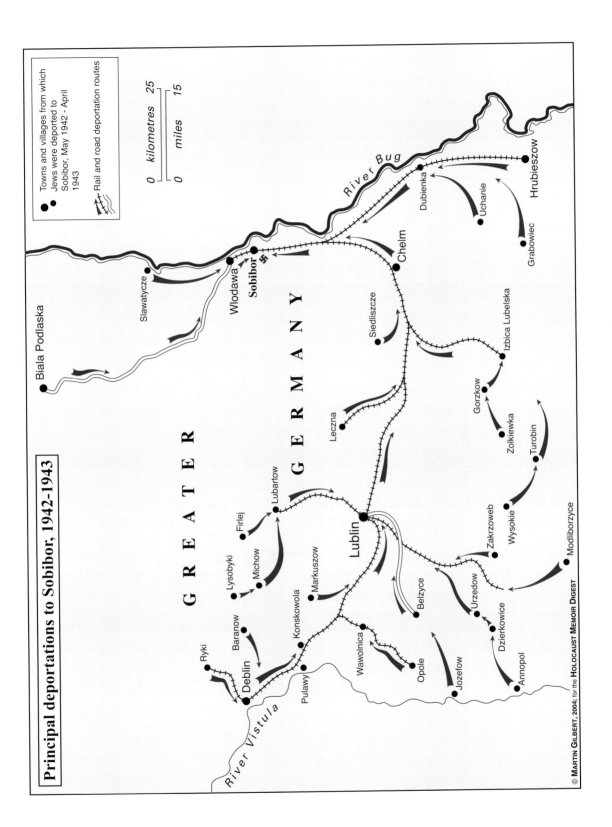

Towns and villages from which Jews were deported to Sobibor, May 1942 - April 1943

Rail and road deportation routes

0 kilometres 25
0 miles 15

Biala Podlaska

Slawatycze

River Bug

GREATER

Wlodawa
Sobibor

Hrubieszow

Uchanie

Dubienka

Grabowiec

GERMANY

Chelm

Siedliszcze

Izbica Lubelska

Leczna

Gorzkow

Zolkiewka

Turobin

Lubartow

Firlej

Lysobyki

Michow

Lublin

Zakrzoweb

Wysokie

Modliborzyce

Markuszow

Belzyce

Urzedow

Ryki

Baranow

Konskowola

Deblin

Pulawy

Wawolnica

Opole

Dzierkowice

Jozefow

Annopol

River Vistula

© MARTIN GILBERT, 2004; for the HOLOCAUST MEMOIR DIGEST

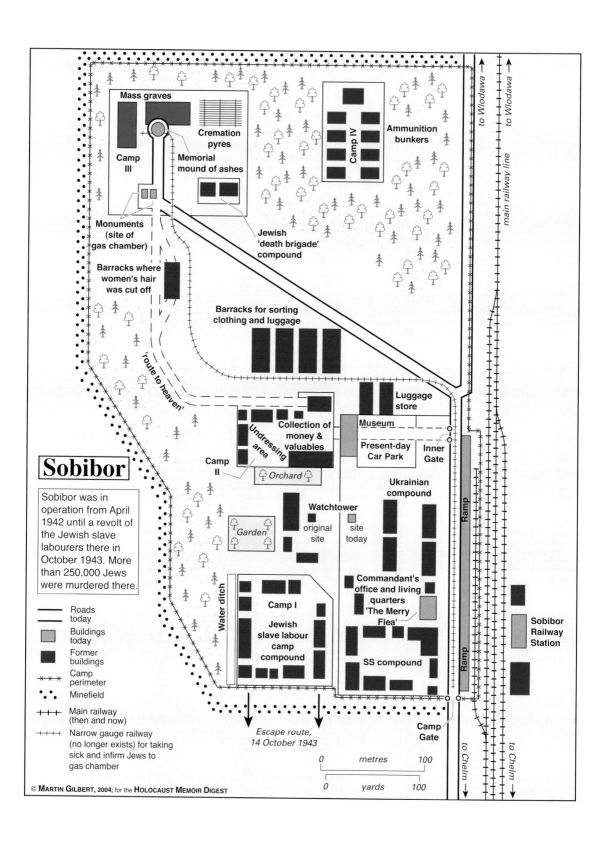

Sobibor

Sobibor was in operation from April 1942 until a revolt of the Jewish slave labourers there in October 1943. More than 250,000 Jews were murdered there.

Mass graves

Cremation pyres

Camp III

Memorial mound of ashes

Monuments (site of gas chamber)

Barracks where women's hair was cut off

Jewish 'death brigade' compound

Camp IV

Ammunition bunkers

Barracks for sorting clothing and luggage

'route to heaven'

Luggage store

Collection of money & valuables

Undressing area

Museum

Present-day Car Park

Inner Gate

Camp II

Orchard

Ukrainian compound

Garden

Watchtower

original site

site today

Water ditch

Camp I

Jewish slave labour camp compound

Commandant's office and living quarters 'The Merry Flea'

SS compound

Ramp

Sobibor Railway Station

Escape route, 14 October 1943

Camp Gate

to Wlodawa

to Wlodawa

main railway line

to Chelm

to Chelm

	Roads today
	Buildings today
	Former buildings
✳✳✳	Camp perimeter
• • •	Minefield
┼┼┼	Main railway (then and now)
┼┼┼┼	Narrow gauge railway (no longer exists) for taking sick and infirm Jews to gas chamber

0   metres   100

0   yards   100

© MARTIN GILBERT, 2004; for the HOLOCAUST MEMOIR DIGEST

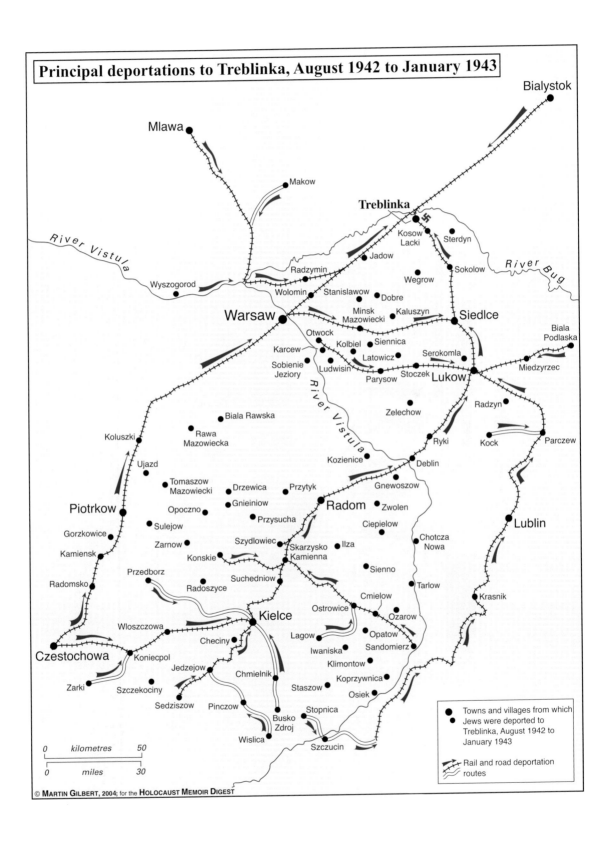

Principal deportations to Treblinka, August 1942 to January 1943

Bialystok

Mlawa

Makow

Treblinka

Kosow
Lacki

Sterdyn

River Vistula

Jadow

River Bug

Wyszogorod

Radzymin

Wegrow

Sokolow

Wolomin

Stanislawow

Dobre

Warsaw

Otwock

Minsk
Mazowiecki

Kaluszyn

Siedlce

Biala
Podlaska

Karcew

Kolbiel

Siennica

Sobienie
Jeziory

Ludwisin

Latowicz

Serokomla

Miedzyrzec

Parysow

Stoczek

Lukow

Biala Rawska

Zelechow

Radzyn

Koluszki

Rawa
Mazowiecka

Kozienice

Ryki

Kock

Parczew

Ujazd

Drzewica

Przytyk

Gnewoszow

Deblin

Piotrkow

Tomaszow
Mazowiecki

Gnieiniow

Radom

Zwolen

Lublin

Gorzkowice

Opoczno

Przysucha

Ciepielow

Sulejow

Chotcza
Nowa

Kamiensk

Zarnow

Szydlowiec

Ilza

Sienno

Radomsko

Konskie

Skarzysko
Kamienna

Przedbozr

Radoszyce

Suchedniow

Tarlow

Krasnik

Cmielow

Ostrowice

Ozarow

Wloszczowa

Kielce

Lagow

Opatow

Checiny

Iwaniska

Sandomierz

Czestochowa

Koniecpol

Jedzejow

Chmielnik

Klimontow

Zarki

Szczekociny

Koprzywnica

Sedziszow

Pinczow

Staszow

Osiek

Busko
Zdroj

Stopnica

Wislica

Szczucin

0   kilometres   50

0   miles   30

Towns and villages from which
Jews were deported to
Treblinka, August 1942 to
January 1943

Rail and road deportation
routes

© MARTIN GILBERT, 2004; for the HOLOCAUST MEMOIR DIGEST

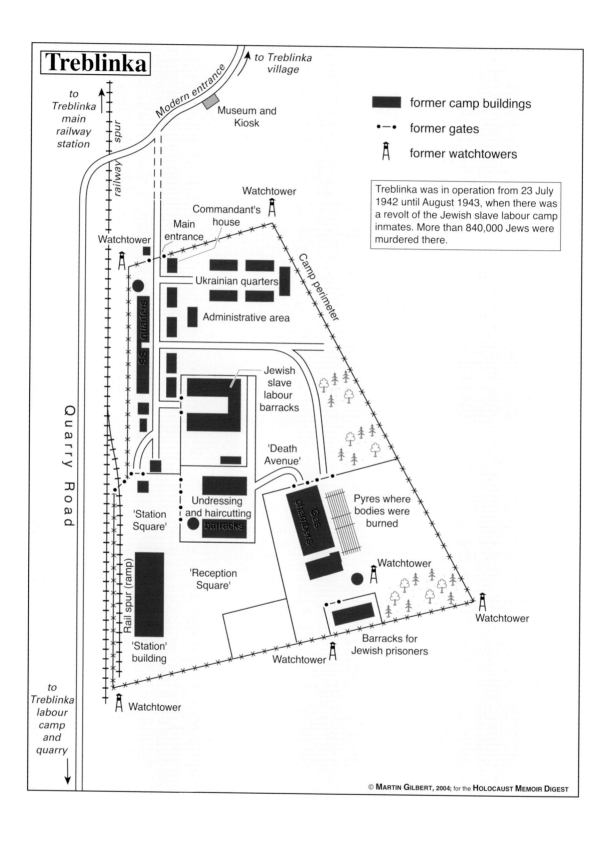

Treblinka

to Treblinka village

to Treblinka main railway station

Modern entrance

Museum and Kiosk

railway spur

■ former camp buildings

•—• former gates

Ⱶ former watchtowers

Treblinka was in operation from 23 July 1942 until August 1943, when there was a revolt of the Jewish slave labour camp inmates. More than 840,000 Jews were murdered there.

Watchtower

Commandant's house

Main entrance

Watchtower

Camp perimeter

SS quarters

Ukrainian quarters

Administrative area

Jewish slave labour barracks

Quarry Road

'Death Avenue'

Rail spur (ramp)

'Station Square'

Undressing and haircutting barracks

Pyres where bodies were burned

Gas Chambers

Watchtower

'Reception Square'

'Station' building

Barracks for Jewish prisoners

Watchtower

Watchtower

to Treblinka labour camp and quarry

Watchtower

© MARTIN GILBERT, 2004; for the HOLOCAUST MEMOIR DIGEST

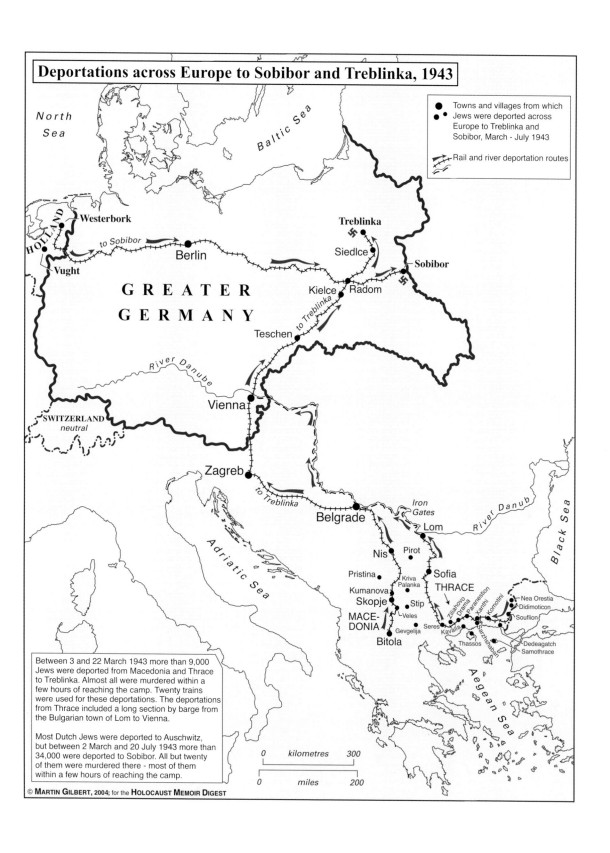

Deportations across Europe to Sobibor and Treblinka, 1943

North Sea

Baltic Sea

HOLLAND

● Westerbork

to Sobibor

● Berlin

● Vught

G R E A T E R
G E R M A N Y

Treblinka

● Siedlce

● Sobibor

Kielce ● Radom

to Treblinka

● Teschen

River Danube

● Vienna

SWITZERLAND
neutral

● Zagreb

to Treblinka

● Belgrade

Iron Gates

River Danub

● Lom

Black Sea

● Nis   ● Pirot

Adriatic Sea

● Pristina   Kriva
Palanka

● Sofia
THRACE

● Kumanova

● Skopje   ● Stip

MACE-
DONIA

● Veles

Zilahovo
Drama   Paranestion
Xanthi   Komotini   ● Nea Orestia
● Didimoticon
● Souflion

Seres ● Kavalla   Starzishaban

● Gevgelija

● Bitola

Thassos

Dedeagatch
Samothrace

Aegean Sea

Between 3 and 22 March 1943 more than 9,000
Jews were deported from Macedonia and Thrace
to Treblinka. Almost all were murdered within a
few hours of reaching the camp. Twenty trains
were used for these deportations. The deportations
from Thrace included a long section by barge from
the Bulgarian town of Lom to Vienna.

Most Dutch Jews were deported to Auschwitz,
but between 2 March and 20 July 1943 more than
34,000 were deported to Sobibor. All but twenty
of them were murdered there - most of them
within a few hours of reaching the camp.

● Towns and villages from which
Jews were deported across
Europe to Treblinka and
Sobibor, March - July 1943

Rail and river deportation routes

0   kilometres   300

0   miles   200

© MARTIN GILBERT, 2004; for the HOLOCAUST MEMOIR DIGEST

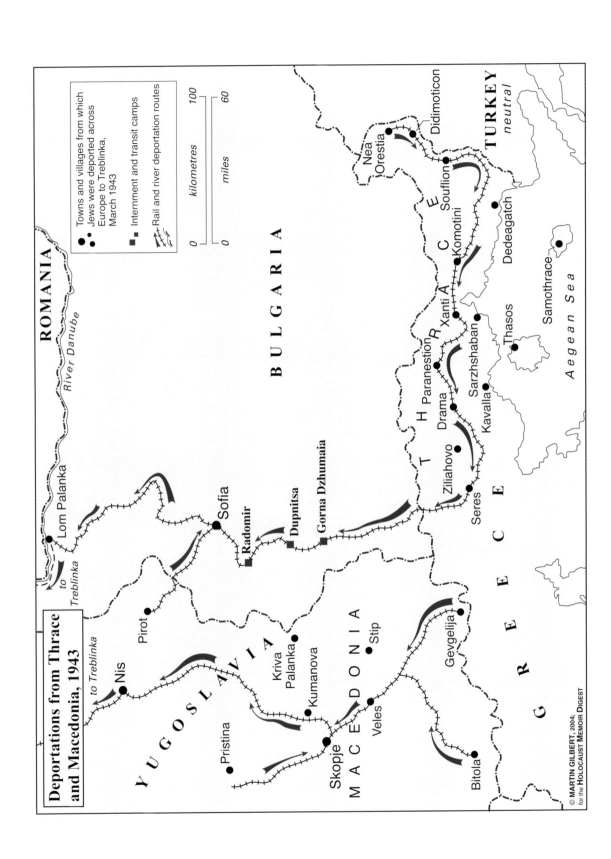

Deportations from Thrace and Macedonia, 1943

Towns and villages from which Jews were deported across Europe to Treblinka, March 1943

■ Internment and transit camps

Rail and river deportation routes

kilometres 0 ————— 100

miles 0 ————— 60

ROMANIA

River Danube

to Treblinka

Lom Palanka

BULGARIA

Sofia

Radomir

Dupnitsa

Gorna Dzhumaia

to Treblinka

Nis

Pirot

Pristina

YUGOSLAVIA

Kriva Palanka

Kumanova

Skopje

Veles

MACEDONIA

Stip

Gevgelija

Bitola

GREECE

T H R A C E

Paranestion

Ziliahovo

Drama

Seres

Sarzhshaban

Kavalla

Xanti

Komotini

Souflion

Nea Orestia

Didimoticon

TURKEY

neutral

Dedeagatch

Thasos

Samothrace

Aegean Sea

© **MARTIN GILBERT**, 2004;
for the **HOLOCAUST MEMOIR DIGEST**

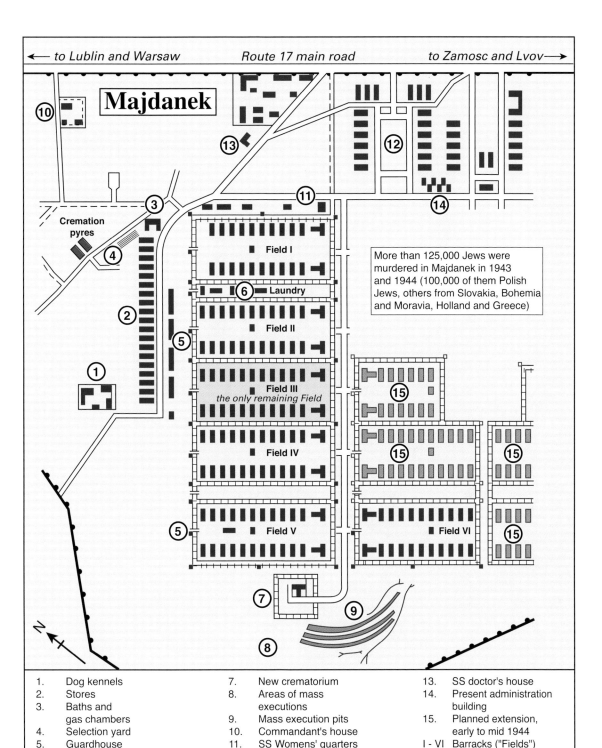

← *to Lublin and Warsaw*   *Route 17 main road*   *to Zamosc and Lvov*→

Majdanek

Cremation pyres

Field I

Laundry

Field II

Field III
the only remaining Field

Field IV

Field V

Field VI

More than 125,000 Jews were murdered in Majdanek in 1943 and 1944 (100,000 of them Polish Jews, others from Slovakia, Bohemia and Moravia, Holland and Greece)

N

1.	Dog kennels	7.	New crematorium	13.	SS doctor's house
2.	Stores	8.	Areas of mass	14.	Present administration
3.	Baths and		executions		building
	gas chambers	9.	Mass execution pits	15.	Planned extension,
4.	Selection yard	10.	Commandant's house		early to mid 1944
5.	Guardhouse	11.	SS Womens' quarters	I - VI	Barracks ("Fields")
6.	Old crematorium	12.	SS quarters and	■■	Watchtowers
			commandant's offices		Camp perimeter

© MARTIN GILBERT, 2004; for the HOLOCAUST MEMOIR DIGEST

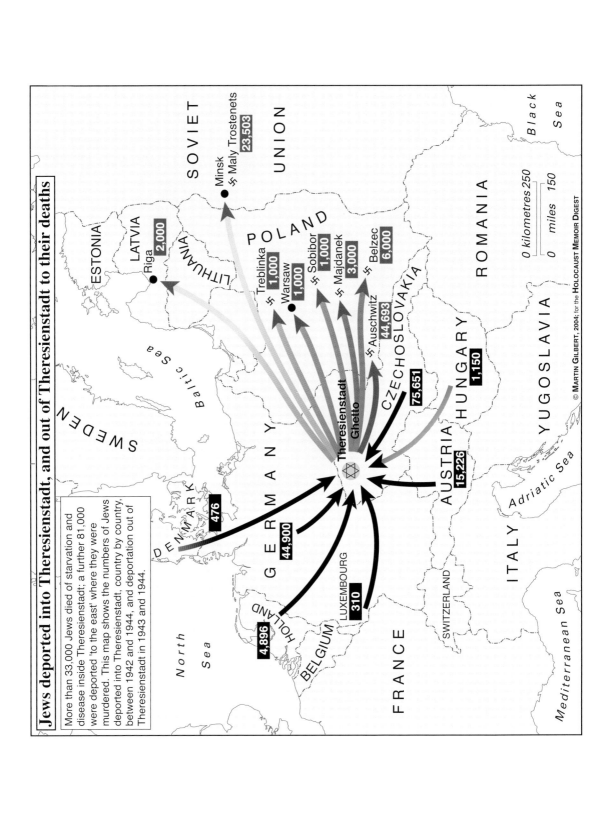

Jews deported into Theresienstadt, and out of Theresienstadt to their deaths

More than 33,000 Jews died of starvation and disease inside Theresienstadt; a further 81,000 were deported 'to the east' where they were murdered. This map shows the numbers of Jews deported into Theresienstadt, country by country, between 1942 and 1944, and deportation out of Theresienstadt in 1943 and 1944.

SOVIET UNION

ESTONIA

LATVIA

Riga **2,000**

LITHUANIA

Minsk
⚐ Maly Trostenets **23,503**

POLAND

⚐ Treblinka **1,000**
Warsaw ● **1,000**
⚐ Sobibor **1,000**
⚐ Majdanek **3,000**
⚐ Belzec **6,000**
⚐ Auschwitz **44,693**

Baltic Sea

SWEDEN

DENMARK **476**

GERMANY **44,900**

HOLLAND **4,896**

BELGIUM

LUXEMBOURG **310**

FRANCE

SWITZERLAND

Theresienstadt Ghetto

CZECHOSLOVAKIA **75,651**

AUSTRIA **15,226**

HUNGARY **1,150**

ROMANIA

YUGOSLAVIA

ITALY

Adriatic Sea

North Sea

Mediterranean Sea

Black Sea

0 kilometres 250
0 miles 150

© MARTIN GILBERT, 2004, for the HOLOCAUST MEMOIR DIGEST

The Theresienstadt Ghetto

More than 33,000 Jews died of starvation and disease inside Theresienstadt; a further 81,000 were deported 'to the east' where they were murdered, 44,693 of them at Auschwitz and 25,503 at Maly Trostenets, outside Minsk.

to Dresden

Ebergasse

PODMOKLY BARRACKS

Postgasse

Brunnenpark

DRESDEN BARRACKS

Berggasse

Stadtpark

to Prague

SUDETEN BARRACKS

Rathausgasse

CAVALRY BARRACKS

Seestrasse

Bahnhofstrasse

Langestrasse

Marktplatz

Hauptstrasse

Parkstrasse

Wallstrasse

Neue Gasse

Badhausgasse

HAMBURG BARRACKS

Westgasse

Jägergasse

HANOVER

MAGDEBURG BARRACKS

Südberg

Kleiner Park

BARRACKS

Bäckergasse

to the cemetery

Südstrasse

railway to the main Dresden-Prague line

1. Children's House and School
2. Post Office, Bank, Theatre
3. Home for young people
4. Home for girls aged eight to sixteen
5. Tent for forced labour tasks (1,000 prisoners)
6. Ghetto shop used for clothing
7. Café, cabaret shows
8. SS Camp Command Headquarters
9. Housing for elderly Jews. Hospital
10. Jewish Ghetto Guard (100 men)
11. Infant school, kitchen, bakery
12. Homes for children and apprentices, and a library
13. Barracks of Czech gendarmes guarding perimeter
14. Craft workshops
15. SS dormitory and restaurant

16. SS Archives brought here from Berlin, 1943
17. Confiscated belongings sorted here
18. Women's barracks, concert performances, football in the yard
19. Housing for mothers and children under three years old
20. Playground for children; only allowed during the making of Nazi propaganda film
21. Central hospital, public baths, showers
22. Home for old and insane deportees

23. Disinfection centre, laundry, shower room
24. Joiners workshop
25. Jewish Council of Elders office and rooms; theatrical performances
26. Men's barracks
27. Bakery and central food store
28. Railway siding
29. Main women's barracks later used for deportees to Auschwitz
30. Barracks for very old deportees
31. Sports arena
32. Earliest deportees lived here
33. Jews with encephalitis housed here. Briefly a culture hall and synagogue during the making of a Nazi propaganda film
34. Columbarium: urns with ashes placed here; the limit of mourners' journey
35. Allotments and a garden - these existed only during the making of the Nazi propaganda film

© MARTIN GILBERT, 2004; for the HOLOCAUST MEMOIR DIGEST

Deportations to Auschwitz-Birkenau, 1942-1944

FINLAND

Helsinki

Narva

Lake Peipus

line of furthest German advance 1942

NORWAY

Bergen

Oslo

SWEDEN *neutral*

North Sea

Baltic Sea

Kovno

Vilna

Grodno

Bialystok   Wolkowysk

Pruzana

BRITAIN

English Channel

Amsterdam

Westerbork

Hamburg

Sachsenhausen

Berlin

Plonsk

Leipzig

Lodz   Radom

Lublin

Vught

Buchenwald

Breslau

Malines

Lille

Brussels

Theresienstadt

Cracow

Luxembourg

Rouen

Nancy

Vienna

Munkacs

Kosice   Beregszasz

Caen

Paris

Munich

Salzburg

Budapest

Eger

Debrecen

Marmarossziget

Angers

Orleans

Dijon

SWITZERLAND *neutral*

Brenner Pass

Beszterce

Szaszregen

Nantes

Tours

Cluj

Lyon

Merano   Padua

Trieste

Zagreb

Pecs

Bonyhad

Mako

Szeged

Septszentgyorgy

Black Sea

Turin

Milan

Fossoli

Bordeaux

Genoa

Florence

Avignon

Pisa

Toulouse

Gurs

Rivesaltes

Marseille

Pyrenees

SPAIN *neutral*

Rome

Adriatic Sea

Veles

Florina

Salonika

Kastoria

Larissa

Aegean Sea

TURKEY *neutral*

CORFU

Arta

Athens

KOS

Ionian Sea

Patras

RHODES

Mediterranean Sea

✡ **Auschwitz**

> Between the summer of 1942 and January 1945 an estimated one million Jews were murdered at Auschwitz.

| 0 | kilometres | 400 |
| 0 | miles | 250 |

© **Martin Gilbert**, 2004; for the **Holocaust Memoir Digest**

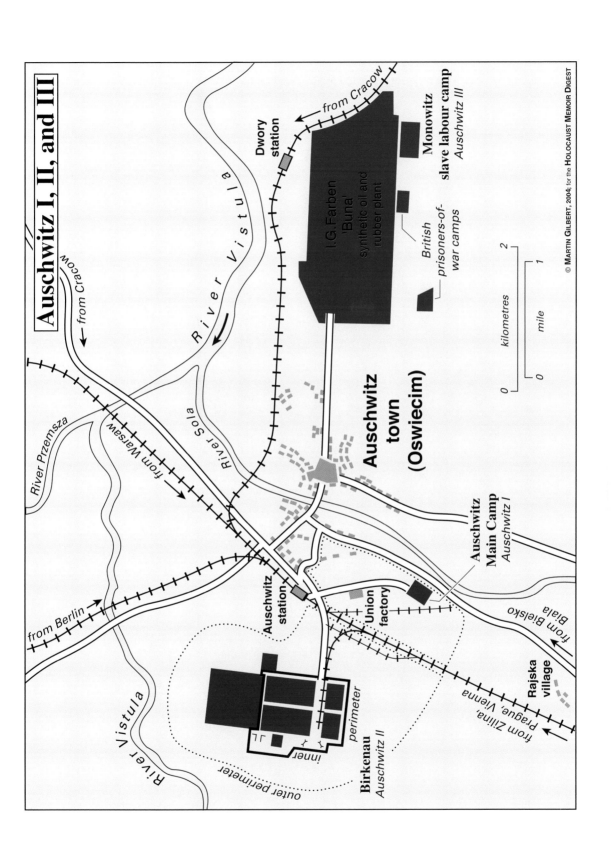

Auschwitz I, II, and III

from Cracow

from Cracow

River Vistula

Dwory station

I.G.Farben 'Buna' synthetic oil and rubber plant

British prisoners-of-war camps

Monowitz slave labour camp *Auschwitz III*

River Sola

from Warsaw

Auschwitz town (Oswiecim)

kilometres

mile

2

1

1

0

0

River Przemsza

from Berlin

River Vistula

Auschwitz station

Union factory

Auschwitz Main Camp *Auschwitz I*

from Bielsko Biala

inner perimeter

outer perimeter

Birkenau *Auschwitz II*

Rajska village

from Zilina, Prague, Vienna

© MARTIN GILBERT, 2004; for the HOLOCAUST MEMOIR DIGEST

Auschwitz Main Camp (Auschwitz I)

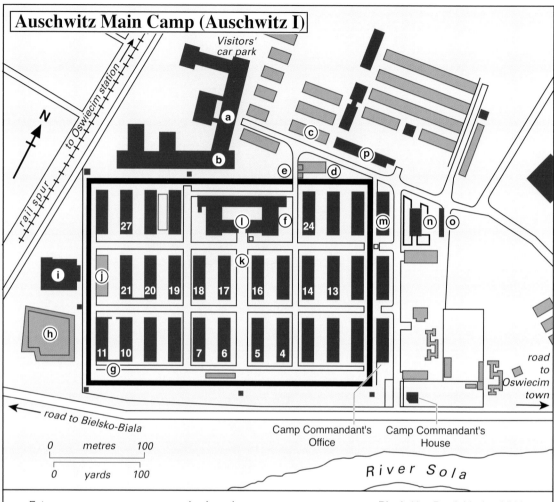

Visitors' car park

to Oswiecim station

rail spur

N

road to Bielsko-Biala

road to Oswiecim town

River Sola

Camp Commandant's Office

Camp Commandant's House

| 0 | metres | 100 |
| 0 | yards | 100 |

a. Entrance
b. Reception building for new prisoners
c. Stores, warehouse, workshops
d. SS Guardroom
e. Entrance gate inscribed 'Arbeit macht frei' (work makes you free)
f. Place where camp orchestra played
g. Wall of Death, where prisoners were executed by shooting
h. Gravel pit, site of executions
i. Warehouse for belongings taken from deportees. The poison gas canisters were also stored here

j. Laundry
k. Assembly Square (Appelplatz)
l. Camp kitchen
m. SS hospital
n. Gas chamber and Crematorium (Crematorium I)
o. Political section (Camp Gestapo)
p. SS garages, stables and stores

Block 4: Extermination exhibition
Block 5: Exhibition of material evidence of crimes
Block 6: Exhibition of everday life of prisoners
Block 7: Exhibition of living and sanitary conditions
Block 10: Exhibition of sterilization experiments

Block 11: Death block exhibition
Block 13: Denmark and Germany exhibitions
Block 14: National exhibition, formerly Soviet exhibition
Block 16: Czechoslovak exhibition
Block 17: Yugoslavia and Austria exhibition
Block 18: Hungarian and Bulgarian exhibitions
Block 19: Prisoners' hospital
Block 20: Prisoners' hospital
Block 21: Prisoners' hospital
Block 24: Museum archive
Block 27: Exhibition, 'Suffering and struggle of Jews'

▬ Brick perimeter wall   ■ Watchtowers

Birkenau (Auschwitz II)

Between the summer of 1942 and November 1944 an estimated one million Jews were murdered at Birkenau.

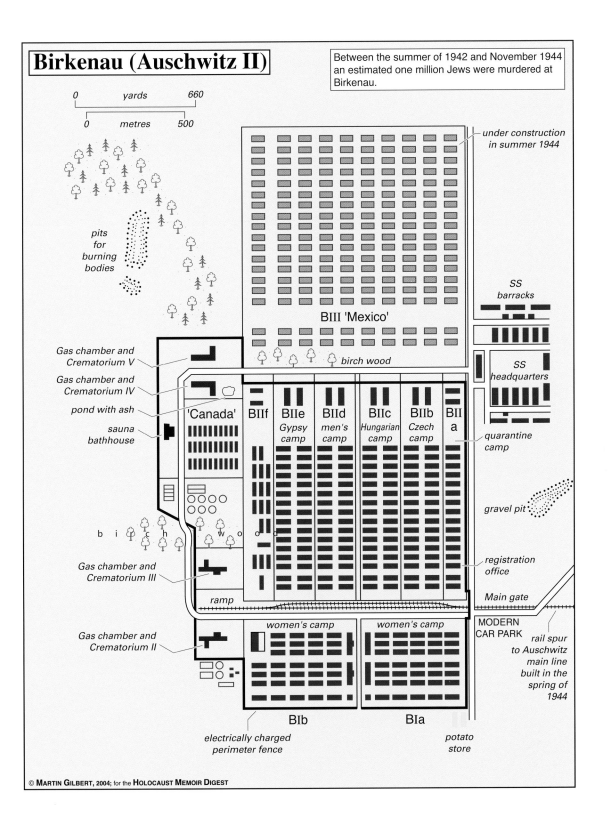

0   yards   660

0   metres   500

pits for burning bodies

under construction in summer 1944

SS barracks

BIII 'Mexico'

birch wood

SS headquarters

Gas chamber and Crematorium V

Gas chamber and Crematorium IV

pond with ash

sauna bathhouse

'Canada'

BIIf

BIIe — Gypsy camp

BIId — men's camp

BIIc — Hungarian camp

BIIb — Czech camp

BIIa

quarantine camp

gravel pit

b i r c h w o o d

registration office

Main gate

Gas chamber and Crematorium III

ramp

MODERN CAR PARK

rail spur to Auschwitz main line built in the spring of 1944

Gas chamber and Crematorium II

women's camp

women's camp

BIb

BIa

electrically charged perimeter fence

potato store

© **Martin Gilbert**, 2004; for the **Holocaust Memoir Digest**

Escape route of Rudolf Vrba and Alfred Wetzler, 7-25 April 1944

Oswiecim

Birkenau

Buna-Monowitz

Auschwitz

E A S T

U P P E R

S I L E S I A

River Vistula

River Sola

P O L A N D

Pisarowice

Porabka

Bielsko-Biala

fired on by a German patrol

Forest

Zywiec

Milowka

Zwardon

Skalite

Sol

Rajcza

Cadca

B e s k i d   M o u n t a i n s

Southward route of the two escapees

Railway from Poland to Slovakia

International borders, 1937

SS-run camps

S L O V A K I A

Zilina

0   kilometres   15

0   miles   10

© MARTIN GILBERT, 2004; for the HOLOCAUST MEMOIR DIGEST

Slave Labour Camps in the Auschwitz Region, 1942 - 1944

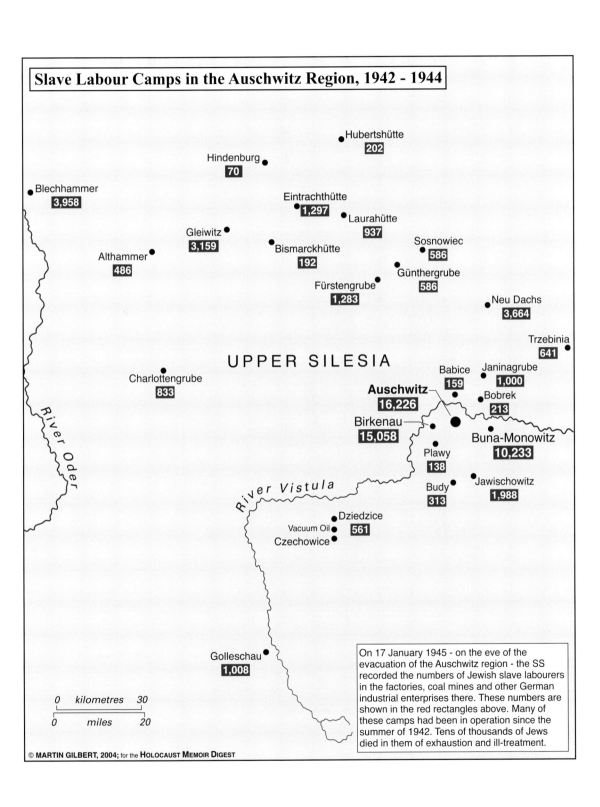

Hubertshütte
202

Hindenburg
70

Blechhammer
3,958

Eintrachthütte
1,297

Laurahütte
937

Gleiwitz
3,159

Bismarckhütte
192

Sosnowiec
586

Althammer
486

Günthergrube
586

Fürstengrube
1,283

Neu Dachs
3,664

Trzebinia
641

UPPER SILESIA

Charlottengrube
833

Babice
159

Janinagrube
1,000

Auschwitz
16,226

Bobrek
213

Birkenau
15,058

Buna-Monowitz
10,233

Plawy
138

Jawischowitz
1,988

Budy
313

River Oder

River Vistula

Dziedzice
561

Vacuum Oil
Czechowice

Golleschau
1,008

| 0 | kilometres | 30 |
| 0 | miles | 20 |

On 17 January 1945 - on the eve of the evacuation of the Auschwitz region - the SS recorded the numbers of Jewish slave labourers in the factories, coal mines and other German industrial enterprises there. These numbers are shown in the red rectangles above. Many of these camps had been in operation since the summer of 1942. Tens of thousands of Jews died in them of exhaustion and ill-treatment.

© MARTIN GILBERT, 2004; for the HOLOCAUST MEMOIR DIGEST

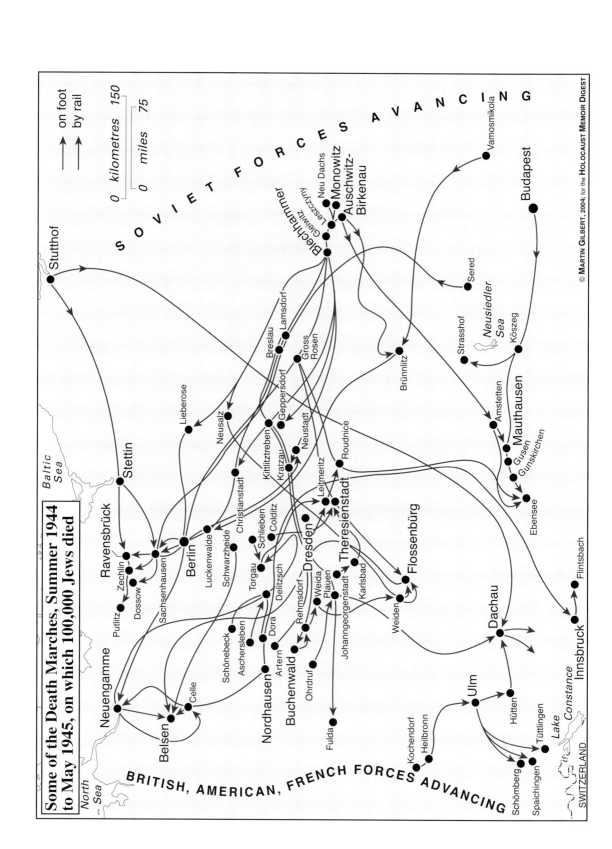

Some of the Death Marches, Summer 1944 to May 1945, on which 100,000 Jews died

SOVIET FORCES AVANCING

BRITISH, AMERICAN, FRENCH FORCES ADVANCING

on foot
by rail

0 kilometres 150
0 miles 75

© MARTIN GILBERT, 2004; for the HOLOCAUST MEMOIR DIGEST

North Sea

Baltic Sea

Stutthof
Budapest
Vamosmikola
Monowitz
Auschwitz-Birkenau
Neu Dachs
Leszczyny
Gleiwitz
Blechhammer
Sered
Neusiedler Sea
Strasshof
Kőszeg
Lamsdorf
Breslau
Gross Rosen
Brünnlitz
Amstetten
Mauthausen
Gusen
Gunskirchen
Ebensee
Lieberose
Neusalz
Geppersdorf
Neustadt
Roudnice
Kittlitztreben
Kratzau
Leitmeritz
Christianstadt
Schlieben
Colditz
Theresienstadt
Flossenbürg
Stettin
Ravensbrück
Berlin
Luckenwalde
Schwarzheide
Torgau
Delitzsch
Dresden
Karlsbad
Dachau
Flintsbach
Putlitz
Zechlin
Dossow
Sachsenhausen
Weida
Plauen
Johanngeorgenstadt
Weiden
Rehmsdorf
Schönebeck
Aschersleben
Dora
Artern
Ohrdruf
Fulda
Ulm
Hütten
Tüttlingen
Lake Constance
Innsbruck
Neuengamme
Celle
Belsen
Nordhausen
Buchenwald
Kochendorf
Heilbronn
Schömberg
Spaichingen
SWITZERLAND

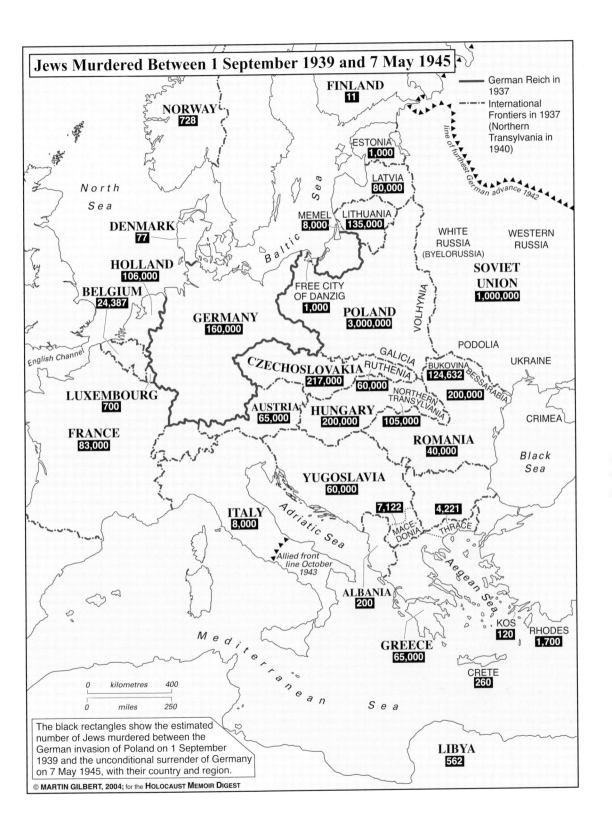

Jews Murdered Between 1 September 1939 and 7 May 1945

German Reich in 1937

International Frontiers in 1937 (Northern Transylvania in 1940)

line of furthest German advance 1942

FINLAND
11

NORWAY
728

ESTONIA
1,000

LATVIA
80,000

North Sea

Baltic Sea

DENMARK
77

MEMEL
8,000

LITHUANIA
135,000

WHITE RUSSIA (BYELORUSSIA)

WESTERN RUSSIA

HOLLAND
106,000

BELGIUM
24,387

FREE CITY OF DANZIG
1,000

GERMANY
160,000

POLAND
3,000,000

VOLHYNIA

SOVIET UNION
1,000,000

English Channel

PODOLIA

UKRAINE

CZECHOSLOVAKIA
217,000

GALICIA

RUTHENIA
60,000

BUKOVINA
124,632

BESSARABIA
200,000

LUXEMBOURG
700

AUSTRIA
65,000

HUNGARY
200,000

NORTHERN TRANSYLVANIA
105,000

CRIMEA

FRANCE
83,000

ROMANIA
40,000

Black Sea

YUGOSLAVIA
60,000

Adriatic Sea

7,122

MACE-DONIA

4,221

THRACE

ITALY
8,000

Allied front line October 1943

Aegean Sea

ALBANIA
200

KOS
120

RHODES
1,700

Mediterranean Sea

GREECE
65,000

CRETE
260

0   kilometres   400

0   miles   250

LIBYA
562

The black rectangles show the estimated number of Jews murdered between the German invasion of Poland on 1 September 1939 and the unconditional surrender of Germany on 7 May 1945, with their country and region.

© **MARTIN GILBERT**, 2004; for the **HOLOCAUST MEMOIR DIGEST**

Non-Jews Recognised For Having Saved Jews From Death, 1939 – 1945

NORWAY 24

SWEDEN 10

ESTONIA 2

RUSSIA 93

North Sea

DENMARK 17

Baltic Sea

LATVIA 93

LITHUANIA 513
• Kaunas

GREAT BRITAIN 13

HOLLAND 4,513

BELARUS 512

Berlin •

GERMANY 376

POLAND 5,733

Kharkov →

BELGIUM 1

LUXEMBOURG

CZECH REPUBLIC 104

UKRAINE 1,881

Vienna •

SLOVAKIA 428

FRANCE 2,262

SWITZ 38

AUSTRIA 84

Budapest •

MOLDOVA 53

HUNGARY 617

Bordeaux •

SLOVENIA 6

CROATIA 93

SERBIA 116

ROMANIA 48

Marseille •

BOSNIA 34

SPAIN 3

ITALY 325

Adriatic Sea

YUGOSLAVIA

BULGARIA 16

Black Sea

MACEDONIA 10

61

ALBANIA

GREECE 253

TURKEY 1

Mediterranean Sea

Aegean Sea

0   kilometres   300

0   miles   200

Rhodes

–·–·– International borders, 1937

·········· Post-1991 divisions of the Soviet Union

© **MARTIN GILBERT, 2004**; for the **HOLOCAUST MEMOIR DIGEST**

The total number of non-Jews who saved Jewish lives during the Holocaust, and have been honoured by the State of Israel and the Yad Vashem Holocaust memorial in Jerusalem since 1953 reached 19,706 on 1 January 2003 (as shown on this map). They are given the title 'Righteous Among the Nations'. They are also known as 'Righteous Gentiles'. This map shows the awards given country by country, during that fifty-year period.

Also shown on the map are the cities where Jewish lives were saved by individuals who have been recognized by Yad

Vashem as Righteous: ten Armenians (including one in Budapest and one in Vienna), two Chinese (one in Kharkov, the other in Vienna), a Brazilian diplomat (in Berlin), a Portuguese diplomat (in Bordeaux), a Japanese diplomat (in Kaunas), and a United States citizen, Varian Fry, who, from Marseille, enabled many hundreds of Jews to leave Europe. The one Turkish citizen indicated on the map was also a diplomat, the Turkish Consul on the island of Rhodes.

At their own request, the Norwegian and Danish resistance movements received their honours collectively.

Survivors of the Holocaust

FINLAND
2,000

NORWAY
1,000

SWEDEN

North
Sea

BALTIC STATES
25,000

DENMARK
5,500

WESTERN
SOVIET
UNION
300,000

HOLLAND
20,000

Baltic Sea

BELGIUM
40,000

DANZIG
8,000

POLAND
225,000

GERMANY
330,000

English Channel

CZECHOSLOVAKIA
44,000

LUXEMBOURG
1,000

AUSTRIA
7,000

HUNGARY
300,000

FRANCE
200,000

SWITZERLAND

ROMANIA
430,000

Black
Sea

YUGOSLAVIA
12,000

BULGARIA
48,000

TURKEY

ITALY
35,000

Adriatic Sea

SPAIN

Aegean Sea

ALBANIA
200

RHODES
161

Mediterranean

GREECE
12,000

CRETE
7

Sea

International
borders, 1937

0   kilometres   400

0   miles   250

© MARTIN GILBERT, 2004; for the HOLOCAUST MEMOIR DIGEST

In addition to the 100,000 survivors of the concentration camps, more than a million and a half European Jews survived Hitler's efforts to destroy them. The numbers are shown on this map, country by country.

Some Jews were fortunate, as in Germany, to escape from Europe before the outbreak of war, or, as in Italy, to be liberated by the Allies before the plans for their destruction could be completed. Others, as in Romania, were saved when their Government, previously anti-Jewish, changed its policy in anticipation of an Allied victory. All 48,000 Jews of Bulgaria were saved by the collective protest of the Bulgarian church, parliament and people.

The majority of the Polish Jews shown here survived because they found refuge at the beginning of the war in Soviet Central Asia. More than 20,000 French, Belgian and Dutch Jews found refuge in Switzerland, Spain and Portugal. Almost all Denmark's 7,000 Jews were smuggled to safety in Sweden. Many Greek Jews found refuge in Turkey.

Some Jews everywhere, particularly in France, Belgium, Holland and Italy, survived because the Germans took longer to deport them than the course of the war allowed: the Allied landings on continental Europe in June 1944 coming while the deportations were still in progress.

As many as 100,000 Jews escaped death because they were hidden by non-Jews who risked their own lives to save Jews.

German-Dominated Europe, 1942; and the United States of America: A Geographic Comparison

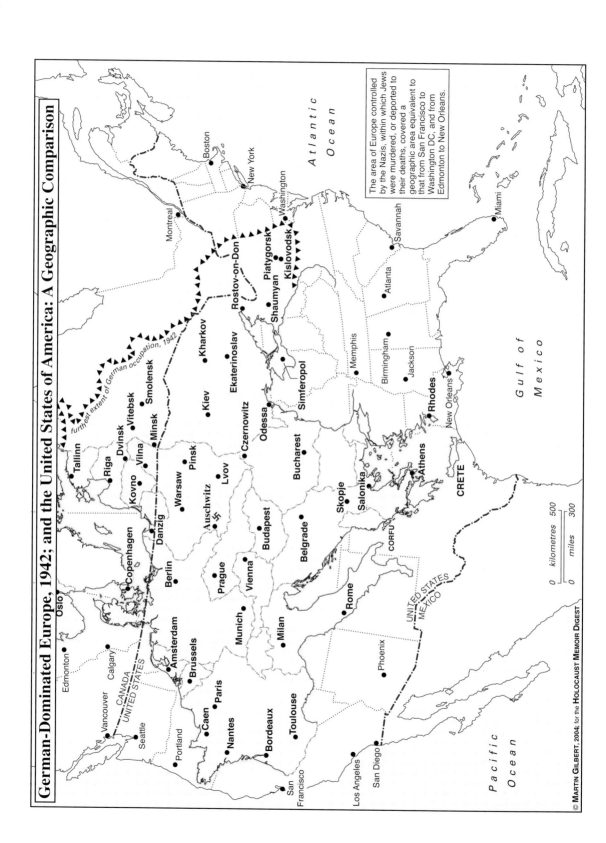

The area of Europe controlled by the Nazis, within which Jews were murdered, or deported to their deaths, covered a geographic area equivalent to that from San Francisco to Washington DC, and from Edmonton to New Orleans.

furthest extent of German occupation, 1942